90 DAYS TO SUCCESS IN GRANT WRITING

Timothy Kachinske

Judith Kachinske

Course Technology PTR
A part of Cengage Learning

COURSE TECHNOLOGY
CENGAGE Learning™

Australia, Brazil, Japan, Korea, Mexico, Singapore, Spain, United Kingdom, United States

COURSE TECHNOLOGY
CENGAGE Learning

90 Days to Success in Grant Writing
Timothy Kachinske
Judith Kachinske

Publisher and General Manager, Course Technology PTR:
Stacy L. Hiquet

Associate Director of Marketing:
Sarah Panella

Manager of Editorial Services:
Heather Talbot

Marketing Manager:
Mark Hughes

Acquisitions Editor:
Mitzi Koontz

Project Editor:
Jenny Davidson

Interior Layout Tech:
Bill Hartman

Cover Designer:
Mike Tanamachi

Indexer:
Sharon Shock

Proofreader:
Sandi Wilson

For product information and technology assistance, contact us at **Cengage Learning Customer & Sales Support, 1-800-354-9706.**

For permission to use material from this text or product, submit all requests online at **cengage.com/permissions**. Further permissions questions can be e-mailed to **permissionrequest@cengage.com**.

All trademarks are the property of their respective owners.

All images © Cengage Learning unless otherwise noted.

Library of Congress Control Number: 2009933300

ISBN-13: 978-1-4354-5486-6

ISBN-10: 1-4354-5486-3

Course Technology, a part of Cengage Learning
20 Channel Center Street
Boston, MA 02210
USA

Cengage Learning is a leading provider of customized learning solutions with office locations around the globe, including Singapore, the United Kingdom, Australia, Mexico, Brazil, and Japan. Locate your local office at: **international.cengage.com/region**.

Cengage Learning products are represented in Canada by Nelson Education, Ltd.

For your lifelong learning solutions, visit **courseptr.com**.

Visit our corporate Web site at **cengage.com**.

Printed in Canada.
1 2 3 4 5 6 7 11 10 09

This book is dedicated to all the people engaged in education and the nonprofit sector who work tirelessly to help others for the common good.

About the Authors

Timothy Kachinske has extensive experience in grant writing. Over a period of 17 years he served as a development officer and grant writer at a number of educational institutions and nonprofit organizations, including a liberal arts college (Ripon College), a research university (The Catholic University of America), an international science organization (The American Institute of Physics), an overseas American college (The American University in Bulgaria), a social services delivery agency (The Lt. Joseph Kennedy Institute) and an independent school (St. Alban's School).

Currently Tim continues development work as a consultant designing contact, grants management, fundraising, and member management database systems for nonprofit organizations and educational institutions. He specializes in using applications designed for sales and marketing and adapting this technology effectively in the nonprofit world.

Tim holds a B.A. from the University of Minnesota, Duluth and an M.A. from the University of Minnesota. He is a veteran of the US Army with 16 months overseas duty. Tim is a Microsoft Certified Professional with core competencies in Microsoft Dynamics CRM and Microsoft SharePoint.

Judith Kachinske has 10 years of experience in grant writing and grants management. She currently serves as an Assistant Instructional Supervisor of Grants and Monitoring for Prince George's County Public Schools in Maryland.

Judith has a B.A. in English from Macalester College and an M.S. in Curriculum and Instruction from Western Maryland College (now McDaniel College).

About the Technical Editors

Lisa Malone is a Partner Account Manager for Microsoft within the Dynamics CRM and ERP product group. Prior to her eight years at Microsoft, she served in various development and marketing roles at the Kennedy Krieger Institute, The Foundation Fighting Blindness, and Big Brothers/Big Sisters of Central Maryland. She is currently leading the Nonprofit & Association Solution Center for Microsoft. You can join this social network at: www.dynamicsnfp.ning.com.

John Abodeely is Program Manager for National Partnerships in the Education Department of the John F. Kennedy Center for the Performing Arts in Washington, DC.

Edward Kachinske is the author of more than 24 Customer Relationship Management books and is a CRM consultant in Washington, DC.

Contents

Chapter 3
Expertise............................. **53**

Chapter 4
Research............................. **65**

Chapter 5
Managing Relationships 109

Chapter 6
Writing 129

Chapter 7
Organizing Information **151**

Chapter 8
Queries and Short Proposals **179**

Chapter 9
Proposals for Projects, Programs, or
Bricks and Mortar **195**

Chapter 10
Proposals for Endowment Support **241**

Chapter 11
Federal Grants........................ **265**

Chapter 12
Managing Grant Awards................. **285**

Chapter 1

Getting Started as a Grant Writer

- Where Do Grant Writers Come From?
- Who Is This Book Intended to Help?
- Where Are Grant-Writing Positions Found?

No one ever grows up thinking "I want to be a grant writer." Still, countless people engaged in education, research, and the nonprofit world have advanced their careers and helped their organizations to survive and flourish as a result of writing successful grant proposals. Schools, colleges, hospitals, and nonprofit organizations count on successful grant applications as a crucial element in their strategic plans. Organizations value grants not only for the dollars they generate, but also for the prestige and respect that accompany those dollars. Grant recipients are winners in a highly competitive environment.

If you have a competitive spirit, you will savor the rewards that come with successful grant writing.

Grant writing is one of those vocations that people tend to either "fall into or get pushed into." Good writers in search of a way to turn that skill into a livelihood will fall into grant writing just to pay the bills and end up staying because of the personal and financial rewards they receive. People who have never thought of themselves as writers may get pushed into grant writing because their organization has a vision for expansion—or because it requires grant funding simply to survive. Sometimes the impetus comes from creative, innovative ideas that are unlikely to be funded any other way.

Grant writing can provide an opportunity to turn a knack for writing or a specialized knowledge base into a productive career.

Grants are a fundamental part of the American story. For some, the American dream has involved becoming so rich that you can afford to give money away. For others, the reality of having accumulated great wealth has brought with it a sense of obligation to society as a whole. Fortunes created in the late nineteenth century by industrial barons such as John D. Rockefeller and Andrew Carnegie gave rise to some of America's great private philanthropic foundations. Many of our museums, parks, libraries, concert halls, colleges, universities, and hospitals exist today because of the generosity of early philanthropists. The tradition has been continued by entrepreneurs such as Bill Gates, whose Bill and Melinda Gates Foundation has given more than 20 billion dollars to worthy causes across the globe over the past 15 years.

To promote the well-being of mankind throughout the world.
—Statement of Purpose of the Rockefeller Foundation (1913)

Federal grant making dates back to the Articles of Confederation, which authorized grants of land. Today, the United States government administers more than 1,800 federal grant programs. Most are competitive, and all involve an application process. These programs are administered by 26 federal agencies, which return hundreds of billions of federal tax dollars each year to state and local governments through grants and cooperative agreements. Grants provide a mechanism to fund projects for the public good carried out on a state or local level.

Even before the Constitution was signed, grants were part of American life.

Grants touch everyone. Grant-funded advances in medicine save lives every day. Whether you were aware of it or not, your education was probably subsidized by grants. You have probably enjoyed grant-funded parks, zoos, and recreation centers. The most recent symphony concert or opera you attended was almost certainly supported by a grant. Your community is undoubtedly protected by a plan made possible by one or more grants from the Department of Homeland Security. The very air you breathe may be affected by grant research funded by the Environmental Protection Agency.

> Today, the lives of all Americans are affected and improved by the efforts of successful grant writers.

Successful grant writers look back on their careers with a profound sense of satisfaction because their work has made good things happen that would not have happened otherwise. Grant writers help to feed the hungry, preserve the environment, find cures for diseases, increase human knowledge, and improve educational opportunities. They make tangible contributions in all walks of life. Grant writers can see the results of their efforts manifested in the programs and institutions they have served. Of course, you have to win the competition to gain the satisfaction. If you have a competitive spirit and a desire to engage in work that can bring measurable rewards, then grant writing may be the niche for you.

Where Do Grant Writers Come From?

High school guidance counselors are unlikely to steer youngsters in the direction of grant-writing careers, for there are no colleges or universities where you can major in grant writing. Degree programs in English, communication, technical writing, and non-profit management all provide useful preparation for a career in grant writing. However, grant writers are just as likely to have degrees in unrelated fields. It may not be necessary to have a degree at all. If you can do the work and do it well, you can be a grant writer regardless of credentials.

> There is no single ideal preparation. Each successful grant writer brings a unique combination of skills and experiences to the profession.

A Variety of Backgrounds

People in the nonprofit world are often prompted to get into grant writing by the lure of new opportunities for support. They hear about a new pie and want a piece of it. Others turn to grant writing out of frustration with the limits their current level of funding imposes on what their organization can accomplish. They see possibilities and want to turn those possibilities into realities. Career advancement is another motivator. Successful grant writing is a prerequisite for career advancement in academe, for example. Still others in the nonprofit world are forced by their organizations' financial situation to engage in grant writing as a means to survival. For them, succeeding in the intense competition for external funding may mean the difference between continued existence and retrenchment or collapse.

Nonprofit staffers can turn to grant writing out of motives as different as altruism, careerism, and fear.

Many professionals enter the field of grant writing as a lateral career move. Educators who gain appropriate experience often are able to transform themselves into full-time grant writers with positions in development offices, sponsored research offices, or other administrative units. Program officers at nonprofit organizations may assume grant-writing responsibilities in addition to their program administration roles. These professionals are able to convey this experience into full-time fundraising positions at their organization or at another nonprofit, sometimes with a promotion and a salary increase. During times of economic uncertainty, professionals with a successful grant-writing track record are able to survive because the demand for experienced grant writers is always greater than the supply.

Uncertain economic times can prompt professionals in a variety of fields to move into grant writing.

The legion of grant writers grows every year. There are lots of ways to get started. Young people can become grant writers through internships or assistantships. Grant writing experience gained through an unpaid position can give a recent college graduate a marketable skill that leads to employment. Graduate research assistants and new university faculty members may take their first steps in grant writing with their own fellowship applications. As their careers progress, they will take on increasingly complex grant proposal projects. Nonprofit or local government employees may turn to colleagues for advice and mentoring, or they may attend grant-writing seminars as a way to get started. Other grant writers simply learn their craft the hard way—on the job. In grant writing, both failure and success are great teachers.

Many paths lead to a career in grant writing.

A Highly Transferable Skill Set

Although grant writers may come to a grant-writing role from various starting points and along divergent pathways, there are two essential types of expertise they must either bring along or develop if they are to be successful. Being able to write reasonably well is one of these, of course. Second, it is essential either to possess expertise in what you write about or to have research skills that will give you the necessary working knowledge reasonably quickly. Communication skills and subject area expertise are both important; one without the other comes up short. If the task at hand is a grant proposal to support a local food bank, just being a wonderful writer will not necessarily win you a grant. Knowledge of specific local circumstances related to hunger and malnutrition and their place in the larger context are essential. By the same token, knowledge of hunger issues and the specific needs of your community will not necessarily be sufficient either. You must be able to communicate effectively with the decision makers who will review your grant proposal in order to prevail, because the needs of competing worthy causes always exceed the grant resources available to meet them.

An investment in knowledge pays the best interest.
—Benjamin Franklin

Fortunately, both writing skills and research skills can be learned. If you are a good wordsmith but you are uneasy about doing research, you can acquire those research skills. If you are already an expert in something but the thought of writing about it sends you into a panic, there are ways to fix that too. Once you have writing and research skills in more or less equal measure, you will have a highly transferable skill set. The successful grant writer can take that combination up the career ladder from one organization to another.

Seasoned grant writers have developed an ability to acquire expert knowledge quickly and in sufficient detail to write a successful proposal on behalf of those who will actually carry out a proposal project. Grant writers who write to support others in teaching, research, or program delivery may be assisted by colleagues who are themselves experts. However, in the end, a proposal is written by a writer. It is the grant writer's craft and expertise that generate a coherent, compelling grant proposal.

Persuasion is often more effectual than force.
—Aesop

It may come as no surprise that a good share of successful grant writers are liberal arts graduates. The writing demands of an American liberal arts education produce good writers in many fields. Because it involves academic study in a variety of disciplines across the arts and sciences, a liberal arts education provides familiarity with a wide range of subject matter. Also, the liberal arts model of learning requires students to write with sufficient clarity and depth to satisfy an instructor who is an expert in the discipline. In practice, the liberal arts curriculum leads naturally to the development of the writing and research skills that are the grant writer's essential equipment.

Other knowledge helpful to grant writing includes familiarity with budgetary and legal matters. Grants are money, after all, so it is necessary to be able to draft a budget and understand the relationship between resources and programs. Rudimentary knowledge of the regulations relevant to your organization and its grant income is also necessary, especially for those who write federal grants. However, a high level of expertise in these areas is not usually essential because you will rely on experts for their advice and input. You do not have to be a financial wizard or a lawyer to be a good grant writer; you do need to know when to seek advice.

Money alone sets all the world in motion.
—Publilius Cyrus
~100 BC

Many grant writers know little about finance and budgeting when they begin writing their first proposals. However, every educational or nonprofit organization has at least one experienced finance officer. Most local government agencies will have a whole staff of finance people. By cultivating professional relationships with the financial side of the organization, a grant writer can access in-house expert assistance in the preparation of proposal budgets and financial statements. Similarly, when tax or other legal issues arise during the preparation of a grant proposal, the grant writer for a nonprofit organization will either turn to in-house counsel or request the advice of an outside attorney.

Who Is This Book Intended to Help?

This book is a primer for anyone who wants to become acquainted with what is involved in grant writing. Whether you are interested in writing proposals to support your own work or the work of others, there is a common body of knowledge you should acquire with respect to determining your needs for support, researching, and cultivating funding prospects and proposal preparation.

It also aims to introduce the aspiring grant writer to the work that must be done before a proposal is submitted. The chapters that follow include nuts-and-bolts suggestions for outlining and drafting a proposal, and provide examples of various types of proposals. They also provide an introduction to the work involved in tracking proposals submitted for decision and ways to approach grant reporting. The grant writing process is a cycle that ideally begins with a winning proposal and ends with a final report to the donor that documents a successful program. Grant writers usually participate in all stages of the cycle.

Jobseekers with Good Writing Skills

Some aspiring grant writers served by this book have a broad career design for learning about grant writing as a profession. Already excellent writers, their aim is to secure a full-time position at an educational institution, nonprofit organization, or government entity where they will write proposals for projects or programs to be implemented by others. There is demand for people who can transform good ideas into coherent proposals for support. Once such an individual establishes a track record of successful grant proposals, it is relatively easy to transfer those skills to other organizations, even if they share little in terms of mission, size, or scope. A record of success in securing support for a local environmental nonprofit might very well serve as the springboard to a position in a national social service organization. Once the requisite skills and processes are firmly in hand, they can be transferred to new situations.

A good track record in one type of writing can easily lead to opportunities in another.

Over the course of a career, it is possible for a good grant writer to work in undergraduate and graduate education, public policy, and social services. Likewise, it is possible for a grant writer to spend an entire career in K-12 education or federal research grants. In fact, the possibilities and opportunities are great and varied for an accomplished writer interested in a grant-writing career.

This book is also intended for good writers who might want to volunteer their skills for an organization that cannot afford grant-writing expertise. Often small, community-based nonprofit organizations do not have staff with grant-writing experience and cannot afford to contract proposals out to independent writers. Even though they might be eligible to compete for grant support, these organizations simply lack the internal capacity to produce proposals and therefore cannot compete. A volunteer with writing skills who is willing to tackle a grant project can make a critical difference.

Experts Who Lack Writing Experience

It is likely that many of the aspiring grant writers this book aims to serve are already employed but have jobs that are not dedicated to grant writing. Instead, they have jobs that may for one reason or another intersect with the grant-writing world. They are engaged in activities that require funding from an outside source. These people already possess a specialized expertise and need

If you already have subject area expertise, you may only need to brush up your writing skills to become an effective grant writer.

only to develop their writing skills in order to be successful grant seekers. They may be teachers, professors, or administrators at educational institutions. They may be program administrators in nonprofit organizations or local government agencies who want to be able to write proposals to support or enhance the programs or projects they intend to direct.

It is often the case that teachers or program delivery experts must write their own grant proposals, even when their organization employs dedicated fundraising staff. Development offices at educational institutions and nonprofit organizations respond to the priorities of the organization's board of directors. Priorities set by a board will generally focus a development operation's activities, leaving few resources for the external fundraising interests of other professional staff. So long as you have the moral support of your executive officer, and any relevant financial or legal support that may be necessary, you should be able to add writing to your professional toolkit and garner the external funding you need to carry out the work you want to do.

Educators Interested in Career Advancement

Supplemental funding can mean the difference between a mediocre education and a great one. Educators with grant writing skills can make that difference.

Grant-writing skills can be a helpful means to career advancement for an ambitious educator. Grant writing is sometimes embedded within a job description. For example, public school administrators may be expected to secure outside funding to support special projects. They may be called upon to develop proposals in response to a Request for Proposal (RFP) published by a public or private funding source. In higher education, a chief academic officer may be required to secure external funding for curriculum redesign or faculty development. Very often, these responsibilities are delegated to administrators who report to the chief academic officer. Staff in such positions need to develop grant writing expertise to advance their careers. There is no better way to get positive attention than by bringing in large sums of money.

On an individual level, every professor, teacher, or teaching assistant can enhance his or her career prospects through successful grant writing. At some research and comprehensive universities, faculty are evaluated for promotion, tenure, salary, and other perks on the basis of external funding received via grant proposals or contracts. There are strong incentives at these institutions for becoming a successful grant writer.

Individual Grant Seekers

This book also aims to serve artists, scholars, and creative writers who are interested in grant opportunities that directly support individuals. Most aspiring grant writers will be writing proposals submitted through a college, university, nonprofit organization, or a government entity. The grant application will include appropriate IRS letters or other documentation proving that the organization is eligible to receive funds, and any grant funds received will go directly to the organization. Most corporate, foundation, and federal grants are made to organizations and not to individuals.

However, people in the arts and academe do have some grant opportunities for direct grant and fellowship support. This means that when a grant or fellowship is awarded, the grant payment checks will be made out to the individual grant applicant rather than to an educational institution or other nonprofit organization. Artists, scholars, and creative writers who qualify for grants to individuals have a highly focused and specialized reason for acquiring grant-writing skills.

> Grants can fill the void left by the disappearance of patronage.

Where Are Grant-Writing Positions Found?

Openings for full-time positions that require grant writing appear every week in newspapers, professional publications, and job websites. Part-time and contract positions are also plentiful. They are found in areas as diverse as education, public policy, social services, child welfare, religion, medical research, animal rights, and environmental preservation. Anyone with a successful track record in grant writing can count on new and frequent job opportunities. Applicants with other types of significant writing experience can often break into a grant-writing job by providing writing samples that are similar to the grant-writing job at hand. Organizations in need of funding are typically well-staffed with people who can't write, hate to write, or don't have time to write. If you can demonstrate that your presence will lift that burden off their shoulders, you will find a position.

> If you can put other people's thoughts and dreams into words, you can find a place as a grant writer.

Tough economic times can actually increase job prospects for good grant writers because of the heightened competition for philanthropic or government resources. The supply of good grant writers rarely exceeds the demand.

Colleges and Universities

College and university development offices offer a huge number of opportunities for grant writers every year. You will frequently find this office called the *advancement* office, a name that captures the concept of moving the institution forward by generating resources. Fundraising positions are typically housed in a development or advancement office, which may also house a broad range of related activities including public relations, special events, and alumni and parent relations. The core fundraising functions found in a typical development or advancement office include annual fund, corporate relations, foundation relations, major gifts, and capital gifts. Writing skills can be a requirement for positions in any of these areas.

You will find grant-writing positions in development or advancement offices.

In the average development office, the primary grant-writing positions are in corporate and foundation relations, but in some cases professionals working in annual fund, major gifts, and capital gift fundraising may be called upon to produce grant proposals. Research universities typically have the largest number of fundraising professionals dedicated to grant writing. It is typical for a large research university to have several dozen people in various positions dedicated to producing successful grant proposals.

The several hundred top research institutions in the United States garner hundreds of millions of dollars a year in external grant support. To accomplish this, the advancement office may contain separate offices dedicated to foundation relations and corporate relations, each with its own director and several associate and assistant directors (as shown in Figure 1.1), all of whom have grant-writing responsibilities. Directors and assistant directors are also likely to have support staff and assistants to help them in the search for grant opportunities and the preparation of proposals. There are opportunities for employment at all levels in these offices. Turnover tends to be frequent because of the opportunities for promotion. One successful grant proposal can be the stepping stone to higher pay and more responsibility.

The reward for work well done is the opportunity to do more.
—Dr. Jonas Salk

Comprehensive universities are not in the same class in terms of dollars generated, but they likewise engage in multimillion-dollar efforts to support research and programs with external grants. Comprehensive universities comprise a large share of new job openings in grant writing and are well worth looking at if you want a grant-writing position.

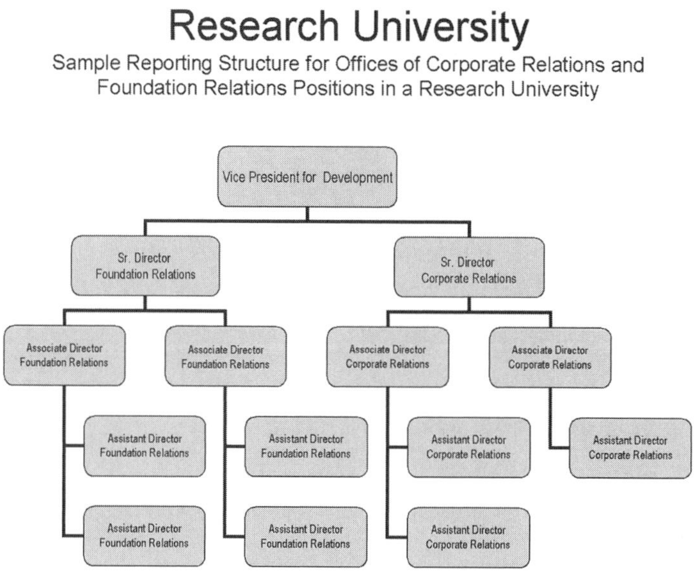

Research University

Sample Reporting Structure for Offices of Corporate Relations and
Foundation Relations Positions in a Research University

Figure 1.1

*Sample reporting
structure in a
research university.*

While professionals in a university's central development office
serve the university as a whole, you will often find additional
development officers serving as grant writers for specific administrators within the management structure. Academic deans in
charge of schools or colleges of law, medicine, engineering, communications, or liberal arts may have their own staff dedicated to
developing new grant proposals for research and educational projects unique to their administrative unit.

*University deans
often run their own
development efforts.*

It is not uncommon for the position announcement for an academic dean to list "grant production" or "increasing external funding" as one of the expectations (as shown in Figure 1.2). Deans
charged with the responsibility of raising funds require significant
grant-writing assistance to be successful. You can be sure that an
academic dean who has proposal production and external funding as measurable goals for her performance will want grant writers on her staff with a reporting channel that goes directly up to
her desk. Given their other responsibilities, few deans have much
time to spend on grants research and writing—as important as it
is to them. They must rely on staff to carry out their ideas.
Theoretically, development professionals working for a constituent school will work cooperatively with the central development office to bring about successful outcomes.

Any institution engaged in a capital campaign—a highly structured effort to achieve major fundraising goals within a specified

SAMPLE POSITION ANNOUNCEMENT: DEAN OF ENGINEERING

University
of the United States

National Search

Dean, School of Engineering

The University of the United States requests nominations and applications for the Dean of Engineering.

Duties: Lead planning and implementation of education and research programs in the School of Engineering. Lead assessment of undergraduate and graduate classroom, laboratory and research experiences. Supervise marketing program of School to include electronic and print materials. Lead faculty and students in collaborative research experiences. Develop a new career day program for science and engineering students, as well as new programs to support local science teachers. Coordinate School of Engineering Alumni Advisory Council. Conduct fundraising and grant writing in support of external funding for School of Engineering initiatives. Lead faculty and staff in implementing a strategic plan for the School of Engineering.

> This dean will be evaluated on fundraising and grants for his school.

Preference will be given to applicants with prior administrative experience at a graduate institution, demonstrated success in obtaining external funding, experience with fundraising and a track record of good relationships with alumni and other potential supporters, and success in teaching.

> With all that is expected of this new dean, you can be certain he or she will be hiring competent grant writers to ramp up the external funding of the school.

Figure 1.2 *Sample position announcement: Dean of Engineering.*

period of time—is likely to need grant writers. At most institutions, the advent of a capital campaign will mean increased hiring in the development office. Constituent colleges, institutes, and programs may well have the need and resources to hire grant writers as well in order to achieve their capital campaign goals. In some large universities, there is significant cooperation between a central development office and constituent colleges, while at others there is intense competition.

Sustaining the momentum of a capital campaign usually requires hiring additional grant writers.

Smaller institutions such as liberal arts colleges or community colleges typically have all of these grant-writing needs on a smaller scale. For example, a small college might have just one grant writer. If you enjoy variety, that might be the perfect setting for you. At liberal arts colleges, the chief grant writer is typically the director of corporate and foundation relations (as shown in Figure 1.3). In small institutions, development functions may be combined with additional responsibilities for federal and state grants. In this type of setting it is possible to gain a wide range of grant-writing experience in a relatively short period of time.

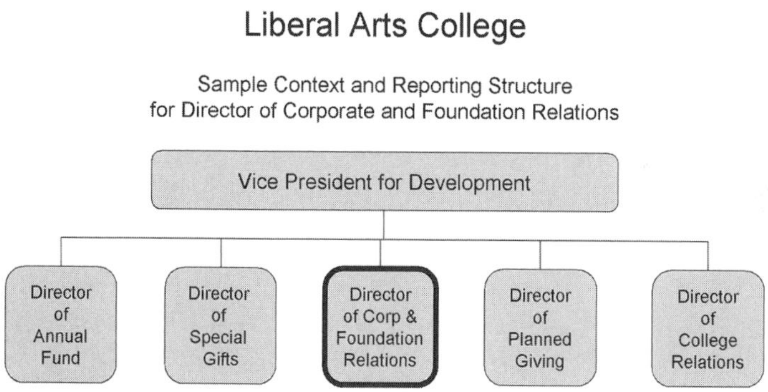

Liberal Arts College

Sample Context and Reporting Structure
for Director of Corporate and Foundation Relations

Figure 1.3
Sample context and reporting structure for director of corporate and foundation relations.

Hospitals and Clinics

All major medical facilities, and many small ones, have development or advancement offices that engage in many of the same types of fundraising activities found in colleges and universities. They solicit funding for such things as program development, new construction, medical research, acquisition of new equipment, and community outreach. Often they will partner with other organizations with which they share common objectives.

There are many opportunities for writers in hospitals and clinics.

Prospective sources of support for medical facilities include corporations, foundations, government agencies, local philanthropic organizations, and grateful patients. Grant writers are needed for all of these types of solicitations. If you enjoy working in a medical setting, you can have a very rewarding grant-writing career in a hospital or clinic.

Sponsored Research Offices

Most sponsored research is funded by public sector funds.

Sponsored research offices at universities, research hospitals, and research institutes comprise another area where grant-writing positions exist. Sometimes these offices are called "sponsored programs," but the function is identical. Whereas a development office is typically involved in securing private sector support, a sponsored research office will be engaged in securing public sector support. Federal grants are normally prepared in a sponsored research office.

In a university, sponsored research offices usually fall under the chief academic officer. All faculty-initiated grant proposals begin at this office. At most research institutions, sponsored research offices have staff dedicated to helping faculty seek potential grant support and prepare proposals for submission. Some institutions even promote sponsored research offices as a place where faculty can get assistance in marketing their ideas for external support. These jobs can result in close professional collaboration and can be rewarding for a competent grant writer.

There is intense competition for sponsored research funds.

Other sponsored research grant writers will be engaged in applying for institutional grants that are driven not by a single individual's research interests but by the institution's leadership. At any research hospital or university, the largest grants as well as the largest number of research grants will be federal grants, which entail a substantially more complex application and reporting procedure than private grants. Grant writers in sponsored research offices are also likely to have more complex reporting responsibilities than their counterparts in development offices. If you are a detail-oriented person, sponsored research grant writing is likely to appeal to you. See Figure 1.4 for a sample reporting structure of grant-writing positions in a university sponsored research office.

Research University
Sample Reporting Structure for Grant Writing Positions in Sponsored Research Offices

Figure 1.4
Sample reporting structure for grant-writing positions in sponsored research offices.

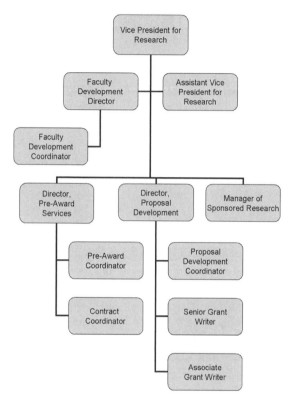

The Nonprofit World

According to the National Center for Charitable Statistics (NCCS), there were 1,515,679 registered nonprofit organizations in the United States in 2008. In terms of sheer numbers, non-profits offer the novice grant writer the best possible hunting ground for employment. These organizations, large and small, need writers who can persuade potential funders to support their causes. If you are willing to start out with the relatively modest salary a small nonprofit organization can provide, you will gain valuable on-the-job experience that can be transferred to higher-paid positions.

A grant-writing position in a small nonprofit organization can be the start of a lucrative career.

15

Nonprofit organiza-
tions that operate
nationwide employ
large numbers of
grant writers.

The very largest nonprofits in the United States have fully staffed development and sponsored programs operations that function much as sponsored research offices do in universities. The country's largest nonprofits tend to be national in scope and to focus on social welfare or disaster relief. These large organizations will have multiple staff positions dedicated to writing proposals for both private and public support.

Countless other grant-writing opportunities can be found in smaller nonprofits, and there is no limit to the causes they support. A genuine, documented passion for the cause can give you great credibility in a small nonprofit organization. If you are interested in turning your convictions into a career, you will find writing grants for a cause you believe in very satisfying. Volunteering is an excellent starting point for the aspiring nonprofit grant writer.

Never doubt that a small group of committed people can change the world. Indeed, it is the only thing that ever has.
—Margaret Mead

Local Government and Tribal Entities

It may seem surprising, but local government and tribal entities are the recipients of millions of federal grant dollars each year. Much of the funding dispensed to local government agencies is passed down through state government agencies and is therefore popularly referred to as "passthrough" funding. Such grants are often called "entitlement" grants, which may give the impression that you don't have to apply for them. Nothing could be further from the truth. The grant application process involved in applying for "entitlement" funds is extensive and employs a lot of people.

A billion here and a billion there—and pretty soon you're talking real money.
—-Senator Everett Dirksen

Federal grant dollars are also awarded on a competitive basis. The federal government offers more than 1,800 grant programs administered by federal departments and agencies. All of these are published in the Catalog of Federal Domestic Assistance (CFDA). Grant writers who acquire the specialized expertise needed to prepare competitive federal grant proposals have a very marketable skill set.

Due to their special status, tribal governments are eligible for special federal programs in addition to those open to state and local government agencies. These grant programs serve 1.9 million American Indians and Alaska Natives from 562 federally recognized tribes. Anyone who is a member of one of these tribes or an advocate on their behalf can play an important role as a grant writer.

Dialogue with a Professional: David Williams

David Williams has been a development officer and fundraising executive for more than 33 years. He began as a grant writer for a liberal arts college, and over the course of his career he has written numerous proposals. As a fundraising executive, he has hired many professionals for positions that required grant-writing skills.

Presently, Williams serves as Vice Chancellor for Advancement and Marketing at the University of Wisconsin-Stout, one of 13 universities in the University of Wisconsin system. Previously, Williams served as Vice President for University Advancement at Minnesota State University and as Vice President for Development at Ripon College.

A graduate of Beloit College, Williams earned his M.A. at the University of Wisconsin. Williams has been called upon for his expertise by many professionals in the United States and elsewhere. He traveled to Britain and Germany on a sabbatical focused on comparative fundraising in the late 1990s, and in 2007 he was the recipient of a Fulbright award directed at sharing U.S. higher education administration and fundraising expertise with German universities. He serves as a volunteer reviewer of applications for the Fulbright Commission.

You began your career in fundraising as a grant writer for a liberal arts college. What drew you to this job?

I moved to the grant-writing position after having served three years in the annual giving office. That was good overall training to understand how vital annual support is in an organization's overall budget. But with it I also saw how special requests for targeted projects could really raise an institution to new heights. By seeking grant opportunities in the corporate, foundation, and government worlds, I could see how my college would get significant notice, and could do things—whether a new research project, or a program for area schools, or to help build a building—that would never be possible from annual budget revenue. I also thought the grant-writing position would give me the chance to have greater and longer-term effect on my college through the projects we could accomplish with grant funds. And it looked like another skill set to help me in the growth of my career in advancement.

When you were starting out in grant writing, what sort of training and mentoring did you receive?

I began reading everything I could get my hands on as I prepared to move into the new role. I learned of the Grantsmanship Center through my reading, and sent away (this was before the days of the internet and web searches!) for all their promotional information. I ultimately signed up for their weeklong grants training workshop, during which they take the group through the whole grant process to the writing of an actual grant.

I was at Ripon College at the time and my boss had a great idea to send me for a few days to shadow a man he knew and respected as a consummate grant writer. I spent those days with Max Smith at Furman University, where he generously shared his mode of operation, hints for success, copies of things which helped and influenced him, draft proposal ideas, and best of all, his willingness to be a resource on call once I returned to my campus. I took advantage of that several times over the next few years. Finding a mentor like Max Smith was the most helpful way to learn the grant-writing profession.

You've worked on many proposals with faculty members and others at the various institutions you've served. Are there any that stand out as particularly rewarding? What was your formula for success?

One special one, not altogether the largest I've dealt with, but interesting in how it changed a community and the faculty members who worked with me on it, happened at Ripon College. I was approached by a husband/wife team of dance instructors at the college, who were sharing a half-time position. They had plenty of time to do more and the energy to use their talent to excite others about movement and dance. We conceived of offering something akin to master's classes in all the elementary schools in our community. That meant we needed first to get our college chief academic officer involved and excited, then the school superintendent, then principals at the schools, and then finally we could explore how we might fund this.

Here's where I made a big novice mistake. I drafted a proposal and we simply sent it off to a local industry plant, which was part of a national corporation, assuming they'd think it was such a great idea, they would bump it up the corporate ladder and the money would come pouring in. We got a summary rejection notice.

That's when we did the right things—we went to visit the local plant manager, shared the school district's enthusiasm for the project, and asked his support as we approached the national corporate office. He gave his endorsement, and I then met with the corporate foundation executive at the company's national headquarters. We then submitted a better proposal. I also went to the Wisconsin Arts Board to describe the project, discuss our other funding efforts, and ask their support. That too required a proposal, but I had an excited ally.

And the rest of the story? Both proposals were funded, and the dancers suddenly found themselves busy meeting grade and middle school classes, getting kids excited about dance and movement skills. The whole community got excited, and the faculty members found themselves new experts in the area of dance for children. As they moved on in their careers, they've copied that model in Montana and Virginia, with similar results. The secret is not so very secret—communicating early with local people who can be advocates as we moved up the funding chain.

Research skills are important to any aspiring grant writer. What would you recommend to a new grant writer that would help develop research skills?

It would probably be helpful to spend a few hours with a reference librarian (I happen to be married to one) to ask how they would go about a methodical search for information. In the early days the resources were all print—directories of foundations and funding priorities. While those still exist in some form, the internet and electronic database searching are critical skills.

Again, those reference librarians are trained to help library patrons with those skills, especially in how to limit searches to find the specific information you may need, or to review other projects which might be similar. Another way is to find that good mentor, someone willing to share how she or he goes at good research. Spending a few hours at that person's elbow could be a tremendous education.

When you set out to draft a proposal, how do you begin?

I begin with thinking through the concept as it has been brought to me, or as I see the need to be served. Asking a lot of questions helps me—I like to think through what an uninformed person would need to know to understand what we're trying to do. Then comes a thorough outline of the project.

The Grantsmanship Center suggests a preferred way to organize a proposal, which helps. But I think it's imperative that you think through everything you can and work it into that outline to make sure your narrative flows logically and effortlessly (for the reader) to the obvious conclusion of funding. What need are you exactly trying to serve? Who perceives this as a need? Who would most logically do the work to solve the need? What steps are probably needed? What resources already exist to help meet the need? What additional resources are needed, and not just financial, to accomplish the plan?

I usually then charge through with a first draft, writing more to meet the broader outline than for final accuracy or style. Then it's redraft time. Write so that your grandmother could understand what you're doing, and be able to tell her friends, was some advice I got early on, and I think still applies. Bounce the draft off that mentor if there's time, or at least off someone local before sending it off.

What advice would you give to a recent graduate who is looking at a position that requires grant-writing skills?

A good grant writer has to have fundamentally good writing skills, which includes understanding of good grammar, and a decent vocabulary. Use the spell check function on your word processor, but don't rely on that alone. Read every other grant you can lay your hands on, especially ones you know to be successful.

I spent a summer as a cub reporter for a daily newspaper during my college years. That job gave me several advantages, beginning with great keyboarding skills. It also gave me the humility of knowing my editor could always find ways to help me improve the prose I turned in—pride of authorship needs to step aside. Even Pulitzer Price novelists work with editors. And the final benefit of that newspaper job was being able to meet a deadline.

It is also important to get to know everything you possibly can about the institution you serve. Sit in on meetings, glean reports, get to know deans, department chairs, or faculty if you're on a college campus. Find out what they're excited about. Good grant writers are always thinking about bringing people and ideas from a variety of disciplines or functional areas together.

If someone is looking at a career change, what kind of positions are available that require grant writing?

Many colleges and universities have such positions, though they aren't always available to people without some other relevant experience. Sometimes serving as a volunteer at a nonprofit in the community can provide a chance to offer to work on a grant to help that nonprofit. Nongovernmental organizations frequently have grant writers to help generate funding for their activities. Service clubs occasionally provide programs that can be packaged into grants for local foundation or corporate funding entities. Any or all such experiences provide great background skills for new grant writers.

Over the course of your career, you've interviewed many professionals seeking a position that requires grant writing. What do you look for in such a person? What sort of things make a candidate particularly strong?

When looking to hire a new grant writer, obviously the ability to write and present well makes all the difference. I usually ask for a writing sample or some sample of programs and grants an individual has put together, and what the results have been. Simply seeing a proposal without the context of the institution it was to serve, or how the project was assembled and presented, isn't as helpful. I want to know what success the person has had with grants submitted.

I also look for good people skills, good relationship-building skills. The grant-writing world still must depend on a writer's ability to connect with people both on the campus or at the institution, who are going to deliver the services the grant will pay for. And that person must be able to connect with the foundation or corporate giving officers to build trust in themselves as the representative of the organization. Do they follow through to get the tasks done in a timely manner?

You have done it all in grant writing, from writing proposals for institutions and individual project directors, to writing successful fellowship applications for your own research and international travel. As a past Fulbright recipient, you now serve as a volunteer for the Fulbright Commission in reviewing new applications. As a reviewer of proposals, what do you look for in a strong application? What might be things to avoid in an application?

A strong application is first and foremost, well written, grammatically correct, with spelling carefully checked—it's amazing how many proposals and applications don't do that kind of elementary final check. It signals to the reviewer that you've exercised care and attention to present yourself or your institution in the best light, and ultimately, it's also a way to signal respect for the reviewer.

A second key issue when I serve as reviewer is whether the person is really writing to answer the questions asked, or to meet the expectations the funding source hopes to fund. Take a moment to consider why the funding source is making its grant money available. What do they want to accomplish, through you or others they fund, to meet the need areas they have identified as important?

Or in the case of the Fulbright applications I've reviewed, what will you bring to the seminar that will put the United States, your institution, and yourself in a positive and helpful light to the new international colleagues you'll be meeting with? Not what's in it for you, but what can you bring to the table?

And be realistic—can you, or your institution, realistically do what you say you will? Can you deliver?

Always make sure the budget reflects accurately what your narrative says you'll be doing. Surprises that pop up in the budget with no explanation in the narrative raise red flags for reviewers.

Be sure you also present a realistic description of how you'll disseminate the knowledge you've gained, or the success your institution shows after receiving a grant. Funding sources always want to know that their money will reach beyond just what you may accomplish. And please be sure to say thank you, both your personal thanks and your institutional leader's thanks. The funding world doesn't appreciate ingrates.

Chapter 2

Finding and Securing a Grant-Writing Position

- Searching for a Position
- Applying for a Position
- Preparing for Interviews

Y ou may already have a job that requires grant-writing skills, and you are reading this book just to improve those skills. Perhaps grant-writing responsibilities have just been added to your job duties, and you are reading this book to jump-start your work because you will be evaluated on your performance in this new role. Perhaps you have had some success at grant writing in your current job and are interested in exploring new possibilities. It's perfectly natural to wonder whether your experience might leverage a better-paying job in another organization. It might just be the time to pursue your interest in a different mission or a move to another location.

On the other hand, you may very well simply need a job. Perhaps you have good general writing skills and you want to break into grant writing, or perhaps you have expertise in an area that has a lot of grant-writing positions. For a small sampling of types of grant-writing jobs, see the position descriptions in Figure 2.1.

This chapter deals with various things you should be doing if you are looking for a position in grant writing. New job opportunities appear daily. Whether you are in the market right now or not, you should be putting some effort into exploiting the multitude of free job resources that are no further away than your keyboard and monitor. By subscribing to feeds and alerts, you can actually keep abreast of new job openings automatically. Even if you are satisfied with your present situation, there's no guarantee that it won't change. After reading the suggestions in this chapter, you will be on top of the job scene for grant writers, and you will be ready to act in the event that you choose to move on or up.

Learning how to organize a job search is the first step toward becoming a grant writer.

Searching for a Position

There are many ways to find a job in grant writing. No single publication or website lists every open position. New positions crop up every day, so last month's information won't be of much use. Staying current is simply a matter of being aware of all the web resources to search for available grant-writing positions. Explore these resources frequently and it will be easy to keep your information up to date. Low-tech methods of job searching are important, too, of course. Who you know is as important in the grant-writing business as in any other field, so think about ways to explore and expand your personal network.

SAMPLE GRANT WRITING POSITION DESCRIPTIONS

Sample Position Description Requiring Research, Travel, and Grant Writing

Position: Director of Corporate and Foundation Relations

The Fr. Meger Foundation for Cancer Research is a non profit organization dedicated to supporting research into the prevention and cure of cancer. Located in Minneapolis, MN. Seeking a **Director of Foundations and Corporate Relations** to develop and direct a strategic plan for foundations and corporate cultivation, prospecting and gift solicitation with the goal of increasing income in order to fulfill the mission of the Fr. Meger Foundation. He/she will represent the Fr. Meger Foundation to foundations, corporations and federal agencies. The ideal candidate will have 3 or more years of experience in Development including substantial experience cultivating foundations. Must be willing to travel up to 30%. Must have experience in reporting, analyzing, researching and writing grant proposals.

Sample Position Description Devoted Primarily to Grant Writing

Position: Grant Writer

The Fr. Meger Foundation for Cancer Research is looking for an expert **Grant Writer** with recent experience in writing grant proposals for corporate, foundation and federal grants. The grant writer would gather statistical and other background information to build the case for support, create evaluation and quality assessment tools, and produce final proposals for submission.

Sample Position Description Potentially Requiring Some Grant Writing

Position: Librarian

The **Special Collections Librarian** will support and manage projects coordinated by the office of Special Collections and Research. Working in a team-based environment and sharing or dividing duties as assignments and skills indicate with a second Special Collections Librarian, the incumbent will research, evaluate, test and recommend various methodologies, standards, and software used in the management of special collections and their long-term preservation; participate in grant writing and external funding initiatives.

Figure 2.1 *Sample grant-writing position descriptions.*

Online Search Engines

Today you can look for a job without leaving your desk.

A little over a decade ago, the vast majority of grant-writing positions were advertised in print media, most of them in newspapers or professional publications. You had to have a subscription or access to a good library in order to know what was available. With the advent of online national search engines, the search for a grant-writing position has become much cheaper and easier.

It is especially helpful to be able to scope out available positions based on geography. If you are confining your search to a specific city, you should always check out online job listings in the local paper as well. Most city newspaper sites now also link to national search engines. *The Washington Post*, for example, has an option for an online job search of the "DC Area" in general, with the option of further refining job location to any of the states and counties in the Washington metropolitan area (see Figure 2.2).

Figure 2.2
Washingtonpost.com.

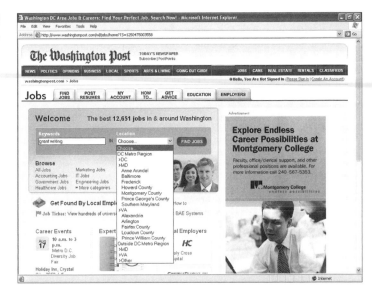

The online edition of a major newspaper close to you is a great place to start your search.

The Washington Post also has an "All US" option that links to Simply Hired, a search engine company in California that claims to be building "the largest online database of jobs on the planet." On a given day, it's possible to search "grant writer" and have several dozen job listings appear for the "DC Area," while an "All US" search will deliver several hundred listings including those in the Washington, DC area (see Figure 2.3).

Figure 2.3
Simply Hired.

Exploring other newspaper sites will give you the option to link to other major job listing search engines. The *New York Times* and *The Boston Globe* link to monster.com (see Figure 2.4).

The *Miami Herald, Chicago Tribune*, and the *Los Angeles Times* all link to careerbuilder.com (see Figure 2.5).

Moving beyond newspapers (and their links to national search engines), you should also explore the meta-search engines that

Figure 2.4
Monster.com.

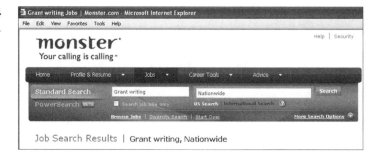

Figure 2.5
Careerbuilder.com.

Meta-search engines pull from many different search engines.

pull job listings from many newspapers and other sources. Juju.com is a descendent of the first online job search engine, and it remains one of the easiest to use. Go to juju.com and type in "grant writer" and your zip code. If you live in a major metropolitan area, many job listings will appear. The default search looks for jobs within 20 miles of your zip code. If not enough listings appear, you can expand your search using the "within miles" drop-down and expand your search up to 100 miles from your stated zip code (see Figure 2.6).

It is also worth giving Craigslist.com a try. City or regional sections on Craigslist have a Jobs category for the nonprofit sector. This is the most productive area to search on Craigslist for grant-writing jobs (see Figure 2.7). Craigslist is one of the few sites that permit searches to be limited to internships only, which is a plus for people with little grant-writing experience but a desire to develop grant-writing skills.

Figure 2.6
Juju.com.

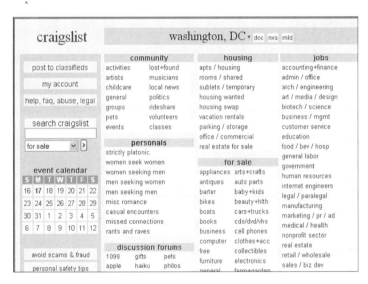

Figure 2.7
Craigslist.com.

Developing Online Search Methods

All online search engines allow you to search for keywords, and most permit you to refine your search by geographical region or states and specific job categories. Begin by experimenting with keywords to see which ones work best. Keywords such as "grant writer" or "grants" are a good start, but you may want to expand your searching with other keywords such as "development," "fundraising," "sponsored research," and "grants administration" to cast your net broadly.

Begin your search with broad criteria and then narrow down to the specifics you are looking for.

In a short time, you will discover the best keywords for each job search website based on the new job opportunities a search engine has revealed to you. Your aim at first should be to pull up a lot of listings. As you sift through them, you will save those hits that are most appealing and relevant to your interests and experience.

Some job search websites offer a free job alert service. This is usually an RSS (Really Simple Syndication) web feed that enables you to set up an automated search by selecting keywords, job categories, and other criteria such as city or state. When a new position that fits your chosen criteria appears on the website, an email with a link to the position announcement is automatically sent to your email address.

RSS feeds send position announcements that fit your search criteria right into your email.

It's a good idea to do manual searches on a job website to learn its indexing, predetermined search terms, and types of categorization before setting up an RSS feed. Understanding that the keyword "grants" will bring up more than five times as many job listings as the keywords "grant writer" will be useful as you set up your search criteria. Remember, at the beginning you will want to do broad searches. Later, after you've set up your alerts and find you're not getting exactly what you want, it's usually easy to cancel the feed, re-do the search criteria, and set up a new RSS feed.

If an RSS feed isn't giving you what you want, it is easy to change the search criteria.

Keep in mind that some sites require a login and password to access your RSS site criteria, so keep good notes as you explore the world of automated job alerts. It would be best to begin your experiments with RSS feeds by using websites devoted exclusively to jobs in the nonprofit sector.

Sites Oriented to the Nonprofit World

There are a number of helpful websites with search engines devoted specifically to the nonprofit world that can assist you in finding the grant-writing job that is right for you. Familiarize yourself with the most important sites and visit their job search services frequently. Because these websites are sponsored by organizations that serve the nonprofit world exclusively, they are likely to have more appropriate search categories for grant writing than other general job search engines. Also, they're likely to deliver job listings that otherwise might not come to your attention.

The Chronicle of Philanthropy (philanthropy.com)

The first site to visit for grant-writing jobs should be philanthropy.com. This site is maintained by *The Chronicle of Philanthropy*, a biweekly national newspaper devoted to issues of interest to fundraising professionals. Many colleges, schools, and nonprofit organizations advertise positions in *The Chronicle's* print edition and separately on its website. Every two weeks hundreds of new fundraising positions are listed in the print version of *The Chronicle*, and every day new positions are added to its website job listings.

> The *Chronicle of Philanthropy* is an indispensible source of information for grant writers.

It costs nothing to use the online search tools and services of philanthropy.com. Nevertheless, you should subscribe to the print version so that you are a regular reader of the country's main newspaper devoted to nonprofit management and resource development. A subscription to the print edition of *The Chronicle of Philanthropy* gives online access to back issues and a host of resources and research tools of use to the grant writer. These tools will be discussed in Chapter 4, "Research."

Both online and print position listings are paid for by advertisers and may not be caught by the meta-search engines of commercial job websites. It's often the case that a position advertised in *The Chronicle* will not appear elsewhere.

Start your first search at philanthropy.com by clicking Jobs. This will take you to the Philanthropy Careers search page. Here, you can browse job listings by position. The categories best suited for a grant writer are the categories Fundraising and Administrative. Searching the broad category Fundraising brings up a further refinement of position categories, including Grant Seeking. Click and in any week you will find anywhere from 75 to 150 jobs listed by date of posting, as shown in Figure 2.8.

Browsing positions, you will notice that they are located in communities across the country. The position listings span everything from internships and entry-level grant-writing jobs to executive positions for seasoned professionals.

> You can search philanthropy.com in a variety of ways.

It's also helpful to check the broad category Administrative, because it will reveal another subset of position categories. You won't find Grant Seeking among these, but if you try Sales and Marketing or Other Administrative, you're likely to find more listings for grant writers under those subcategories. It's important to try a variety of browse terms in a job search. Browsing through

Figure 2.8

Grant-writing job listings at philanthropy.com.

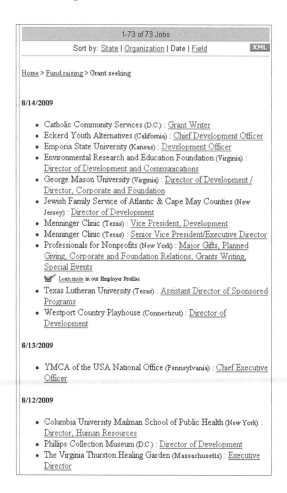

the philanthropy.com listings is perhaps the easiest and quickest way on the web to get a picture of the employment marketplace for professional grant writers.

Browsing nationwide openings will give you a helpful view of the big picture, but unless you are willing to relocate, you will eventually want to restrict your searches to a specific community or region. Try using the Search Jobs feature by entering "grant writing" in the keyword field placeholder, and entering your zip code. The default zip code search limits to listings within 60 miles of your zip code, but a drop-down enables you to expand to as many as 180 miles, as shown in Figure 2.9. Click Go and you will find a selection of listings that are within a geographical range tailored to your interest. You may find a very long list of positions. Practice sorting the list by position, field, organization, and relevance.

Figure 2.9

Geographical search at philanthropy.com.

Once you feel comfortable doing simple searches, it is time to explore advanced searches. To see how this works, set up an advanced search for the keyword "grant seeking" in the Positions category, and further restrict the Fields category to an area that interests you. You can also restrict your advanced search to one of five national regions or any one of the 50 states. It is a good idea to experiment with advanced searches a bit before setting up an RSS feed. Verify that your search criteria will produce some existing job listings before setting up automated alerts for future job listings.

Advanced searches allow you to retrieve only the jobs that are likely to interest you in places you want to live.

When you're ready to automate philanthropy.com to alert you to new grant-writing positions, do a search that you know works for you. When the results are shown, click the Create Search Agent button. The Create Search Agent page will open. Enter your email address and name the search to remind you of the selection criteria used. The frequency allows you to choose to have alerts sent once a week or daily as the site receives new listings. You can also choose between HTML and plain text as the email format of your alerts. Click Save This Agent, and you have automated your grant-writing job search. Philanthropy.com will send you an email for each agent you create. Click on a link in the message to activate your agent. It's that simple.

Most job seekers experiment with agents. Some like to be made aware of a broad range of new job listings, while others prefer to have more focus and control over what comes into their email inboxes. It is very easy to cancel an agent, so don't hesitate to experiment based on your knowledge after you have manually browsed and searched philanthropy.com.

The Chronicle of Higher Education (chronicle.com)

People who want to limit their grant-writing job searches to higher education should visit *The Chronicle of Higher Education's* website, chronicle.com. *The Chronicle of Higher Education* is a sister publication to *The Chronicle of Philanthropy*, and as you would expect, serves the higher education community exclusively. *The Chronicle of Philanthropy* grew out of *The Chronicle of Higher Education* as a separate publication when the demand from the nonprofit world became apparent.

The Chronicle of Higher Education is the premier marketplace for job listings in colleges and universities.

Some colleges and universities still prefer to advertise development positions in *The Chronicle of Higher Education*, which a generation ago was the only national biweekly regularly presenting fundraising and grant-writing job opportunities. While the overall search services are more limited than philanthropy.com, the focus is very specific. For example, some job searchers may be attracted to chronicle.com's ability to search exclusively among the nation's community colleges or specifically for jobs in higher education grants and contracts.

If a career in higher education is your first choice, you will want to subscribe to the *Chronicle of Higher Education*. Reading it regularly will keep you abreast of news as well as jobs.

Job searches are free on chronicle.com, but if you are at all interested in grant-writing jobs in research and higher education, you should definitely subscribe to the print version of *The Chronicle of Higher Education*. There are many tools useful to a grant writer available on the website that are available only to print subscribers.

The basic search criteria on chronicle.com include keywords, a position category with a drop-down basically to separate teaching positions from administrative positions, and a location category offering a drop-down of U.S. regions and the 50 states. A location alternative search by zip code offers a limitation drop-down from 10 to 150 miles (see Figure 2.10). At the time of writing, chronicle.com does not offer an RSS feed service based on job search criteria, but the publication is revamping its job site and will undoubtedly offer RSS feeds in the future.

Idealist.org

Idealist.org is a clearinghouse for nonprofit jobs and news from all over the world.

Idealist.org offers some features that are unique among the job search sites for nonprofit professionals. An international site maintained by the nonprofit Action Without Borders, it contains a vast number of grant-writing job listings—probably more than any other site devoted to the nonprofit world. The default search language is English, but you can also search in Spanish, French, and Portuguese.

Figure 2.10
*Grant-writing job
search at
chronicle.com.*

Idealist.org offers special searches for internships, which is a boon for inexperienced aspiring grant writers. Of the thousands of nonprofit internships listed, several hundred will typically include grant-writing duties. College students and recent graduates will find idealist.org internship listings to be a goldmine of opportunities to gain experience quickly. Many experienced development officers and sponsored research officers have begun their grant-writing careers as interns; it is a logical place to start.

Internships are posted on idealist.org, which sets it apart from many other sites.

However, idealist.org is also an important site for experienced grant writers. On any given day, approximately 5,000 nonprofit jobs are posted. Because idealist.org is international in scope and includes government as well as nonprofit jobs, you will probably not want to browse but instead go directly to the Find Jobs feature to limit your search by country, state, or city as shown in Figure 2.11. Keywords such as "grant writer" or predetermined job categories such as Grants Administration or Fundraising and Development are helpful to get your searches going.

Association of Fundraising Professionals (afpnet.org)

The Association of Fundraising Professionals sponsors the website afpnet.org, which is free to job seekers. Jobs that are not advertised elsewhere or picked up by meta-search engines will appear on afpnet.com. AFP is the premier national membership organization for professional fundraisers. This membership is loyal, and many administrators and executives choose to advertise only on afpnet.com when looking for new hires.

It is important to check out AFP because it contains listings not found elsewhere.

It's easy to use afpnet.org. Click on the Jobs feature to find Job Seekers, a search service shown in Figure 2.12. You can browse jobs by predetermined fundraising categories such as Grants, Foundation, and Marketing, to get an overview of the national scope and the types of nonprofits listing grant-writing openings on afpnet.org. You can do keyword searches on "grant writer" to narrow your searching, and you can further refine any search by predetermined categories such a job level (entry, internship, experienced). Searches can be refined to one or more U.S. states as well.

Once you have explored a search to your satisfaction, save it by clicking the Job Agent button to set up an RSS feed based on that search. The setup process is similar to that used by chronicle.com. Keep in mind you will need to set up a profile (a free login account) before you can save search criteria and create Job Agents on afpnet.org. Searching jobs manually requires no login account.

HigherEdJobs.com

HigherEdJobs is a useful website for grant writers interested in jobs in higher education and research. Many of the grant-writing jobs at HigherEdJobs are in sponsored research and

Figure 2.12
Afpnet.org.

sponsored program offices, making this yet another search site posting positions unlikely to be picked up by search engines or duplicated by other sites.

Advanced searches on HigherEdJobs offer a host of predetermined job categories, most of which are for teaching positions at colleges and universities. However, two categories found under Administrative Positions are very useful. Click on Development and Fundraising for general grant-writing jobs or Sponsored Programs, Grants and Contracts if you are interested in federal grant writing. Several options are offered for refining searches by state, region, and full-time or part-time. You can also limit your search to four-year or two-year institutions, as shown in Figure 2.13.

Searching HigherEdJobs is free, but in order to save your searches and set up a Job Agent for an RSS feed, you will need to create a free Job Seeker login account. Other features available free of charge to account holders include a tracking system for the account holder's applications and a place on the site to post a resume that only prospective employers can read.

HigherEdJobs is a good place to search for federal grant-writing positions.

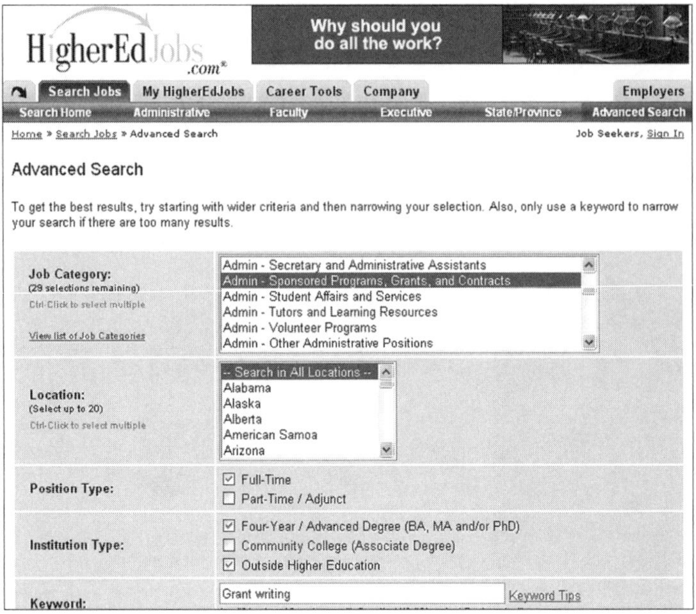

Figure 2.13
HigherEdJobs.com.

Foundation Center

The Foundation Center is the major source of all types of information about private foundations and private sector grantsmanship.

The Foundation Center is a national nonprofit service organization working for the benefit of grant seekers and grant makers alike. Since 1956, it has served as our country's clearinghouse for information about private foundations. For grant writers seeking information about jobs, the Foundation Center's Philanthropy News Digest service offers a Job Corner. Go to www.foundation-center.org/pnd/jobs to find it.

The prestige of the Foundation Center prompts many organizations to post their positions in the Job Corner.

The Job Corner offers free job listings to nonprofits, which attracts many organizations that would not otherwise post openings on a national site. Prospective nonprofit employers are also motivated to use the Job Corner because of the sterling reputation of the Foundation Center. Again, this is an important site that might have job listings that do not appear on other sites and are not picked up by commercial meta-search engines. Anyone looking for a grant-writing job should have this site bookmarked.

A simple keyword search on "grant writer" will pull open job listings from across the nation, as shown in Figure 2.14. Refining this search is easy. A Browse Jobs feature contains a set of drop-downs for organization type, job function, and states. You could, for example, choose Educational Institutions in the organization type drop-down, select Grant Writing in the job functions drop-down, and then further narrow your search by selecting just one state.

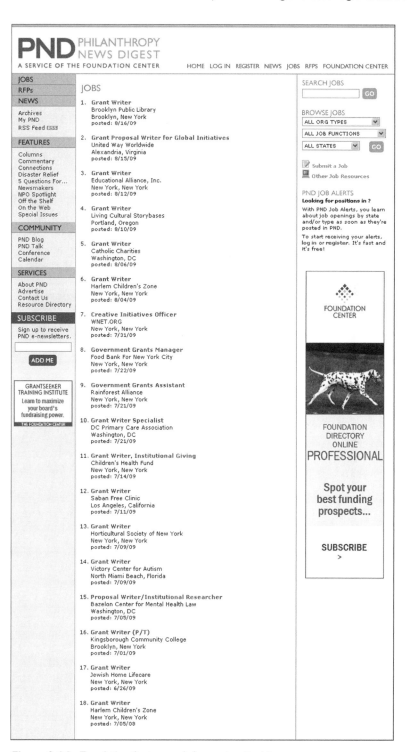

Figure 2.14 *Foundation Center search for grant-writer jobs.*

You will want to sign up for a free account at Philanthropy News Digest.

An RSS feed is available on the Job Corner once you sign up for a free account at Philanthropy News Digest (PND). When you sign up for an account you will be presented with a matrix of checkbox fields comprised of the predetermined categories in the search drop-downs. Simply sign in to your account and go to the PND Job Alerts section. Look through the Job State and Job Type checkboxes and select the categories you need as shown in Figure 2.15. Then log out and wait for new job listings to appear in your inbox.

Altering your Job Alerts criteria is as simple as logging in to your PND account and unchecking the boxes you have previously checked. Checking new checkboxes will change your alert criteria. There are a host of other services on this site, and any experienced grant writer will become familiar with most of them.

Figure 2.15
Profile category selection for automated Job Alerts on Foundation Center's Job Corner.

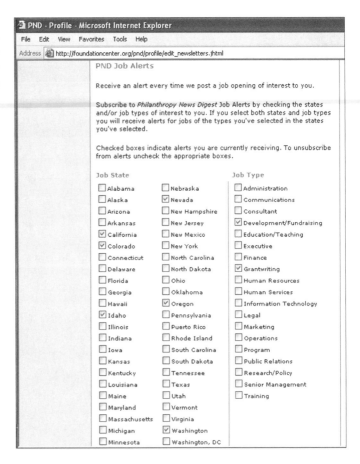

Create a Favorites Folder for Job Search Links

As you explore the many online search services available, it is a good idea to bookmark sites so that you have them at your fingertips with the click of a mouse. Literally hundreds of search engines are available online. If you explore just the services covered in this chapter, you will want to retain links to most if not all of them.

Create an Explorer Favorites folder called Nonprofit Jobs Only for the search services that exclusively deal with jobs at colleges, universities, schools, and nonprofit organizations. To get a handle on commercial online job search services, use Microsoft's search browser Bing. Go to Bing and search on "grant-writing jobs." Bing will return many thousands of hits on any given day, as shown in Figure 2.16. Doing this search through Bing will reveal many more search services and engines than you can possibly use.

An organized Favorites list will save time and ensure that your searching is comprehensive.

The first page or two of your Bing search will reveal all the major commercial meta-search engines with household names such as monster.com, indeed.com, and jobster.com. Browse and locate these search engines, and bookmark them in an Internet Explorer Favorites folder called Grant-Writing Job Engines so that you can refer to these search services easily. You can also refine your keywords and do additional Bing searches to look for sites that have a specific geographic or organizational focus.

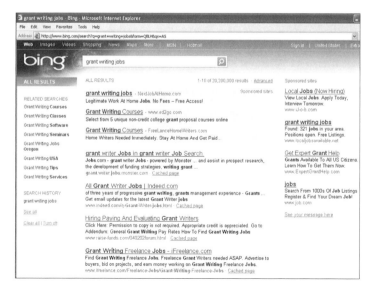

Figure 2.16
Bing search on grant-writing jobs.

Networking

Online search engines are indispensible, but you should also take care not to neglect more traditional job hunting methods. First and foremost is your own personal network. If you are acquainted with people who write grant proposals, talk to them. Sometimes new openings are in the works long before they are made public. It's possible to learn about a new position before it is even advertised if you talk to the right person.

Advances in technology have not replaced the need for personal contacts.

If you don't have any contacts in the grant-writing world, create your own network of advisors from scratch. Even if you do, it is wise to expand your network of professional acquaintances. There are a number of ways to go about this. First, if you are not already doing so, consider volunteering at a nonprofit organization. Volunteering will expose you to staff professionals in the nonprofit world who could be potential mentors and career advisors. You might attend fundraising and sponsored research conferences to broaden your knowledge and meet recruiters as well as professionals in the field.

If you don't already have contacts in the grant-writing world, begin to build a network.

National gatherings tend to be costly, but local and regional meetings are less so. An affordable option would be to attend local or regional workshops and events sponsored by the Foundation Center and targeted specifically for professionals engaged in grant writing. These events are usually offered free or at a minimal cost. Find out what is happening in your area and start attending and networking. More information about the Foundation Center and its regional affiliates is provided in Chapter 4.

Retaining or reviving contacts from your alma mater can be both enjoyable and helpful.

You should also be in contact with people at your alma mater, seeking out contacts who are working in grant-writing positions. If you volunteer in an annual fund campaign, the staff you deal with will probably not be involved in grant writing but they will know those at the institution who do work in that area. An interested alumnus is usually a welcome voice or face to college administrative staff.

Start out your networking with institutions and nonprofits you are connected to and expand from there. Building a personal network of nonprofit professionals will help to get your name out among people who at some point will be hiring a grant writer.

Applying for a Position

Once your job research is underway, the next step is to organize the job application process. Initially, every application should be approached with two important things in mind: what will you submit as documentation, and who are the people who will serve as your references? It is likely that your searches will result in a number of good prospects. It is important to approach each application individually so that when you are preparing an application, your attention is clearly focused on the specifics of a particular position.

> Approach every job application individually. Do not send every prospective employer exactly the same packet.

Because grant writers are always in demand, an experienced grant writer in a large urban area will typically find more than a handful of open positions at any given time. As you sort through job listings and begin to assemble applications, it's a good idea to put all the important factors you can collect about each job on a matrix as you go through the application process. You can create this matrix by hand on a writing tablet, or in an Excel spreadsheet or a Word table, as shown in the sample in Figure 2.17.

A matrix aids the decision-making process by giving an instant view of the pluses and minuses of each possible choice. If you have the good fortune to be offered more than one position, a matrix will help you to make a well-balanced decision at a time when rational thought is important.

> A matrix will enable you to compare jobs against the criteria that matter to you.

Some information on your matrix may not be available until you reach the interview stage, but much you might want to consider is public information—such as commuting distance and time, health insurance coverage, tuition benefits, or retirement benefits. If an advertisement doesn't include a salary range (and many of them don't), you will need to wait until the interview to learn about that. Other information not available until the interview stage could include physical conditions in the office, budget resources for travel and equipment, prospects for internal advancement, what prospective colleagues are like, and whether your expenses would be covered for professional meetings and conferences. Whatever you think is important from a personal or professional perspective should go on your matrix.

		SAMPLE MATRIX FOR TRACKING & EVALUATING MULTIPLE JOB APPLICATIONS					
	Salary	**Commute**	**Retirement**	**Health Ins.**	**Best things**	**Worst**
The University of the United States	$45k-60K Range	Mass transit; easy half hour; 20 minute drive with parking	TIAA-CREF 10% employer contribution	Immediate Full coverage, $25 co-payments, 20% employee contribution	+Big Office! +Easy commute +free tuition for grad school courses	-Competitive colleagues -Expectations too high for new multi-million $ grants
Civil Policy Association	$35K	Grueling drive one hour on freeway each way	No retirement plan until first 5 years served	Don't understand yet	+Very nice colleagues +They like me!	-LOW salary! -Cubicle among 12 people
Methodius College	Don't yet know	Not bad, 45 minute mass transit	TIAA-CREF 4% employer contribution, 4% required of employee	$10 co-payments, 25% employee contribution	+Free tuition for dependents +Nice, old fashioned office with window to college quadrangle	-Everything is old-fashioned. Will this lose its charm?
Denham Memorial Hospital	$50-60K range	Pretty bad, daily one hour on interstate; difficult parking	Private 401k with 6% employer contribution	Don't know yet	+Potential for quick salary increases	-Terrible commute
The Fr. Meger Academy	$45-55 range	Not bad, 30 minute drive by no jams or interstate	TIAA-CREF 3% employer contribution matched by 3% employee	Nicest plan around, no co-payments, no employee contribution	+Best Catholic school for my son in a six state radius. $17K/yr of free tuition	-Boys high school environment, could get tiring

Tips: Don't hesitate to expand a matrix to a wider format. You may want to include more objective categories about the qualities of each organization such as its financial situation or technology resources. Also, you may want to categorize some more subjective thoughts, such as what your prospects might be for promotion within the organization.

Figure 2.17 *Sample matrix for tracking and evaluating multiple job applications.*

Communicating with Your References

Simultaneous with your job opportunity research, you should be communicating with potential references. Never leave this until the last minute. Sending an application before you talk to your reference is not a good idea. For one thing, it creates the impression that you take your reference for granted; it is discourteous. It can also have unintended negative consequences. Perhaps your reference does not have a good relationship with your prospective employer or feels you are not an appropriate candidate.

Stay in close contact with your references.

Discussing your application with a reference before you send it off can yield important information. She may give valuable advice on what to include or exclude from your application materials. You should ask your references to review and criticize your resume for every application. In fact, you will want to ensure that all your references have a copy of the resume you are sending to a prospective employer and the position description of the job you are seeking. A well-informed reference is always the strongest reference.

The more your reference knows about you and the position you are applying for, the better advocate she can be.

Making a Good Impression

Having made a good impression on your references by discussing your application well in advance of submitting it, you will also want to make a good impression with your prospective employer. The first rule in making a good impression is to follow all instructions.

If an advertisement asks for a paper application to be sent to a human resources department, do not send your resume as an email attachment to someone in the department where the position will be filled. Follow instructions in the position announcement to the letter. If requested to file additional papers in the mail or online with a human resources department, be sure to follow through.

Follow the instructions in the job listing exactly. Not doing so sends the potential employer a very bad message.

Many job listings specify "no phone calls." Even when phone inquiries are not expressly forbidden, the applicant should never be the one to make the first call.

Crafting a Resume

The primary aim of a resume is to land an invitation for an interview. Here again, it's essential to make a good impression. There are a tremendous number of services and aids to help you write

Draft a resume that will make the reader eager to meet you.

a good resume. Good resume writing books are available in every Kinko's store as well as any conventional bookshop. A Bing search on "resume writing" will pull up a multitude of articles on resume writing tips as well as links to free resume writing templates, as shown in Figure 2.18.

Figure 2.18
A search on Microsoft's Bing will reveal thousands of links for resume writing tips.

Enlist friends and colleagues to critique your resume.

The best resume tips you can get will be from friends and acquaintances working in nonprofit organizations or higher education. These people understand the audience you are trying to impress. If you have three or four friends in nonprofits who can critique your resume, you will be hard pressed to find better advice. If they happen themselves to be engaged in writing grants or hiring grant writers, they can provide the critical perspective you need well before you fire off resumes.

Consider revising your resume for each application you submit. This does not mean, of course, that you can reinvent your education or job history each time you apply for a job. It does mean that you should emphasize talents and experience that are relevant to each application. A thorough review of the position description and application requirements is a must to ensure that all information required by a prospective employer is included. A one-page resume is ideal, but that is not always possible. When you need to go to a multi-page resume, make sure that someone who looks only at the first page will get all the salient information.

> A multi-page resume should be designed for readers who only look at the first page.

Two items are essential for a grant-writer's resume: educational background and employment or internship history. The education section should include not only degrees but also any training relevant to grant writing, and the employment section should emphasize any experiences you have had that can be connected to grant writing. Personal interests and volunteer work are secondary unless they have a bearing on your qualifications for the specific position you are applying for, in which case they could be very important. A long history of active involvement in animal welfare causes, for example, might send your resume to the top of a stack if the grant-writing position is at a nonprofit dedicated to animal welfare.

> Don't discount the importance of personal or volunteer experiences. They might provide the expertise that will make you a credible candidate for a grant-writing position.

Another item to consider placing on your resume is an offer of "writing samples available on request." Anything you have published or written for a class is yours to share. However, be aware that grant proposals written for another employer are confidential. See the discussion of writing samples later in this chapter.

Make sure your resume pleases the eye. A simple, easy-to-read design is best. If you are submitting a paper application, use a good laser printer and high-quality white paper. Experts in resume writing usually recommend using a standard font such as Arial or Times New Roman at 12 point. If your resume will be sent via email as an attached Word document, send the attachment to a friend first and ask her to print a copy for you. You will want to know what your resume looks like when printed by strangers. Sending a resume in a portable document format (pdf) is usually fine, but if the position announcement specifies a particular software, be sure to use it.

> Be sure that your resume not only reads well but looks good.

Writing Your Cover Letter

Whether the cover letter of your application is on paper or submitted online, it should be brief. A one-page business letter will suffice. The letter can begin with the simple statement, "I would like to be considered for the position of _____ in the _____ department at _____." You might add a sentence stating that you are enclosing or attaching a resume and that you look forward to hearing from your addressee. Writing an elaborate cover letter is unnecessary, unless the job listing has specified certain information that the cover letter should contain. Occasionally a prospective employer will request that cover letters explain the applicant's reasons for being interested in the position. In that case, include a few concise sentences that make your suitability for the position very clear. Still, the rule is to keep your cover letter brief.

Preparing for Interviews

A prospective employer should not hear your favorite music or an inside joke when leaving you a message on voicemail.

The immediate purpose of a job application is to get a job interview. If your application packet perks the reader's interest, you will receive an email message or a phone call to set up an interview. Interviews may be arranged by a human resources staffer or the person actually making the decision. Record a crisp, professional greeting, and check to see that your voicemail is working properly before you send out your first application.

While most organizations prefer to bring at least three candidates to the interview stage for consideration, it's not always the case that three qualified applicants turn up for grant-writing positions. However, assume that the situation is competitive and act accordingly. Even if you know yourself to be the only qualified candidate, you should still act as though the situation is competitive—because it is. They do not have to hire you.

When an interviewer asks what questions YOU have about the organization, display your knowledge—not your ignorance.

Once an interview is scheduled, move full steam ahead into researching the prospective employer. Now is the time to obtain and read annual reports, periodical publications, and any other public sources of information about your prospective employer. The objective of this research is to go into the interview knowing enough about the organization that you don't ask any questions that could be answered with publicly available information.

Interview Formats

Interviews can be conducted in a variety of different ways. Be prepared for all of them.

Interviewing situations can be organized by institutions or nonprofit organizations in a variety of ways. At some large organizations, a human resources officer will be responsible for organizing and setting up an interview. Sometimes the person actually making the hiring decision will set things up. You may meet with only one person, or you may meet with a dozen people. You should be prepared for a variety of interview formats because you may not know what to expect until you arrive for the interview.

Sometimes you will meet with just one person. In this case, the person doing the hiring has set up the interview and has probably not involved anyone else in planning it, so it is unlikely that anyone else will be involved in the hiring decision. Meeting with one person generally is less stressful than meeting with several people. If you get on well with the interviewer, this is the easiest type of interview to do. Of course, if you step off on the wrong foot, it can be the most difficult.

The round-robin interview is a more frequently used interview format. Typically, you will be called in first to meet with the primary interviewer, usually the person who will be making the final hiring decision. Then you will be sent to a series of appointments with other persons at the organization. Sometimes these are colleagues in the primary interviewer's department, and sometimes they are people elsewhere in the organization who have his trust. Eventually you will make it back to the primary interviewer for one last interview of the day. Meeting and interviewing with many people in the course of a day is exhausting. It is important to start with a high energy level and maintain it throughout the process. Plan to use whatever helps you maintain your energy, whether it be coffee, energy snacks, or taking a few deep breaths during the few private moments you will have during breaks in the interview schedule.

> If you have a round-robin interview, it is vital to keep your enthusiasm up—even when a succession of different people all ask you the same questions.

Another common interview format is the panel interview, often used when candidates are all asked identical questions and scored on their responses. This procedure establishes a paper trail for hiring decisions that can protect the organization from charges of favoritism or biased hiring practices. In this rather formal format, the candidate is brought in to a room to meet and interview with a group of people who ask questions in turn. You may have a brief private interview with the decision-maker before the group interview, in which case it is important when meeting with the group not to focus solely on the decision-maker you have already met. Practice forcing yourself to direct your responses to everyone in the room. If you know you will be facing a panel interview, do a mock run through with a group of friends and ask them to critique your eye contact and mannerisms. It is important, of course, to make eye contact with the person asking you a question, but you will need to pull other panel members in to connect with your response as well. Be sure to spread your enthusiasm for the job equally among the people in the room.

> Panel interviews ensure that the interview process is transparent and can be documented.

The aim of your interview is to get a job offer. You are not likely to be given an offer on the day of the interview. However, since unfilled grant-writing jobs translate into unwritten proposals, it is usually in the interest of the employer to fill a position quickly. Don't raise salary issues in an interview; leave that discussion for when the job is offered. However, if your primary interviewer brings up salary you must be prepared to respond. Salary averages at educational institutions and nonprofit organizations are published annually in *The Chronicle of Philanthropy* and *The Chronicle of Higher Education*. Salary averages are categorized by title and institutions by mission and size. You will get a sense of what is reasonable from these comparisons.

If at all possible, don't talk salary until you get an offer.

Writing Samples

A writing sample is sometimes requested of applicants in grant-writing position announcements. Even if this is not part of the application packet itself, you should anticipate being asked for samples at some point. It is important to do this part of the application and interview process well.

Your writing portfolio should showcase what you are capable of doing. It should "sell you" as a writer and an advocate for a cause.

If you are trying to "break into" grant writing, you will need a portfolio of writing samples that show you can communicate clearly using the conventions of standard written English. A run-on sentence, dangling modifier, or misspelled word can send your application straight to the circular file. Writing samples a newcomer might use include successful scholarship application essays, published articles or editorials, or any marketing pieces you might have written in the private sector. If you know an experienced grant writer, ask her for advice about what you might present as a writing sample and then have her review it.

Experienced writers should prepare a portfolio containing writing samples selected to appeal to a variety of employers. Sharing past grant proposals raises ethical issues. Successful federal grant proposals are fine to copy and share in any way when they become public documents. However, proposals prepared for private foundations and corporations are not public documents. If you wish to share them, you need permission. To demonstrate that you can do the work, you may want to assemble a portfolio that you can share for reading in your presence and take away when the interview is over.

90-Day Checklist for Finding and Securing a Grant-Writing Position

✓ Become thoroughly familiar with national job search engines such as monster.com and meta-search engines such as Simply Hired and Juju.

✓ Practice keyword searches that yield grant-writing job announcements.

✓ Subscribe to at least six job alert services or RSS feeds.

✓ Create a well-organized set of job-finding websites on your browser that you visit weekly.

✓ Develop a solid resume that has been critiqued by at least three reliable readers.

✓ Line up five references, all of whom know you well and can speak to your suitability for a grant-writing position.

✓ Assemble a portfolio of writing samples to showcase your skills.

✓ Conduct a mock interview with friends or colleagues you trust to give honest feedback on your performance.

✓ Join at least three professional organizations related to grant writing, fundraising, or nonprofit management.

✓ Attend at least three professional gatherings or conferences related to grant writing, fundraising, or nonprofit management.

✓ Add at least three grant writers to your professional network.

✓ Subscribe to *The Chronicle of Philanthropy* and read it faithfully.

✓ Submit applications for all of the positions that interest you.

Chapter 3

Expertise

- Knowledge of Your Subject Area
- Knowledge of Your Organization and Its Needs
- Identifying Needs

Unless you come to grant writing with a high level of subject area and organizational knowledge already in your toolbox, one of your first tasks will be to develop sufficient expertise to be able to be an effective advocate. You can't write about what you don't know. While it is unlikely that you will become an expert in 90 days, it is very possible in that span of time to develop a level of expertise that will serve you well as a beginning grant writer.

Three types of expertise are prerequisites for success as a grant writer: familiarity with the subject area, understanding of the organization and its needs, and basic information about funding sources. Familiarity with the subject area can usually be acquired through research, reading, and conversations with the right people. In order to write an effective grant for species preservation, for example, you would need a grasp of the science involved and the economic factors contributing to species endangerment.

An understanding of your organization and its needs may be more of a challenge to acquire, since it requires access to internal sources. However, it is critical. This chapter will give you a number of strategies for acquiring the type of information that leads to an understanding of an organization and its funding needs. Chapter 4 covers the search for funding resources and potential grants in great detail.

External funding should never drive your organization. Your organization's mission should drive your organization.

It is important not to put the cart before the horse. Your understanding of your funding needs must be in place before you begin to seek out funding sources. Never look around for funders and then try to develop a project or program based on funding opportunities. It is always counter-productive to allow external funding to drive the development of educational, research, and social programs or projects. The needs articulated to potential funders in grant proposals must be intrinsic to your organization and should always evolve from its mission in a logical, authentic way.

If you invent a need in order to capitalize on the availability of a pot of grant funds, it is usually very easy for grant makers to see through the ruse. Program staffers at grant-making entities typically review hundreds or perhaps even thousands of proposals and inquiries, and in the process they acquire considerable knowledge about the organizations whose work they support. They are likely to possess both subject area expertise and a deep understanding of what their organization is committed to funding. You can count on them already knowing quite a bit about your organization and your competitors for funding.

Grant makers set their priorities and then solicit proposals that fit what they want to accomplish. Your needs must fit their priorities. It's as simple as that.

Knowledge of Your Subject Area

Since you can assume that anyone reviewing a grant proposal will have some expertise on the subject of funding, as a grant writer you likewise will need a good working knowledge of the subject area. If you are professionally engaged in the subject you are writing about, your education and professional experience will serve you well. If not, you may need to become a "quick study" of the background knowledge and specialized vocabulary needed to communicate effectively about the subject.

Don't be intimidated. You don't have to be a veterinarian to write a compelling proposal to secure funding for an animal hospital. In fact, in terms of communicating with a lay audience it might be an advantage *not* to be a veterinarian. A good grant writer is able to speak in the authoritative voice of the expert but in a way that an ordinary reader can understand. Sometimes the experts themselves find it difficult to communicate with anyone other than experts.

Many grant proposal writers are not actually engaged in the research, teaching, medical, or social service project area that might be the subject of a grant proposal. Instead, these writers are brought in specifically for their ability to organize and communicate. They will work closely with project directors or teams who do possess a high level of subject area expertise, and based on this collaboration they will develop a proposal designed to communicate with a specific audience.

It is perhaps not surprising that many grant writers have a background in the liberal arts. Exposure to a wide range of disciplines is helpful, as is the capacity for independent learning that typifies those grounded in a traditional liberal arts curriculum. However, a liberal arts background is not by any means a prerequisite for success as a grant writer. So long as you have curiosity and a willingness to learn new things, you can develop subject expertise sufficient to write grant proposals.

Educational institutions and nonprofit organizations employ grant writers in development, sponsored research, or other offices to assist in developing proposals for grant support. These grant

---

Grant seekers are looking for funders interested in supporting their mission. Grant makers are looking for projects aligned with their priorities. The secret is to find a match.

Vast technical knowledge is not usually required in order to write grants. The ability to communicate the subject matter is essential.

A liberal arts background will serve the aspiring grant writer well.

Expertise can be acquired through curiosity and hard work.

writers may not have an educational background that would qualify them as experts on the subject of a proposal. Thousands of successful grant writers are engaged in such work. They are successful because they have the initiative and wherewithal to find out whatever they need to know.

Knowledge of Your Organization and Its Needs

Whatever the specific need addressed in a grant proposal, it is vital to articulate that need in the overall context of your institution or nonprofit organization. You must be able to place your grant ideas within the context of the whole. If you are new to your organization, this means that you will need to develop organizational expertise quickly.

Sources of Institutional Knowledge

Some grant proposals will require a significant amount of information on the background of your organization or institution. If you are new to your organization, seek out professionals who have been working there for years. If your organization is relatively new, you may be able to reach out to an executive officer or other professional involved in its formation. Knowledge of the informal history of the organization is invaluable. Seek out staff members who can give you their perspective. Ask permission to take notes, and send them a copy of your notes for review to ensure accuracy. Individuals who possess institutional knowledge will enable you to fill in gaps that you can't fill with recorded or published sources.

Long-time staffers can be a valuable source of institutional knowledge.

If historical information is needed for a proposal, you will want to read any and all published histories, chronologies, and other narratives that may be available. Collect as much of this type of information as you can early on for future reference. In addition, ask if you can read through office files. You can gain understanding and perspective reading through records that document an organization's history, particularly as it relates to successful and unsuccessful grant proposals.

Most colleges, universities, and schools have one or more published histories, and often a professional associated with the institution will function as its historian. If your institution has an archivist, get to know that person and her work early on in your new role as a grant writer.

Nonprofit organizations in social services tend to be preoccupied with present activities as opposed to documentation of their past, so if you work with such a nonprofit you may need to rely on oral history you collect yourself. Don't ignore volunteers in the search for information about your organization's past. Often volunteers have a longer association with a nonprofit than the professional staff you will encounter as new colleagues.

Read anything and everything that has been published about your institution or organization.

Long-Range Planning Processes

Planning and institutional review documents provide insight into the conceptual framework of an organization as well as detailed information about its past and vision for the future. These documents will be invaluable as you work on proposals. Often grant makers will want to have evidence showing where a proposed project fits in your organization's priorities. Typically, they will want to see a proposed need high among your organization's priorities and prominent in your long-range planning, and sometimes they will require documentation to back up claims made in a grant proposal.

Almost all educational institutions and most nonprofit organizations belong to one or more accrediting associations. Most universities belong to one of the six regional U.S. accrediting associations for overall institutional accreditation, while constituent colleges and departments in medicine, engineering, law, and other disciplines may belong to other accrediting organizations that specialize in a relevant professional activity. Nonprofits engaged in social welfare and health care also have accrediting organizations that are relevant for their membership.

Accrediting associations are authorized to assess and determine the legitimacy and status of an organization based on an external review process.

Build a list of all of your organization's association memberships. Track down any reports, reviews, and studies prepared by your organization for submission to an accreditation association. Accreditation associations require frequent internal long-range planning and external evaluation reviews performed by outside experts. The documentation of a formal accreditation review process will yield a great deal of helpful information, including an objective evaluation of your organization's strengths and weaknesses.

Accreditation documents provide detailed information related to established criteria.

Planning and evaluation documents will provide you with information about the past performance of your organization and its plans for the future. To place accreditation reviews in context, go to the website of the accrediting organization and look for the criteria of standards on which evaluation reviews are based. To give you an example of what you will find, Figure 3.1 shows the web page of the North Central Association of Colleges and Schools containing the federal laws and regulations that drive reviews conducted by agencies accredited by the United States Department of Education. You will see that these criteria cover most of the questions you might have about the quality of a college or university. Any recognized accrediting agency will have similar published criteria.

Information contained in an accreditation review will be recognized as valid and objective because it has been generated by a respected agency.

Accreditation studies and reviews are likely to be regarded as highly confidential, so you may need to earn the trust of the custodians of your organization's accreditation reports in order to see them. It is worth the effort, because these documents can provide invaluable background information for a grant writer. In addition, accreditation documentation (if it is positive) can serve as credible evidence of strength. A reference to an accreditation document will be viewed by a grant maker as more reliable and substantial than a reference to a document prepared internally.

Public or Media Relations Information

Another important source of institutional or organizational knowledge is your PR operation. It might be called public relations or media relations or community outreach. In a big organization, there might be a whole department dedicated to these functions. In higher education, it will be called university relations or college relations, and you can count on these offices to be staffed by experienced professionals. In a small nonprofit, public relations may occupy one line in one individual's job description. Whatever it is called and wherever it is housed, PR records are a goldmine of organizational information.

A review of your organization's PR efforts and successes will give you a panoramic snapshot of its relationship to the outside world.

Traditional print resources you should review include press kits, news releases, published articles, speeches, and newsletters. If your organization has the capacity to produce them, you may also find audio and video news releases. Publicity surrounding special events is helpful, as is any media coverage such events may generate. Letters sent to constituents or stakeholders will also help you to get a sense of how your organization relates to and is perceived by the external environment.

The Higher Learning Commission

Serving the common good by assuring and advancing the quality of higher learning.

A Commission of the
North Central Association
of Colleges and Schools

Search this site: [   ] | Search |

HLC Home
AQIP Home Page
Downloads
File Third-Party Comments

Assessment Academy
Peer Review Corps

About the Commission
Opportunities to Participate
Affiliated Institutions
Member Resources

Overview of Accreditation
Handbook of Accreditation
HLC Policy Information
Commission Rosters

Annual Meeting
Events / Meetings
Projects / Initiatives
Politics and Government

Publications
Staff Directory

Employment

Contact Us
Glossary
Search

Site Map
Links

▸HLC Home ▸ About the Commission ▸ Law & Regulations for Accrediting Agencies (USDOE)

Law & Regulations for Accrediting Agencies (USDOE)   Print   Refer a Friend

LAW AND REGULATIONS FOR ACCREDITING AGENCIES
RECOGNIZED
BY THE U.S. DEPARTMENT OF EDUCATION

U.S. CODE requires the following for recognized accrediting agencies:

the standards for accreditation of the agency or association assess the institution's -

(**A**) success with respect to student achievement in relation to the institution's mission, including, as appropriate, consideration of course completion, State licensing examinations, and job placement rates;

(**B**) curricula;

(**C**) faculty;

(**D**) facilities, equipment, and supplies;

(**E**) fiscal and administrative capacity as appropriate to the specified scale of operations;

(**F**) student support services;

(**G**) recruiting and admissions practices, academic calendars, catalogs, publications, grading and advertising;

(**H**) measures of program length and the objectives of the degrees or credentials offered;

(**I**) record of student complaints received by, or available to, the agency or association; and

(**J**) record of compliance with its program responsibilities under this subchapter and part C of subchapter I of chapter 34 of title 42 based on the most recent student loan default rate data provided by the Secretary,

Figure 3.1 *Criteria of standards for evaluating colleges and universities shown on the website of the North Central Association of Colleges and Schools.*

As you collect PR artifacts, build a multi-year calendar for your own reference, showing the chronology of events. A quick mastery of this type of information will enable you to come across as interested, informed, and committed to the organization.

Identifying Needs

You should have a clear understanding of your needs before you begin searching for external funding. If you are a new institutional grant writer working in a development or sponsored programs office, you will undoubtedly be given priorities that have already been established. If funding priorities are not spelled out for you, it will be necessary to pull together a profile of financial and descriptive information related to your organization's needs and priorities. You will use this information as a basis for searching out potential grant opportunities and strategizing with your colleagues about potential matches and approaches for grant applications. The object is to match your organization's needs with the interests and eligibility requirements of a grant maker (see Figure 3.2).

Grant writers need to establish good working relationships with both the finance people and the program people.

As you pull together a profile of your organization, talk with the financial officer for budgetary input and with program staff about the substance of the needs. If your organization has a relatively sophisticated strategic planning process in place, this may already have been done. In that case, study the strategic plan and then discuss it with the finance and program people.

Figure 3.2
Ultimately, your aim will be to match your organization's needs with a grant maker's stated interests and requirements of eligibility.

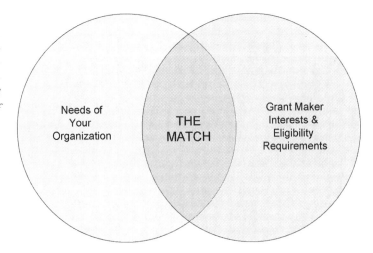

60

If your organization has planned for a capital campaign, then the organization and prioritization of needs will already be well documented. Capital campaign planning documents such as feasibility studies, campaign committee and subcommittee notes and minutes, and a draft or published case statement will give you a wealth of financial and programmatic information. If no such planning has taken place to formulate your organization's needs for external support, it will fall to you to develop this in cooperation with your organization's officers and other staff. Look on this as an opportunity to shine.

Don't be dismayed if your organization doesn't have a strategic plan for external support. You can be instrumental in developing one.

Restricted and Unrestricted Support

Financial information is required on some level for every grant proposal. To be a successful grant writer you need not be an MBA or a CPA, but you do need to understand clearly how every grant proposal you write fits into your organization's budget. At first, you may need to rely on a financial officer at your organization to assist you with the preparation of proposal budgets. As you become comfortable with the budget process, you may develop your own expertise to the point that you are more or less self-sufficient. New grant writers with little or no experience developing budgets find it useful and economical to take a course in nonprofit accounting at a community college. Keep in mind that even if you draft grant budgets yourself, it is essential for them to be reviewed and approved by your organization's financial officer well in advance of submission.

Grants are money: You need to be able to translate your organization's needs into dollars and cents.

Every nonprofit organization categorizes its annual budget in terms of restricted and unrestricted funds. Restricted funds can only be used for a specific purpose. These funds appear as specific line items in your organization's annual budget. When you look for a grant prospect, you may find a match by narrowing down your organization's needs to a specific restricted purpose. For example, a youth organization might seek support specifically for the purchase of sports equipment. A college might seek funding for a new physics laboratory. In either case, funding given for such a specific purpose can only be used for that specific purpose; it is *restricted funding*.

All grant funds have strings attached. Restricted grant funds have MULTIPLE strings attached very tightly.

Unrestricted funds are not designated for a specific purpose and can usually be expended with discretion. Unrestricted grant support can be used to further the overall goals and objectives of your organization. A youth organization or a college might use

Unrestricted grant support is given out of a grantor's commitment to the overall goals and objectives of the recipient organization. This type of commitment is rare.

unrestricted support to fund staff salaries and general operating expenses. Unrestricted support may be the most desirable type of support from the point of view of your board and executives, but it is not easily obtained. Unrestricted grants are rare; the majority of grant dollars awarded each year are restricted.

New Program and New Project Support

The nature of the grants culture is such that a good share of your applications for support will involve new program development. While it is true that occasionally you will find a corporation or a foundation that does make grants of unrestricted or general support, the overwhelming majority of grant making entities will require that your organization propose something new or innovative.

Grant makers are interested in funding programs that they consider to be new and innovative.

As a grant writer, you probably will not be designing and implementing new programs. However, you will be in a position to bring a fresh perspective to the executive and program staff in your organization, based on your knowledge of what grant makers are looking for and what they will consider to be new and innovative. No grant-making entity will be interested in simply maintaining the status quo. Don't expect, for example, that when the grant funding for a successful program runs out you will be able to interest a new grant maker in picking up where the last one left off.

The grants culture focuses on making relatively small grant "investments" in order to leverage significant and long-term change. The education and nonprofit cultures, on the other hand, are often preoccupied with survival. You may find yourself poised between opposing cultural values and norms, and it will be your job as a grant writer to structure a "win-win" for both sides.

If you can identify the passions that drive the commitment of program staff, you will know what is most likely to move the organization forward.

You may be able to come up with program development ideas by reviewing internal planning documents. If these are made available to you, this is a good place to start out. Also, make a point of getting to know your colleagues on a personal level and finding out what their passions are. It is their passions that will generate excitement and drive grant success. With luck and perseverance, you should be able to identify new program possibilities that will fit both the grant-making culture and the vision of your organization.

A good grant writer must understand, quantify, and articulate an organization's needs. In order to do this well, it is helpful to communicate directly with the executive decision makers and program staff of the organization about the potential for developing new and innovative project ideas. Draw them out. It may be that their wildest dreams have more funding potential than their day-to-day expectations. If you can tap into what the program people would do if money were no object, you may be on your way to developing the type of cutting-edge program that grant makers want to support.

Connecting with the vision of your organization's leaders can pave the way to the development of new and innovative programming.

90-Day Checklist for Developing Expertise

✓ Read enough about the subject area you will be supporting to discuss it intelligently.

✓ Develop your own personal glossary of vocabulary essential to the subject areas you will be supporting.

✓ Have at least three extended conversations with experts in the subject areas you will be supporting.

✓ Familiarize yourself with the history and development of your organization.

✓ Review your organization's strategic plan and accreditation documents.

✓ Collect several years' worth of PR artifacts such as press kits, news releases, published articles, and videos, and organize them chronologically.

✓ Develop working relationships with your organization's finance staff.

✓ Review your organization's budgets for the past five years and be able to discuss trends for restricted and unrestricted support over this period.

✓ Develop professional and personal relationships with program staff and become aware of what their passions are in terms of the mission of the organization.

✓ Identify or develop one or more program ideas that a grant maker would consider new and innovative.

✓ Be able to respond quickly and effectively to these questions: "What are your organization's current funding priorities? Why?"

Chapter 4

Research

- What Is Grants Research?
- Researching Foundation Support
- Finding IRS Form 990-PF
- Researching Corporate Support
- Grant-Seeking Resources
- Managing Grants Research
- Presenting Grants Research Internally

All grant writers need research skills. Some people seem to be born with a gift to do research, and spend their spare time collecting and organizing information in libraries or on the web. Others acquire research skills in school or college, often mentored by a special teacher, professor, or librarian.

Any determined person can acquire the basic skills of a good grants researcher. To start, all you need is curiosity and access to the Internet.

Not everyone has had the good fortune to work under the tutelage of a role model capable of seeking out information and using it systematically for great benefit. Fortunately, research skills can be acquired on your own. The ability to do good research is learned behavior. There are many resources available for developing research skills to support grant writing. Any reader of this book can learn enough about research resources and methods to get started as a grant writer.

Research skills are always required for grant-writing positions.

Figure 4.1 shows a position description for a senior grants writer. This is a typical grant-writing job description that lists a number of required functions, including proposal and report writing, interfacing with colleagues, organizing, recordkeeping, and developing internal procedures. The ability to conduct research is also included among the required skills.

This position description summarizes what a successful grant writer needs to be able to do. Although it is offered by a nonprofit membership association, the duties and responsibilities are similar to what you would encounter in a position for a development officer at a college, university, or social service agency.

Research underpins everything grant writers do.

Every single one of the skills associated with the required duties listed in this position description must be supported by good research. As a grant writer, your research will be the basis for selecting the corporations, foundations, and government agencies to which you will submit proposals. The content and organization of every proposal you write will be informed by your research. Any discussions you have about potential proposals with colleagues and volunteers will be backed up by research you have conducted beforehand. If you are successful with a proposal submission, everything you do to implement the grant successfully will be driven by your research. Even the tracking systems and procedures you develop will be guided by what you turn up in your research. In short, research is essential to all aspects and stages of the grant-writing process. Research is what enables you to be smart about what you do.

SAMPLE POSITION DESCRIPTION: GRANT WRITER

for immediate posting

Civil Policy
Association

Position Open: Grant Writer

Function and Scope:

Reporting to the Senior Vice President of Business Development, the Grant Writer will oversee and write proposals for grants submitted to corporations, foundations, industry groups and government agencies for support of programs of the Civil Policy Association. This new position will proactively and aggressively seek out corporate and foundation funding opportunities and generate new grant awards. The Grant Writer will conduct research and write successful grant proposals.

Major Duties and Responsibilities:

• Write grant proposals and status reports, ensuring high quality standards and meeting all deadlines.

• Express complex program activity in clear, convincing language, in writing and verbally, to motivate funders to support our work and deepen their relationship with our organization.

• Research new funding opportunities, connecting our organization's mission and potential funders.

• Maintain up-to-date records and files.

• Plan and maintain grants calendar of all funders.

• Develop and maintain formal procedures for proposal preparation and submission.

• Work with staff and volunteers of the Civil Policy Association to develop new proposals of support.

Figure 4.1 *Sample grant-writing position description.*

What Is Grants Research?

Research on prospective funders is called "prospect research." In small organizations, grant writers usually do their own prospect research.

Grants research is the systematic collection and analysis of information that will lead to the submission of a proposal. It is often called "prospect research" because this phrase captures the objective of this type of research, which is identification of grant makers that might award a grant to your organization. Grants research involves collecting information about prospective grant makers such as corporations, foundations, or government agencies.

Your prospect research should focus on finding a match between your organization's need for support and a grant-making entity's stated interest in that need. You will also need to establish that your organization is eligible to apply for support according to the published guidelines of the grant maker.

An efficient grant writer is able to find, store, and retrieve research about grant opportunities.

Generally, this information is available to the public. The grant-writer's task is to learn how to find it, how to store it so that information is retrievable when needed, and how to present it to colleagues in a way that is meaningful and useful.

The term "prospect research" encompasses the collection of information about any prospective donor to an organization. When development officers use this phrase, they are often referring to research on individuals. Most prospect research, in fact, is devoted to information about individuals, who usually comprise the majority of donors to an organization. This type of information is always treated with strict confidentiality, even though most of it is usually available in public sources.

Prospect research on corporations and foundations usually involves public information. Prospect research on individuals should be regarded as confidential, even when it is derived from public sources.

In grants research, the prospective donors are not individuals but rather are grant-making entities such as private foundations, companies, or government agencies. Most of the information that you will uncover about grant-making entities will be public information. Occasionally grants research involves collecting biographical information about individuals associated with a grant maker. For example, your organization's president or executive director might be meeting with a foundation president, and it will be your job to provide that individual with background information about the person she is meeting with. However, for the most part a grant writer is seeking institutional information about companies and foundations with the aim of making that all-important match between the interests of the grantor and the needs of the grantee.

The purpose of assembling research about potential grants and grant makers is to acquire enough information to determine whether it is worthwhile to develop a proposal to submit for funding. Grants research results are used to ensure that your organization is eligible for funding, that the grant maker is likely to be interested in your organization or a proposed project idea, and that your organization is fully capable of accepting the funding and utilizing a grant for its designated purpose.

> The purpose of grants research is to find grant makers likely to be interested in supporting the work of your organization.

Internal Research

Internal grants research will provide you with information about previous grants awarded to your organization. Grant makers that have supported your organization in the past should always be on your list of potential future supporters. Of course, this does not mean you will always be able to match a new need with a grant maker that has supported a previously proposed need or project. In fact, many foundations and corporations will support only one proposal from an organization at a time. If you currently have a grant from such a grant maker, you can't approach them again until the project has concluded. Nevertheless, you should be aware of your current funding and be considering what you might propose after the successful completion of your current grant.

> Always consider past supporters as potential future supporters.

If you are new to your organization, you might find that your predecessor has researched past funders and left such impeccable records that moving forward all you need to do is keep the information up-to-date. This is ideal, because it will save you considerable time. However, it is just as likely that your predecessor left little behind. You will need to do some backtracking even if you find the remnants of past research. In the event that you have nothing to work with, you will need to start from scratch.

If you have worked for your organization for some time and are now stepping into grant-writing responsibilities, find out whether anyone has done systematic research on previous grants to your organization. Here again, it will be necessary to do the research yourself if it has not been done.

Research on Past Support (Quantifiable Data)

Begin your internal grants research by assembling quantifiable data. The best-case scenario would be to receive a spreadsheet from your business officer showing all grants received by your

If your predecessor did not leave good records behind, you will need to pull together a record of past grant support.

organization over the past several years. However, such a spreadsheet may not be available. Be prepared to dig in and have a look at many spreadsheets and reports in order to pull this information into one complete and coherent record of past grants.

Create your own grant support spreadsheet so that you have the information in a format that you can easily analyze and frequently revisit, as shown in Figure 4.2. Essential pieces of information to pull together for your internal grants research include the name of the grantor, the date a grant was awarded, the dollar amount of the grant, the purpose of the grant, the name of a contact at the grant-making organization, the project director of the grant, and the grant writer.

Entering all past grant-support information into a spreadsheet will make it easy to sort and filter it.

Your finance officer will have all the financial information, but you will probably need to go elsewhere for the program and contact information you will need. Keeping all of this in a spreadsheet rather than a text document will enable you to sort and filter it later. As you add new grants received to your grant-support spreadsheet, you will find that it forms the basis of a valuable report that the officers of your organization should also be systematically reviewing. The grant-support spreadsheet will enable you to showcase your own productivity in the context of your organization's grant-support history.

Record of Past Support

Grantor	Year Awarded	Amount ($)	Purpose	Grantor Contact	Project Director	Grant Writer
Alphabet Foundation	2012	220,000	Capital campaign, endowment	E. Dawes	Jones	Glass
Dept. of Energy	2012	41,520	Conservation project	J. Billinngsley	Stanley	Brown
Tee Corp.Foundation	2012	75,000	Scholarships	R. Williams	Jones	Brown
Dept. of Justice	2012	21,900	Police education	L. Mason	Moronis	Brown
Zeta Foundation	2012	100,000	Scholarships	A. Goode	Jones	Glass
Theta Foundation	2012	250,000	Capital campaign, unrestricted	E. Kelly	Jones	Glass
AlphaFoundation	2012	7,000	Disability education program	I. Johnson	Bennettoon	Brown
Tee Company	2012	100,000	Research in pre-K education	R. Williams	Hanley	Brown
Forma Foundation	2012	13,224	Community outreach, internships	T. Taylor	Post	Brown
Best Company	2012	222,222	Summer internships	A. Wilder	Rosen, Harfield	Winters
Zoto Foundation	2012	38,972	New computer laboratory	J. Ferguson	Fontinalis	Church
Largest Corporation	2013	98,449	Market research education	S. Morton	George	Brown
Omega Foundation	2013	250,000	Unrestricted support	Z. Fitzgerald	President	Glass
Dept. of VA Affairs	2013	175,000	Outreach K-12 project	G., Lukoff	A. Morrow	Brown
Alphabet Foundation	2013	29,500	Photographic exhibit in gallery	E. Dawes	C. Handy	Peretti
Dept. of Interior	2013	73,200	Game warden education	K. Sweet	George	Brown
Chi Foundation	2013	75,000	History of Stamps exhibit	U. Igbo	Smith	Peretti
Hart Company	2014	125,500	New computer laboratory	H. Salim	Hansen	Church
Tee Company	2014	12,300	Conference on new designs	R. Williams	Grove	Peretti
Beta Foundation	2014	7,500	Outreach K-12 project	J. Tucker	Blumberger	Brown
Tee Corp.Foundation	2014	90,000	National gala	R. Williams	Kozenowski	Glass
Omicron Foundation	2014	25,000	Summer internships	S. Halvorsen	Rosen, Harfield,	Winters
Alphabet Foundation	2014	75,000	Conference on new designs	E. Dawes	Ferritti	Church
Bee Company	2014	101,456	Outreach K-12 project	N. Sachez	Washington	Brown
Omega Foundation	2014	9,300	Summer internships	Z. Fitzgerald	Rosen, Harfield	Winters

Figure 4.2 *Sample spreadsheet of past grant support.*

As you begin researching your organization's grants history, keep in mind that all organizations consider information about their donors to be confidential to some degree. While this confidentiality is pervasive when it comes to individual donors, some organizations are also reluctant to share information about all grants received with the general public. Initially, you should only be sharing your research with your superior and officers of the organization. You may be given permission to share your research with selected other staff.

All government grants are a matter of public record, and information about them is easily available on the Internet. For example, TAGGS (Tracking Accountability in Government Grants System) allows you to search government grants awarded by type or recipient. Although foundations are private entities, the grants they award can be found in their tax returns, which are open to public review and easily accessible through the Foundation Center's 990 Finder (http://foundationcenter.org/findfunders/990finder/). Corporations often make grants through a corporate foundation, and these records likewise are open to public review. Annual reports are another source of public information about grants awarded and received.

Research on Relationships (Qualitative Data)

Another important aspect of internal grants research involves piecing together information on relationships. People at your organization who were involved in preparing successful proposals or implementing the projects or programs that past grants have supported are an important potential source of qualitative data. As you learn the names of people associated with past grants, ask to meet with them. Find out their views on what has and has not been done well in the past, and solicit their advice on what needs to be accomplished. Most people enjoy being asked for advice, so this shouldn't be difficult. Ideally, you will establish good working relationships with key people who will serve as a resource for information that goes beyond quantifiable data.

In many cases, people who have worked on successful grant projects have maintained contact with the grant maker long after a grant has been completed. These people will be useful as you plan to return to the corporation or foundation for another grant. They will know about the relationship your organization has with the grant maker, and this knowledge will supplement what you

Consider donor information as confidential until you know otherwise.

Relationships are often the key to success for grant writers.

Seek the advice of colleagues to find out about your organization's relationships with former grant makers.

might find in paper or electronic files. Often the most important relationship information isn't recorded anywhere. Colleagues who have a history with a grant maker will know of any pitfalls or special circumstances that occurred with a past grant. For example, they may let you know who does and doesn't get along, sparing you the discomfort of finding out such things the hard way.

Make sure that your colleagues know that you are committed to help them to be successful.

A significant share of a grant writer's work involves managing relationships between key people at your organization and key people at a grant-making entity. As you begin your research inquiries with your new colleagues, make certain that your research and inquiries are aimed at helping them and that they understand that you are a facilitator. A more detailed discussion of managing relationships with colleagues who are involved in a proposal can be found in Chapter 5 (Managing Relationships).

Researching the Competition

If you know yourself but not your enemy, for every victory gained you will also suffer a defeat.
—*Sun Tzu, The Art of War*

In the course of collecting information about past grants to your organization, it would be wise also to begin doing research on grants awarded to your peer organizations. Keeping a close watch on the competition is always a good idea. It is surprising that many grant writers neglect this fertile ground of prospect research. Keeping track of competitive grants awarded to organizations that have comparable missions and goals will reveal prospective grant possibilities for your organization that you might not have otherwise identified.

Find out who you are competing against for funding.

Finding a list of comparable organizations and institutions is the first step. Most organizations belong to consortia, associations, or conferences that will give you a start at identifying competitive educational institutions or nonprofit organizations. This could turn out to be a list of 100 or 1,000 organizations, in which case you will need to refine it. If you are an aspiring grant writer in higher education, you will already know your athletic conference—and that may be a good start because it tends to be based on size and geographic location. Your chief academic officer will be able to tell you who the institution itself considers to be its top competitors. Most institutions maintain an informal list of competitors with which they compare themselves for faculty and staff salaries, enrollment, endowment, academic quality, and budget.

If you are starting out in a grant-writing position at a nonprofit organization, you will probably find that top administrators maintain an informal list of competitors used for comparisons of such things as membership, service delivery, educational program development, and staff salaries and benefits. Nonprofit executives and senior education administrators use these informal lists in discussions with their governing boards. Such lists might not be public knowledge even within the organization, but they will be invaluable to you as a way to winnow your list of competitors.

Once you have a reasonable list of competitive organizations (more than 10 but less than 100), start out collecting their annual gift and grant reports, donor lists, and other publications. Press releases found on competitors' websites are a source of information about grant awards. If you are diligent, you should find enough grant information to develop and maintain a grant support spreadsheet similar to the one in Figure 4.2. Be sure to update it regularly. Current information on your competitors' successes will be a valuable contribution to grant planning and strategy sessions with your colleagues.

Create a grant-support spreadsheet and update it regularly.

Researching Foundation Support

Philanthropic foundations form the backbone of the nonprofit sector, and it is essential that any aspiring grant writer understand the context of foundations in the search for private external funding. The foundation world has its own culture, and you will want to understand this culture. However, it is also vital to study each foundation you hope to approach as a unique, individual organization. Long before you submit a proposal to any foundation, you should have done sufficient research on that foundation to ensure that your proposal is welcome for review and consideration.

Foundations and the Public Good

Since the late 19th century, private charitable foundations have had a prominent leadership role in shaping American society as we know it. They have not only supported existing social and educational needs but have also helped to define problems and their solutions.

In the early 20th century, great American family fortunes gave rise to philanthropic giants like the Ford Foundation, the Rockefeller foundations, and the various Carnegie foundations. The financial power of these foundations enabled them at times to be a force equal to the public sector. The tradition of such organized philanthropy continues today as successful

The United States has a longstanding tradition of powerful private philanthropy.

entrepreneurs like Bill Gates and Warren Buffet turn their attention to serving the public good.

As a grant writer, you will be dedicating your efforts to matching the specific financial needs of your nonprofit organization with foundations that are likely to be interested in funding those needs. Very likely, you will be the point person in your organization charged with managing the relationships with foundations considered to be prospective sources of support.

Foundation funding is so important that most colleges, universities, and large nonprofits have staff dedicated solely to researching and writing proposals for foundations. In smaller organizations, writing proposals for foundations may be just one of a wide range of responsibilities assigned to a grant writer.

Grant writers often manage relationships with prospective funders.

Building Background Knowledge about Foundations

If the foundation world is new to you, a logical place to begin is simply to do some reading. A lot has been written about America's great philanthropists, and reading their stories will give you invaluable insights into the history of American philanthropy and how its culture has developed over the last hundred years or so. You can find biographies of America's great philanthropists in most large libraries. Many books have been written about the families of great fortunes, and the most prominent foundations have been the subject of books and articles.

Great 19th century fortunes gave rise to great philanthropic enterprises that have shaped our country's cultural landscape.

This foundation culture has given us great museums, parks, hospitals, and research centers. Our National Gallery of Art was given to the nation by Pittsburgh banker Andrew W. Mellon. Chicago's great Field Museum owes its existence to its first major benefactor, department store magnate Marshall Field. We would not have the glories of Colonial Williamsburg were it not for the vision and generosity of John D. Rockefeller, Jr. and his wife, Abby Aldrich Rockefeller.

Andrew Carnegie, whose name graces the portals of libraries across the country, also was responsible for establishing the first secure and attractive pension system for college and university professors. You may find that your own nonprofit pension plan can be traced directly to Andrew Carnegie's fortune. It is probable that the more you learn about American philanthropy, the more fascinated you will become. As a grant writer new to the foundation culture, you will be entering an interesting and exciting world.

Categorizing Foundations

There are many types of foundations. This means you will need a methodology and structure to guide your work. Foundations reflect the intentions, interests, and relative wealth of their donors, heirs, and trustees. Grant seekers often face eligibility restrictions based on these intentions and interests.

Foundations typically impose restrictions with respect to the programs or activities they will support based on interests determined by their donors or trustees. One foundation may restrict its grant making to biomedical education and research, for example. Another may restrict its support exclusively to private secondary education. Yet another may make grants only to organizations that provide programs for people with developmental disabilities. Your job is to know these interests and restrictions.

Foundations are formed to support specific causes and therefore place restrictions on what they will fund.

Foundations may also restrict their grant making based on factors such as geography or type of grantee. A foundation may make grants only within a specific region, state, or city. It may focus on a particular type of nonprofit, such as organizations that provide community services. Such a foundation would typically decline all proposals from schools and colleges, unless the project or need proposed was perceived as a community service. Other foundations may make their grants exclusively to institutions of higher education.

To be efficient in your foundation research, you will need to focus first on restrictions. If your organization is not eligible based on a foundation's restrictions, there is no point in investing the time to do detailed research.

It is important to take note of a foundation's restrictions because they define eligibility.

Depending on the grant-making year you are researching, you can count on between 80,000 and 100,000 private charitable foundations having awarded grants to nonprofit organizations and institutions. The total number of grant-making foundations varies from year to year. New foundations are created every day, and foundations are also closed down, often due to a founding donor's request that the foundation expend all its resources on grants by the end of a specified number of years.

Researching all existing foundations would be an overwhelming task. Your research will be manageable and productive if you develop a system of categorizing foundations. Categories and subcategories will enable you to winnow your list of research subjects and identify the foundations that are your organization's best prospects for support.

Categorize foundation prospects so that you can easily identify those that match your organization's needs.

National Foundations

National foundations are a good place to start because they can be easily researched. The phrase "national foundations" is not a legal description, so you are not likely to find it useful as a search term in online databases. National foundations are the largest foundations in the U.S., and most tend to place few if any geographical restrictions or limitations on their grant making. This makes them worth looking at, no matter where your organization is located.

Consult The Foundation Directory *to develop a list of foundations to focus on as possible sources of support for your organization.*

A list of the nation's largest foundations, in assets and grant dollars awarded, can be easily be found in the Foundation Center's print edition of *The Foundation Directory*, or in its online edition. The list of largest foundations varies in number depending on which year of the *Directory* you are consulting, but you are likely to encounter a list of 400 foundations. Using eligibility and program interests as your criteria, you should be able to develop a watch list of 25 to 50 foundations that you should study further.

Don't ever expect that a foundation will make an exception to their rules in order to accommodate your need.

If you find that according to a foundation's guidelines your organization is ineligible for any reason, put your research on hold. Foundations almost never make exceptions to their rules, which are normally set by the trustees of a foundation.

Regional and Local Foundations

Regional and local foundations limit their grant making to a specific area. Most states and many communities have at one time or another published their own foundation directories. These publications tend to be updated sporadically, so you may find out about one that is relevant to your research but out of print. It's worth tracking down such publications in local libraries or second-hand bookstores because even if they are not current, they will give you a place to start your research.

State and local foundation directories are an important source of grant possibilities restricted to a particular geographic area.

General searches for foundations by city and or state can quickly be done on the Foundation Center's website www.foundationcenter.org at no charge. Under the FIND FUNDERS tab, you will see a Foundation Finder feature with search boxes for the fields Name, State, and ZIP Code, as shown in Figure 4.3. If, for example, you would like to identify all the foundations in Minnesota, just open the State drop-down menu and select Minnesota, and click the SEARCH arrow.

Figure 4.3
The Foundation Center online FIND FUNDERS feature enables you to search for foundations by name, state, or ZIP code.

This simple and free search will reveal a list of all the foundations that have office addresses in Minnesota. You cannot assume that your organization is eligible for support simply because it is in Minnesota. That might seem likely, but do not make that assumption. Nor should you assume that because your organization is not in Minnesota, it is therefore not eligible for support.

One way to find specific information about geographical and other restrictions is to consult the publications of each foundation. A more efficient and systematic search can be done through the Foundation Center's *Foundation Directory Online*, which requires a modest but worthwhile subscription fee. As a subscriber, you will be able go beyond the three simple search criteria and include "Geographic Focus" in your search. You will also be able to narrow your searches by other criteria such as "Types of Support" and "Fields of Interest."

The Foundation Center's *Foundation Directory Online* is an indispensible resource for grant writers.

Family Foundations

Family foundations are usually small, and they tend to maintain a very low profile. They are driven by the interests of immediate family members. Often, family foundations do not publish an annual report or provide information on their grant-making interests beyond what is required by law. They may have very specific interests that may be impossible to determine from published sources. There are many thousands of these foundations.

Relationships are all-important when approaching a family foundation. Do not be discouraged by the size of a family foundation's assets. If you can discern a connection between your organization and the family (ideally someone on the foundation's board), you should regard that foundation as a potential grant prospect even if it is across the country and most of the grant making

Relationships are the key to securing grant support from family foundations.

appears to be random. A relatively small family foundation may have far more discretion than a large foundation that requires a more formal method for requesting and reviewing proposals. Your challenge as a grants researcher will be first to identify any family foundations that have a link to your organization and then to orchestrate the relationships in a way that will benefit both the family interests and the needs of your organization.

Community Foundations

It is practical to consider community foundations as a separate category, since they typically are not included in foundation grant resources. Technically, community foundations are not private charitable foundations like those previously discussed. They are classified as a public charity and generally raise more money for their endowment in a given year than they actually make in gifts and grants to nonprofits. Still, you should be aware of community foundations as they may be a potential source of grant support.

Don't ignore community foundations as a potential source of support.

Community foundations are created by local leaders as a means to pool private assets to benefit a specific community. In this sense, a community foundation functions as a local foundation. The assets of some of the oldest community foundations in the United States rival those of the country's largest private charitable foundations. Typically, a community foundation seeks donations from individuals to establish funds in perpetuity, and a portion of these funds is disbursed annually in the form of gifts and grants to local charities. Some donors restrict the giving of their funds to specific types of organizations or charitable work, while other donors create unrestricted funds.

Community foundations raise a lot of money each year by means of planned giving programs that offer individual donors a way to make a large gift of cash or securities and in return benefit from a substantial tax deduction. Community foundations may therefore be your competitors, but they are also prospective grant makers.

If you are a school, college, or other educational organization, you should be looking beyond your immediate community foundation. For example, funds held by a community foundation are frequently restricted to scholarships for needy local residents. If you have a high enrollment of students who fit the community foundation's definition of needy local residents, you may be eligible for grant support even though your organization itself is not "local" according to the community foundation's definition.

Community foundations are sometimes the rock that is unturned. Don't neglect to research the possibilities a community foundation might offer your organization.

Non-Grant-Making Foundations

Technically the word "foundation" has no special legal status. You may find many organizations with the word "foundation" in their name, even though they have neither the capacity nor the intention to award grants to nonprofit organizations. You will want to be able to distinguish these organizations from private charitable foundations, which by law must make grants every year.

Most public colleges and universities have a foundation. Many public school districts have a foundation. These are set up in order to take in gifts and grants in the same way that your own 501(c)(3) is set up to accept gifts and grants, and they do their own fundraising. Such foundations as these are your competitors in grant seeking.

Also, some organizations that are called "foundations," principally in the areas of causes and diseases, do their own fundraising but also make grants for research and projects. These organizations are basically engaged in re-granting gifts that were given to them. These foundations also are likely to be your competitors in the grant-seeking world. In some cases, these foundations have created endowments, and they use that income to make modest grants. This enables them to do new and innovative projects without actually having the research or program staff on their payroll.

Someone in your organization may have a research project or other program that could be funded by one of these foundations. If you are involved in areas such as cause advocacy, health care, or medical research, you will want to be aware of these foundations. They will not, however, constitute a major or consistent source of grant funds for your organization.

You may be in competition with community foundations for donor support while at the same time being potential beneficiaries of community foundation grant programs.

Be aware that just because an organization has the word "foundation" in their name, it does not mean they make grants.

Some foundations raise funds and also engage in limited grant making.

Nonprofit organizations engaged in cause or disease advocacy frequently carry the word "foundation" in their names, but they are not usually a potential source of major grant support.

Finding IRS Form 990-PF

The most valuable and revealing document about any grant-making foundation is IRS Form 990-PF, officially entitled "Return of Private Foundation or Section 4947 (a) (1) Nonexempt Charitable Trust Treated as a Private Foundation." The IRS Form 990-PF is the counterpart to the IRS Form 1040 filed by individuals each year. Like the 1040, the 990-PF must be filed annually. Unlike the 1040, the 990-PF is freely available as public information. In the case of some foundations, it may be the only place where you can find current information on the assets of the foundation, who runs the foundation, and grants awarded.

IRS Form 990-PF is the single-most valuable and revealing source of information about a grant-making foundation.

Many years ago, the phrase "available to the public" meant only that a foundation was obligated by law to give a copy of its 990-PF to any person who physically entered the foundation office and asked for a copy. You can still do that, but it is not common practice among grant seekers. A few decades ago, 990s were systematically put on microfiche and sold by the federal government. It could take many months to receive microfiche requests. A few regional libraries of the Foundation Center stocked these fiche files, as did a few public libraries in the country. Although this represented progress, microfiche was a physically difficult and time-consuming medium to work with, and researching on microfiche usually required travel.

Using the 990 Finder

The Foundation Center's website offers an online 990 Finder for locating copies of recent 990 returns.

Today, your role as a foundation grants researcher has been made easier. The Foundation Center's website offers an online "990 Finder," as shown in Figure 4.4. The 990 Finder enables you to search through recent filings and quickly locate a PDF copy of a foundation's 990-PF. You can even save this PDF to your computer or onto storage media such as a memory stick.

Take a look at the search options available in the 990 Finder depicted in Figure 4.4. Your first selection is comprised of three buttons offering options to search for IRS Form 990-PF, IRS Form 990, or both. You will want to select only 990-PF. The option to search on 990 will include any nonprofit organizations that filed IRS Form 990 Return of Organization Exempt from Income Tax, which is the tax return that charities, colleges, universities, and other nonprofits must file each year. Right now, you are interested only in foundations that make grants and file an IRS Form 990-PF.

Use the 990 Finder to restrict your searches to grant-making foundations only.

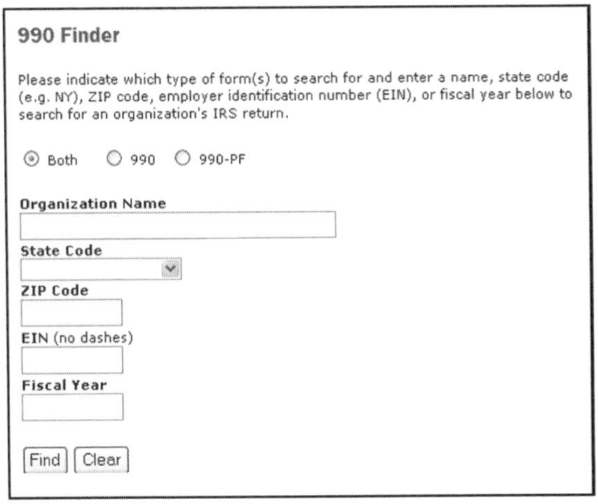

990 Finder

Please indicate which type of form(s) to search for and enter a name, state code (e.g. NY), ZIP code, employer identification number (EIN), or fiscal year below to search for an organization's IRS return.

◉ Both   ○ 990   ○ 990-PF

Organization Name

State Code

ZIP Code

EIN (no dashes)

Fiscal Year

[Find] [Clear]

Figure 4.4
Foundation Center website online 990 Finder.

Since right now you are looking only for private charitable foundations that make grants, you will want to change the 990 Finder default setting from Both to 990-PF. Later you may want to try searching for other nonprofits' 990s. If you work for a nonprofit, chances are your own organization's return can be found using the 990 button.

Next, take a look at the field placeholder under Organization Name. This is in effect a keyword search, so it won't always be necessary to know the exact legal name of a foundation to locate its 990-PF. For example, try entering "Rockefeller" in the Organization Name field placeholder, then click the 990 button, and then click the Find button. This will execute your search and 990 Finder will refresh and deliver an itemized list of more than 60 IRS Form 990s available to you for review. See Figure 4.5 for a partial list. You will see that about a dozen private grant-making foundations comprise the results of your search, with several years of returns for each foundation. Note, too, that the word "foundation" does not exist in the legal names of all the entities you have discovered. A grant-making private charitable foundation is not required by law to call itself a "foundation."

In the 990 Finder, enter the name of foundation in the Organizational Name field placeholder.

Other search options in the 990 Finder include State Code, which searches for the state of the address on the return. This search is an address of record search only, and it is not related to the stated geographic grant-making interests of a foundation.

You can also search for a 990 by ZIP Code and Fiscal Year of the return. While it is always good to look at several recent years of

FOUNDATION CENTER
Knowledge to build on.

Home   Profile   Search   Site Map   Ask
About Us   Locations   Newsletters   Press Room   P

Get Started   Find Funders   Gain Knowledge   View Events   Shop

FIND FUNDERS

990 Finder

Fact Finder
- Foundation Finder
- 990 Finder
- Trend Tracker

Identify Funding Sources
- Foundation Directory Online
- Corporate Giving Online
- Foundation Grants to Individuals Online
- Print and CD Funding Directories
- Requests for Proposals
- Associates Program

Related Tools
- Common Grant Application Forms
- Prospect Worksheets
- Grants Classification

Check Statistics
- Top Funders
- Grantmaker Stats
- Grants Stats

Local Resources
- Atlanta
- Cleveland
- New York
- San Francisco
- Washington, DC
- Cooperating Collections

Your query: (Organization Name: *rockefeller* , State: None Chosen , Zip: None Chosen , EIN: None Chosen , Fiscal Year: None Chosen)

67 documents matched. 67 documents displayed.

ORGANIZATION NAME	STATE	YEAR	TOTAL ASSETS	FORM	PAGES	EIN
Government W Rockefeller Charitable Corp.	AR	2004	$7,400,000	990PF	18	47-0863973
Laurance S Rockefeller Fund	DE	2006	$0	990PF	19	20-4192256
Rockefeller Archive Center	NY	2008	$0	990PF	16	20-8030810
Rockefeller Archive Center	NY	2007	$0	990PF	15	20-8030810
Rockefeller Brothers Fund, Inc.	NY	2007	$983,499,647	990PF	200	13-1760106
Rockefeller Brothers Fund, Inc.	NY	2006	$918,583,236	990PF	196	13-1760106
Rockefeller Brothers Fund, Inc.	NY	2005	$815,561,407	990PF	179	13-1760106
Rockefeller Brothers Fund, Inc.	NY	2004	$773,436,060	990PF	248	13-1760106
Rockefeller Brothers Fund, Inc.	NY	2003	$709,681,522	990PF	223	13-1760106
Rockefeller Brothers Fund, Inc.	NY	2002	$622,583,676	990PF	208	13-1760106
Rockefeller Brothers Fund, Inc.	NY	2001	$684,464,383	990PF	229	13-1760106
Rockefeller Charitable Corporation, Gov. W.	AR	2005	$7,400,090	990PF	14	47-0863973
Rockefeller Charitable Corporation, Governor Winthrop	AR	2008	$7,770,205	990PF	15	47-0863973
Rockefeller Charitable Corporation, Governor Winthrop	AR	2007	$777,052	990PF	15	47-0863973
Rockefeller Charitable Corporation, Governor Winthrop	AR	2006	$7,770,010	990PF	18	47-0863973
Rockefeller Charitable Trust, Laurance S.	NY	2007	$8,140	990PF	20	13-3618404

Figure 4.5 *Partial list of foundations with the name "Rockefeller" delivered by searching the Foundation Center's 990 Finder search service.*

giving for each foundation, there may be instances when you want to confine your search to a specific year. Keep in mind that IRS Form 990-PF covers the filing foundation's fiscal year, and that many foundations do not start their fiscal year on January 1. A foundation has 6 months to file after the fiscal year, so don't expect current year information to be available to you for analysis.

An additional EIN field placeholder allows for searches on a foundation's IRS Employee Identification Number. This is a number assigned to a foundation by the IRS and it is rarely used in searches. If you already know the EIN, chances are you already have a copy of the 990-PF. However, the EIN appears with each return in a list of search results. The EIN can be helpful if several foundations have similar names. No two foundations can have the same EIN. You can use combinations of any search options in 990 Finder to refine and target your searches, and it costs nothing for your search or for obtaining copies of IRS Form 990-PF.

Analyzing IRS Form 990-PF

Once you have downloaded a 990-PF, you may feel the urge to print it out right away so that you can read the fine print in hard copy. Resist this urge, because sometimes 990-PFs can be hundreds of pages long and you may really need only a few pages for your research. The printed form itself is only a few pages long, but some foundations attach lists as appendices to provide detailed information that does not fit in the small spaces on the form. Sometimes called "schedules," these appendices may contain the most important information a grant seeker is searching for. Browse through the PDF file just to get a sense of the length of the document, and then go back to page 1.

The IRS Form 990-PF can change slightly from year to year, depending on changes in reporting requirements. Do not assume that information contained on specific pages on the form will be consistent from year to year. What will remain consistent is that somewhere on every return, information can be found detailing all grants made by the foundation during the tax year. The name of the nonprofit receiving each grant will be included, as will the dollar amount of each grant. You can also count on finding any grant commitments made for future years shown in dollar

990 Finder allows you to search by state, fiscal year, or ZIP code.

Searching 990 Finder by EIN is possible only if you know the unique number assigned to a foundation by the IRS.

Read through a 990 return before printing because the document could be several hundred pages long.

Be aware that although the IRS Form 990-PF may change slightly from year to year, you can still count on finding essential information you need.

amounts along with the names of the nonprofits receiving the commitment. IRS 990-PF returns also consistently contain the names of foundation trustees and top staff persons and information about grant application procedures.

Page one of IRS 990-PF has changed very little over the years. Here is where you will find basic information such as the foundation's mailing address, total assets, and the total dollar amount of grants paid out for the tax year. See Figure 4.6 for an example of page one of IRS Form 990-PF. Knowing the market value of a foundation's assets at tax time will give you a reasonable sense of the foundation's total grant-making capacity. The law requires that a charitable foundation give away at least 5% of its assets every year, but some foundations actually make grants in excess of the 5% rule. Some make well over the 5% rule in annual grants and spend themselves out of existence. Still, the 5% of assets formula is a good way to estimate a foundation's overall potential grant making.

Page one of IRS 990-PF contains a foundation's mailing address, total assets, and the total dollar amount of grants paid out during the tax year.

Most of page one's information consists of dollar figures about investments and administrative expenses, none of which is very interesting to a grant writer. However, near the very bottom of page one of IRS Form 990-PF is a very important line called "Contributions, gifts, grants paid." This figure will be the total dollar amount of grants paid out in the tax year reported.

The 990-PF will tell you what top individuals in a foundation have received as compensation.

Moving beyond page one of IRS Form 990-PF, the next vital information revealed will be the people who actually run the foundation. In recent years, this information has been on page six, as shown in Figure 4.7. Midway down the page, you will find a section called "Part VIII Information about Officers, Directors, Trustees, Foundation Managers, High Paid Employees, and Contractors." Over the years, this heading and Roman numeral have remained consistent, but the section has not always been on page six. This section will list the name and title of anyone who is on the foundation's governing board, as well as any compensation provided to these individuals by the foundation.

The trustees listed in Part VIII are the people who ultimately decide whether to approve your proposal or not. Part VIII also has a section called "Compensation for the Five Highest-Paid Employees," which will display the names of the five top staff members of the foundation. You will see in Part VIII that there is very little room for a long list. If the foundation's board has more than four individuals, you may see a notation, "See Schedule 17," that serves as an appendix to the return. The actual number of the schedule will vary from one return to another, depending on how many "schedules" precede it in the return. Scroll through the return to the appropriate schedule to review the trustees of the foundation.

Further down IRS Form 990-PF in Part XV (Supplementary Information) you will find an area for grant application information, as shown in Figure 4.8. Very likely for many foundations you will have obtained this information from a foundation's own publications. However, if you are researching obscure, family, or small foundations, this section could be your only reliable source of information about application information such as deadlines for submission and the form in which applications are accepted.

The most important information to a grant seeker is actually quite far down in the 990-PF in a section called "Part XV Supplementary Information, 3, Grants and Contributions Paid During the Year or Approved for Future Payments," as shown in Figure 4.9. Here you will find a list of the dollar amount of every grant paid during the tax year along with the name of the recipient nonprofit organization and the purpose of the grant. You will find another list of grant amounts and their recipients if the foundation has approved grants for a future year but deferred the payment for the year of the tax return. If the foundation awards many grants during the course of a tax year, you will most likely see a reference directing you to another "schedule" where you will find the full list of grants by dollar and recipient.

The IRS Form 990-PF is the most important source you can consult for information about a private charitable foundation, but there many more print and online services and reference works available for research into grant opportunities.

Part VIII of IRS Form 990-PF lists names and titles of trustees. These are the people who have the authority to approve or reject a proposal.

Part XV (Supplementary Information) of the IRS Form 990-PF gives detailed information about how to apply for funding.

Part XV (Supplementary Information) of the IRS Form 990-PF lists all grants awarded during the tax year, as well as the purpose, dollar amount, and recipient of each grant.

Be prepared to search through the appended documents of an IRS 990-PF return for complete lists of grants awarded.

Form **990-PF**	**Return of Private Foundation** or Section 4947(a)(1) Nonexempt Charitable Trust Treated as a Private Foundation	OMB No. 1545-0052
Department of the Treasury Internal Revenue Service	**Note:** *The foundation may be able to use a copy of this return to satisfy state reporting requirements.*	2007

For calendar year 2007, or tax year beginning , 2007, and ending , 20

G Check all that apply: ☐ Initial return ☐ Final return ☐ Amended return ☐ Address change ☐ Name change

Use the IRS label. Otherwise, print or type. See Specific Instructions.	Name of foundation **NAME**	**A** Employer identification number
	Number and street (or P.O. box number if mail is not delivered to street address) Room/suite **ADDRESS**	**B** Telephone number (see page 10 of the instructions) ( )
	City or town, state, and ZIP code	**C** If exemption application is pending, check here ► ☐
		D 1. Foreign organizations, check here . . ► ☐

H Check type of organization: ☐ Section 501(c)(3) exempt private foundation
☐ Section 4947(a)(1) nonexempt charitable trust ☐ Other taxable private foundation

2. Foreign organizations meeting the 85% test, check here and attach computation . ► ☐

I Fair market value of all assets at end of year (*from Part II, col. (c), line 16*) ► $ **ASSETS**

J Accounting method: ☐ Cash ☐ Accrual
☐ Other (specify) ....
(*Part I, column (d) must be on cash basis.*)

E If private foundation status was terminated under section 507(b)(1)(A), check here . ► ☐

F If the foundation is in a 60-month termination under section 507(b)(1)(B), check here . ► ☐

Part I Analysis of Revenue and Expenses (*The total of amounts in columns (b), (c), and (d) may not necessarily equal the amounts in column (a) (see page 11 of the instructions).*)

		(a) Revenue and expenses per books	(b) Net investment income	(c) Adjusted net income	(d) Disbursements for charitable purposes (cash basis only)
Revenue	1 Contributions, gifts, grants, etc., received (attach schedule)				
	2 Check ► ☐ if the foundation is **not** required to attach Sch. B				
	3 Interest on savings and temporary cash investments				
	4 Dividends and interest from securities				
	5a Gross rents				
	b Net rental income or (loss) _____				
	6a Net gain or (loss) from sale of assets not on line 10				
	b Gross sales price for all assets on line 6a _____				
	7 Capital gain net income (from Part IV, line 2) . .				
	8 Net short-term capital gain				
	9 Income modifications				
	10a Gross sales less returns and allowances _____				
	b Less: Cost of goods sold .				
	c Gross profit or (loss) (attach schedule)				
	11 Other income (attach schedule)				
	12 **Total.** Add lines 1 through 11				
Operating and Administrative Expenses	13 Compensation of officers, directors, trustees, etc.				
	14 Other employee salaries and wages				
	15 Pension plans, employee benefits				
	16a Legal fees (attach schedule)				
	b Accounting fees (attach schedule)				
	c Other professional fees (attach schedule) . .				
	17 Interest				
	18 Taxes (attach schedule) (see page 14 of the instructions)				
	19 Depreciation (attach schedule) and depletion .				
	20 Occupancy				
	21 Travel, conferences, and meetings				
	22 Printing and publications				
	23 Other expenses (attach schedule)				
	24 **Total operating and administrative expenses.** Add lines 13 through 23				
	25 Contributions, gifts, grants paid	**GRANTS PAID**			
	26 **Total expenses and disbursements.** Add lines 24 and 25				
	27 Subtract line 26 from line 12:				
	a **Excess of revenue over expenses and disbursements**				
	b **Net investment income** (if negative, enter -0-)				
	c **Adjusted net income** (if negative, enter -0-) .				

For Privacy Act and Paperwork Reduction Act Notice, see page 30 of the instructions. Cat. No. 11289X Form **990-PF** (2007)

Figure 4.6 *Page 1 of IRS Form 990-PF contains important information about a foundation's total assets and the total amount paid out in grants during the year of the tax return.*

Part VII-B **Statements Regarding Activities for Which Form 4720 May Be Required** *(continued)*

5a During the year did the foundation pay or incur any amount to:

(1) Carry on propaganda, or otherwise attempt to influence legislation (section 4945(e))? . ☐ Yes ☐ No

(2) Influence the outcome of any specific public election (see section 4955); or to carry on, directly or indirectly, any voter registration drive? . . . . ☐ Yes ☐ No

(3) Provide a grant to an individual for travel, study, or other similar purposes? . . . . ☐ Yes ☐ No

(4) Provide a grant to an organization other than a charitable, etc., organization described in section 509(a)(1), (2), or (3), or section 4940(d)(2)? (see page 22 of the instructions) . . . ☐ Yes ☐ No

(5) Provide for any purpose other than religious, charitable, scientific, literary, or educational purposes, or for the prevention of cruelty to children or animals? . ☐ Yes ☐ No

b If any answer is "Yes" to 5a(1)–(5), did **any** of the transactions fail to qualify under the exceptions described in Regulations section 53.4945 or in a current notice regarding disaster assistance (see page 22 of the instructions)? | **5b**

Organizations relying on a current notice regarding disaster assistance check here . . . . . . ▶ ☐

c If the answer is "Yes" to question 5a(4), does the foundation claim exemption from the tax because it maintained expenditure responsibility for the grant? . . . . ☐ Yes ☐ No

If "Yes," attach the statement required by Regulations section 53.4945–5(d).

6a Did the foundation, during the year, receive any funds, directly or indirectly, to pay premiums on a personal benefit contract? . . . . ☐ Yes ☐ No

b Did the foundation, during the year, pay premiums, directly or indirectly, on a personal benefit contract? . . | **6b**

If you answered "Yes" to 6b, also file Form 8870.

7a At any time during the tax year, was the foundation a party to a prohibited tax shelter transaction? . ☐ Yes ☐ No

b If yes, did the foundation receive any proceeds or have any net income attributable to the transaction? . . . | **7b**

Part VIII **Information About Officers, Directors, Trustees, Foundation Managers, Highly Paid Employees, and Contractors**

1 List all officers, directors, trustees, foundation managers and their compensation (see page 23 of the instructions).

(a) Name and address	**(b)** Title, and average hours per week devoted to position	**(c)** Compensation **(If not paid, enter -0-)**	**(d)** Contributions to employee benefit plans and deferred compensation	**(e)** Expense account, other allowances
OFFICERS				

2 Compensation of five highest-paid employees (other than those included on line 1—see page 23 of the instructions). If none, enter "NONE."

(a) Name and address of each employee paid more than $50,000	**(b)** Title, and average hours per week devoted to position	**(c)** Compensation	**(d)** Contributions to employee benefit plans and deferred compensation	**(e)** Expense account, other allowances

Total number of other employees paid over $50,000 . . . . ▶ |

Form **990-PF** (2007)

Figure 4.7 *Page 6 of IRS Form 990-PF (Part VIII Information About Officers, Directors, Trustees, Foundation Managers, High Paid Employees, and Contractors) contains information about a foundation's board and top staff.*

Form 990-PF (2007)   Page **10**

| **Part XIV** | Private Operating Foundations (see page 27 of the instructions and Part VII-A, question 9) |

1a If the foundation has received a ruling or determination letter that it is a private operating
foundation, and the ruling is effective for 2007, enter the date of the ruling . . . . ▶
b Check box to indicate whether the foundation is a private operating foundation described in section ☐ 4942(j)(3) or ☐ 4942(j)(5)

	Tax year	Prior 3 years			(e) Total
	(a) 2007	(b) 2006	(c) 2005	(d) 2004	
2a Enter the lesser of the adjusted net income from Part I or the minimum investment return from Part X for each year listed					
b 85% of line 2a					
c Qualifying distributions from Part XII, line 4 for each year listed . .					
d Amounts included in line 2c not used directly for active conduct of exempt activities . .					
e Qualifying distributions made directly for active conduct of exempt activities. Subtract line 2d from line 2c . .					
3 Complete 3a, b, or c for the alternative test relied upon:					
a "Assets" alternative test—enter:					
(1) Value of all assets					
(2) Value of assets qualifying under section 4942(j)(3)(B)(i)					
b "Endowment" alternative test—enter ⅔ of minimum investment return shown in Part X, line 6 for each year listed . . .					
c "Support" alternative test—enter:					
(1) Total support other than gross investment income (interest, dividends, rents, payments on securities loans (section 512(a)(5)), or royalties) . . .					
(2) Support from general public and 5 or more exempt organizations as provided in section 4942(j)(3)(B)(iii) . . .					
(3) Largest amount of support from an exempt organization . . .					
(4) Gross investment income . . .					

| **Part XV** | Supplementary Information (Complete this part only if the foundation had $5,000 or more in assets at any time during the year—see page 28 of the instructions.) |

1 Information Regarding Foundation Managers:
a List any managers of the foundation who have contributed more than 2% of the total contributions received by the foundation before the close of any tax year (but only if they have contributed more than $5,000). (See section 507(d)(2).)

b List any managers of the foundation who own 10% or more of the stock of a corporation (or an equally large portion of the ownership of a partnership or other entity) of which the foundation has a 10% or greater interest.

2 Information Regarding Contribution, Grant, Gift, Loan, Scholarship, etc., Programs:

Check here ▶ ☐ if the foundation only makes contributions to preselected charitable organizations and does not accept unsolicited requests for funds. If the foundation makes gifts, grants, etc. (see page 28 of the instructions) to individuals or organizations under other conditions, complete items 2a, b, c, and d.

a The name, address, and telephone number of the person to whom applications should be addressed:

b The form in which applications should be submitted and information and materials they should include:

APPLICATION INFORMATION

c Any submission deadlines:

d Any restrictions or limitations on awards, such as by geographical areas, charitable fields, kinds of institutions, or other factors:

Form **990-PF** (2007)

Figure 4.8 *Page 10 of IRS Form 990-PF contains Part XV (Supplementary Information) offering information about grant application procedures and timelines.*

Part XV **Supplementary Information** (continued)

3   **Grants and Contributions Paid During the Year or Approved for Future Payment**

Recipient	If recipient is an individual, show any relationship to any foundation manager or substantial contributor	Foundation status of recipient	Purpose of grant or contribution	Amount
Name and address (home or business)				
a Paid during the year				

GRANTS PAID

Total . . . . ▶ **3a**

b Approved for future payment

FUTURE GRANTS

Total . . . . ▶ **3b**

Figure 4.9 *Page 11 of IRS Form 990-PF lists all grants awarded during the year of the return, including the amount, purpose, and recipient nonprofit organization.*

Foundation Publications

If a foundation has a website, read it thoroughly for information about funding interests, grant proposal guidelines, and restrictions in grant making.

Many foundations publish periodicals, guidelines, and reports on their grant-making activities. Try to collect everything published by the foundations on your watch list. Most publish their guidelines in print and also on their web page. Foundation guidelines will cite specific kinds of programs or nonprofit organizations that the foundation will and will not support, as shown in Figure 4.10. Often a foundation will prescribe a method of approach, such as requiring a letter of inquiry prior to considering a proposal.

Figure 4.10

Sample grant guidelines from a page of a major foundation's website.

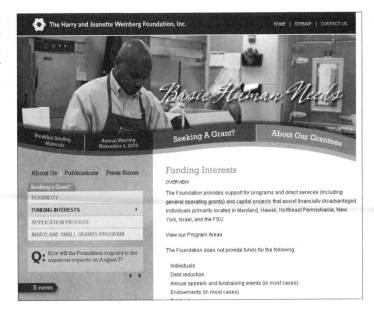

Grant seeking and grant making involve cycles and timelines. Scour the publications you collect for information about each foundation's grant-making calendar. Do not assume that you can send off proposals at your own convenience or that decisions about grant awards will be made quickly. In fact, foundations typically work in cycles during the year and make final decisions on proposals at trustee meetings. These meetings may be held quarterly or annually. A grant writer must always be thinking ahead when it comes to proposal submission, and anticipating a foundation's decision cycle is an important aspect of strategizing. Knowing the deadlines for submission is crucial.

As you review foundation publications, record all relevant application information. Assume that each foundation has its own distinct interests, eligibility requirements, and timeline. You will want to be able to access this information later.

If you have identified a foundation of interest, and you are unable to find grant guidelines on the web, send the foundation a simple one-line letter requesting current guidelines and application information. You can count on a timely reply. It is better to write than call. A cold telephone call can be perceived as intrusive, and this is a time when you do not want to be intrusive. Sometimes writing a foundation to request guidelines will put you on its mailing list for future updates, but don't count on it. Review your research regularly to make sure that the grant guidelines you have on file are current. Foundations can and do change their grant-making interests, application procedures, and even their locations.

Request foundation application information by mail rather than by telephone.

A great number of foundations with a national or international grant-making scope publish paper reports and periodicals. Try to obtain these publications even if you think you are ineligible, for reading them will keep you abreast of what is happening at the top levels of the foundation world. Subscribe to magazines published by national foundations. These publications are free, and they typically offer feature articles about social and educational issues of interest to anyone involved in grant seeking.

Trust Magazine, published three times a year by The Pew Charitable Trusts, is an excellent example of a periodical worthy of any grant-writer's attention. National foundations such as the Pew Charitable Trusts tend to support the latest innovations in social and public policy as well as education and social service delivery. Reading *Trust Magazine* is an enjoyable way to keep up to date on current concerns, issues, and trends in the nonprofit sector. Magazines published by national foundations usually contain articles of substance written by experts. Even though you may not be in a position to apply to a particular national foundation, reading its magazine may assist you in developing strategies and proposals for other funders. Many national foundations allow you to subscribe online. In the case of *Trust Magazine*, you can even order free back issues, as shown in Figure 4.11.

Many foundations publish magazines that are free to the public. An aspiring grant writer should subscribe to everything that might possibly yield useful information or advice.

Some foundations send out e-alerts or e-updates as a service to grant seekers and the press. The Ford Foundation offers such a service, as shown in the online subscription form in Figure 4.12. If you subscribe to several foundations' e-updates, you may want to create a "Foundations" folder in Outlook to save all your updates in one place. It costs nothing to subscribe to these online updates. In time, you will find that they are helpful in your research and strategy, and in electronic form they will be easy to share with colleagues collaborating with you on a grant proposal project.

If a foundation offers funding e-alerts, you will be able to subscribe online.

http://www.pewtrusts.org - Publications Request Form - The Pew Charitable Trusts - Microsoft Internet Explorer

File Edit View Favorites Tools Help

THE PEW CHARITABLE TRUSTS

Site Map Resource Library

Home Our Work Experts Events Program Investments Giving News R

TRUST MAGAZINE

Past Issues

Publications Request Form

Home / Trust Magazine / Publication Request Form

Publications Request Form

Please complete the form below.

Red Asterisks * indicate required information.

*Trust Magazine Issue

Trust Magazine, Summer 2009

Other Publication Title

* First Name

Tim

* Last Name

Kachinske

* E-mail Address

tim@methodiuscollege.edu

Example: name@company.com

* Confirm E-mail Address

methodiuscollege.edu

Figure 4.11
Online request form for back issues of a foundation's magazine.

FORD FOUNDATION

eUpdates

Receive announcements from the Ford Foundation

Fields in **bold** are required.

First Name Tim

Last Name Kachinske

E-mail Address tim@usuniversity.edu

Country United States of Amer

Choose one

I am a member of the press
If yes, the following fields are required

Outlet

Beat

I am a grantee
If yes, the following information is required

Organization

The University of the United States

Other
If yes, the following information is required

Affiliation Select One

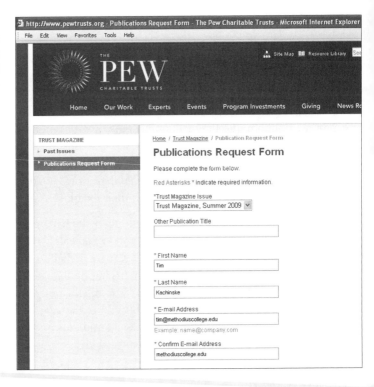

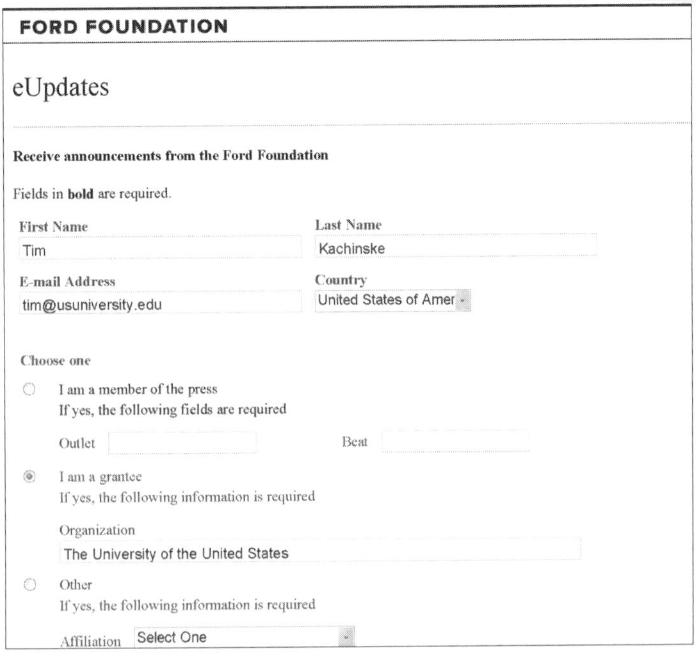

Figure 4.12
Online subscription form for e-updates on the Ford Foundation website.

Researching Corporate Support

Like foundations, corporations are an important source of grant support for educational institutions and the nonprofit sector. A grant writer just beginning to search for corporate grant opportunities will employ methods analogous to those used in foundation research. However, as you progress, you will find that the methodology, sources of information, and strategies that lead to corporate grant support differ significantly from those utilized for foundation support. Funding goals may be the same, but the motivation behind corporate support is usually grounded in the profit motive. Nevertheless, the purpose of a grant-writer's corporate research is to identify prospective funders and submit successful proposals for grant support.

Corporate grant makers provide significant support for the private sector.

The Culture of Corporate Philanthropy

A fundamental difference that distinguishes corporations from foundations in terms of their philanthropic activity is that the law does not require companies to give money to nonprofit organizations. Still, like foundations, corporations are an important source of grant support for the nonprofit sector. Knowing how this has come to be will help you to understand the nature of corporate philanthropy and improve your success at securing corporate grant support.

Foundations are required by law to make grants. Corporations are under no obligation to make grants; they do it for their own reasons.

Early manifestations of corporate grant making were often efforts of "enlightened" corporate self-interest related to the benefit of a company's workforce. For example, in the first half of the 20th century, the great iron mining companies in northern Minnesota built magnificent schools on the Iron Range for the children of their huge, multi-national immigrant workforce. In Duluth, the U.S. Steel Corporation built an entire town for their workers. Morgan Park was a planned community, complete with steel-reinforced concrete housing, community centers, and public buildings. These amenities were available only to employees of U.S. Steel's massive concrete and steel production plants.

Today, a living example of this tradition of corporate philanthropy can be seen in Columbus, Indiana. Over the past 50 years, corporate philanthropies of the Cummins Engine Company have directed and funded a remarkable architecture grant program in Columbus. This small town in Indiana, site of the Cummins Engine Company's corporate headquarters, boasts buildings designed by giants of modern architecture such as Eliel Saarinen, Eero Saarinen, Richard Meier, Cesar Pelli, and I.M. Pei. No other town with a population under 40,000 has such a collection of 20th century architecture.

In order to be successful at writing grants for corporate support, it is essential to understand the corporation's motive for giving.

As a new grant writer researching corporate grant opportunities, you will dedicate your efforts toward matching the specific needs of your organization with companies that are likely to be interested in making grants in support of those needs. You might even be the point person in your organization charged with coordinating relationships with corporations. In order to be successful in this role, you will need to understand the motivation behind the corporate giving programs you have identified as potential sources of support.

Universities and large nonprofit organizations typically separate corporate and foundation relations into separate dedicated positions. Sometimes corporate and foundation relations are separated into multi-person departments that coordinate but do not do the same work. However, more often than not the roles are combined into one position. In a small organization, a grant writer may be the person who fulfills both corporate and foundation grant-seeking functions.

Understanding Corporate Philanthropy and Grant Making

Corporate giving programs typically support corporate interests.

Like foundations, corporations designate specific areas of interest for grant making. Unlike foundations, corporations are not always looking to fund programs that are new and innovative. Instead, their intent is often to make grants that support the corporation and its surrounding community in a direct and tangible way.

You may be able to find a corporation that gives unrestricted grant support to categories of organizations you happen to fit. More often than not, a corporation will focus on a specific area of program support. For example, over the past 20 years the Exxon Corporation has supported mathematics education in a variety of ways. Outdoor retail giant REI makes grants to support environmental stewardship. American Express gives grants to support projects designed to preserve tourism sites.

If you have noticed a link between what these companies support and the type of business activities they are engaged in, you are on your way to understanding corporate philanthropy and grant making.

Building Your Knowledge about Corporations

As you begin your search for corporate grant opportunities, it will be helpful to do some reading. If you are not yet a reader of *The Wall Street Journal*, get a subscription and read it front to back every day. It is a good idea also to subscribe to *Business Week*, *Fortune*, and *Forbes*. Read an assortment of national business periodicals religiously for a period of several months and you will have a good start on understanding the corporate world.

Business periodicals should become part of your required background reading in the search for corporate grant opportunities. *Fortune* and *Forbes* will give you a handle on the country's most important public and private companies. If you have online subscriptions to these periodicals, you will be able to download lists and articles as you work on your corporate research. There are many other good business magazines. You should be aware of them and consistently read the ones you find to be relevant to your work.

Reading national business periodicals regularly will give you the background information you need to understand the corporate environment.

It is important to keep up with general reading on current business affairs so that eventually you will be able to carry on conversations with corporate people on their own terms. There will be times when you may be one of the few persons, or perhaps the only person, in your nonprofit organization who can do this, which will make you an invaluable resource to your colleagues.

Local and regional business journals, usually published as tabloid weeklies or monthlies, are also essential reading because they will bring you up to speed on the immediate business environment surrounding your organization. These journals often sponsor breakfasts or luncheons on business issues of particular interest to area executives. Someone from your nonprofit should aim to begin attending such events in order to build relationships in the local business community. Business journals publish lists, such as the "25 largest manufacturers" in your area, that will help you in your research efforts and in your understanding of the environment.

Reading local and regional business periodicals will put you in touch with your local business community.

If at all possible, read at least one "business book" a month. Autobiographies and biographies of industry leaders are a good place to start. Books on business management strategies and organization are also helpful. If you work in an area where particular industries are concentrated, such as paper manufacturing or automobile manufacturing, it would behoove you to bone up on those local industries.

You don't need to have an MBA to write successful grants for corporations; you just need to understand the corporate environment.

This is not to suggest that a crash MBA course is needed in order to be successful at grant writing for corporations. However, a personal reading program will help you to understand the culture of business and be successful at your job. An English major who reads the right stuff can be very successful in developing corporate grant opportunities and writing successful proposals.

Identifying Corporations for Research

If you are starting from scratch as a grant writer searching for corporate grant opportunities, it makes sense to begin with categories as the basis for identifying companies worthy of further research. Building lists is an ongoing part of the search for grant support. Consider starting with a list of all the companies you can identify that have in some way or another supported your organization in the past.

Knowing the companies that support your competitors is an important first step in securing their support for your organization.

It is helpful also to build a list of companies that support your competitors in the nonprofit sector. You will want to examine your competitors' newsletters, annual reports, and magazines for any donor lists or stories that recognize corporate support. Keep your colleagues informed about your interest in competing organizations because they will often be able to pass on publications or first-hand stories that wouldn't otherwise come to your desk.

Before developing a national or regional list of companies worth looking at for grant support, look to the companies within commuting distance of your organization. Begin by checking out your local business journal. American City Business Journals publishes more than 50 weekly local business newspapers, each of which publishes a weekly list of the 25-100 largest local businesses based on categories of size, audience, or business activity. Each city's weekly also publishes an annual *Book of Lists*, and this information is readily available online for subscribers. See Figure 4.13 for a sampling of lists on the publisher's website www.bizjournals.com . The sample displays the Book of Lists for Milwaukee, showing 78 business lists and more than 2,300 business contacts. Each city or region will have different totals, but you can count on the Book of Lists as being the most accessible information for the newcomer beginning to research local or regional companies.

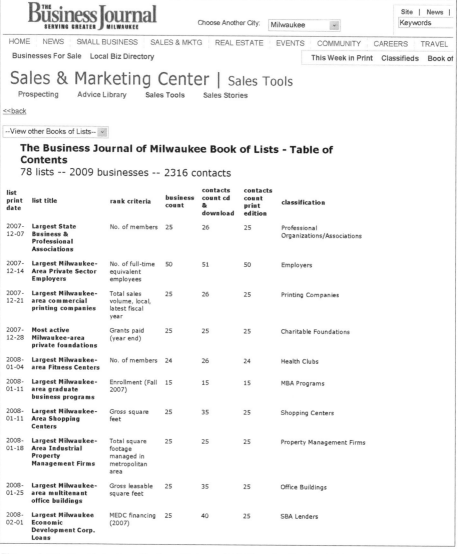

Figure 4.13 *Sample business list from Bizjournals' Milwaukee* Book of Lists.

Researching Corporate Foundations

Once you have identified companies to research, finding that all-important match between your needs and a corporation's funding priorities will be your next step in finding grant opportunities.

Corporate founda-
tions are created as
a vehicle for making
grant awards.

Corporate foundations are an excellent place to find important information on corporate grant programs. Not all corporations have a foundation. In fact, there are less than 3,000 corporate foundations out of a total of 80,000 foundations. Nevertheless, these corporate foundations are significant and worth researching because almost 30% of all corporate contributions are given through corporate foundations.

Corporate foundations file the same annual tax return as private foundations, the IRS Form 990-PF. The 990 PF for a corporate foundation will yield exactly the same important information that you would find for a private charitable foundation. See the sections "Finding IRS Form 990" and "Analyzing IRS Form 990-PF" earlier in this chapter.

A well-endowed
corporate founda-
tion will normally
be able to maintain
giving levels regard-
less of whether or
not the company
has made a profit in
a given year.

Like private charitable foundations, a corporate foundation may have significant assets in the form of an endowment. Such endowments are usually comprised of real estate or securities. At the end of the year, all assets are added up and the corporate foundation is required to spend at least 5% of the assets on grants and administration of the foundation. Corporate foundations with endowments are dependent on their investment market, and in years of good return, they can increase their grant award dollars. An endowment can enable a company to maintain corporate giving even when the company itself has had a difficult financial year.

Other corporate foundations are pass-through foundations, which means that each year the company transfers funds from the corporation to its foundation. These funds, less any administrative expenses, comprise the total grant dollars available in the forthcoming year. The amount of funds transferred will depend on the company's financial success in the previous year. Some companies will maintain a foundation with an endowment and also transfer funds in good years, thereby maximizing the ways in which their foundation can receive funds.

The giving pro-
grams of corpo-
rate pass-through
foundations tend
to vary depending
on profitability.

You can get a good sense of potential future grant dollars available to a corporate foundation based on the previous year's income and grants awarded. All of this information is available on the 990.

If your corporate prospect has a corporate foundation, then that would be a good place start your research. The dollar grant amounts on a 990 are cash grants, whereas in corporate publicity about corporate support the dollar amounts noted could include in-kind contributions as well. Many corporations have giving programs that extend well beyond the grants of cash awarded by their foundations, including contributions from marketing budgets, services, materials, and equipment in total amounts well beyond the foundation's annual total grant awards.

Some corporate foundations have an endowment that provides additional income for their corporate giving program. Other corporate foundations are set up to receive funds transferred from the company and passed through the foundation to grant recipients.

Researching Corporate Giving Programs

Sometimes large corporations have a dedicated corporate giving staff that maintains web pages and publishes reports and magazines detailing a corporate giving program and grant-making activities. It's important to collect and update this information. No two corporations will have an identical corporate grant program. As you do your research, you will be collecting the information needed to determine whether your organization is eligible for funding and of possible interest to the company.

Procedures for contact and applications will be a routine item to collect in your research on corporations. In some cases, you will find that the awards of corporate grants are centralized in one office. Other large corporations with facilities and offices across the country may centralize some basic information about corporate giving in guidelines and other publications, but require that all steps taken toward submitting a proposal take place at a local facility or office level. Decisions about grant proposals would then be made at the local level.

The procedures for applying for corporate funding vary depending on a variety of factors, including size and organizational structure.

Often in medium-sized companies a corporate giving program, including the administration of a corporate foundation, is assigned to an office that also has other significant corporate responsibilities. Most often these offices are human relations or public relations.

Knowing where a corporate giving program is housed can be crucial to your strategy, because it will give you important clues regarding corporate motivation. For example, a program administered out of human resources may be designed to ensure continued availability of a highly trained workforce able to meet the company's hiring needs. If you are working for a college or university that has a reputation for turning out first-rate engineering graduates, your institution may be of interest to the company. A program administered out of a public relations office may exist to generate publicity and goodwill. With this knowledge you will make certain that your approach for funding includes substantial "incentives" in terms of such things as press coverage, signage, and public acknowledgement. You may even include these things in your proposal.

The smart grant writer will pay close attention to where a corporate giving program is housed. A program run out of the CEO's office is likely to be critical to the organization's strategic mission.

Occasionally a corporate grant program will be administered out of a company's executive offices. In such cases, corporate grants represent a relatively small responsibility mixed in with the myriad of other executive functions. When executives involve themselves personally in a corporate grants program, you can assume that it is very closely tied to the company's overall strategy. This placement puts corporate grant making in close proximity to the board. If anyone at your organization has connections to the board, they may be able to assist you as you develop a proposal.

Grant-Seeking Resources

The Foundation Center offers far more than the information on private foundation tax returns covered earlier in this chapter. Whether you are seeking foundation grant opportunities, or corporate grant opportunities, or both, you should become familiar with all aspects of the Foundation Center's web resources.

Major research libraries of interest to grant writers are located in New York, Washington DC, and Chicago.

The New York and Washington DC Foundation Centers have substantial research libraries. The Donors Forum of Chicago is another outstanding reference library. Keep them in mind when you travel these cities for other reasons, and work in a visit if at all possible.

Today there are regional Foundation Centers in a number of other cities that also offer a reference library and database access to all visitors. These centers also offer free or inexpensive training seminars. If you are new to seeking foundation or corporate grants, you should look up your closest Foundation Center office, get on their mailing list (both snail mail and email), and visit them at your earliest opportunity.

Most of your resources for information on corporate grant programs will be online. The one indispensable reference book you will want to purchase is the Foundation Center's annual *National Directory of Corporate Giving*, which is the most comprehensive directory in print. You may prefer to subscribe to the online version called *Corporate Giving Online* to take advantage of the Foundation Center's continuous updating of this information. Both resources will give you information on nearly 4,000 corporate foundations and corporate giving programs as well as details on more than 250,000 recent corporate grants.

The National Directory of Corporate Giving and Corporate Giving Online are vital sources for corporate grant information.

Conferences and Workshops

It is important to develop your grant-writing frame of reference beyond the books and online services you use in your day-to-day research. Workshops, seminars, and conferences especially designed for grant writers will constitute an important part of your training. Typically instructors and speakers are either seasoned grant writers or representatives from grant-making foundations, corporations, or agencies. There is obvious value in the substance of such presentations, whether it is an expert's view on new methods or services, or current information about grant-making programs. In addition to giving you access to information and methodologies, attendance at workshops and conferences will also give you valuable opportunities to meet grant writers from other organizations.

Attending workshops and conferences with like-minded people aiming to develop their grant-seeking or grant-writing skills will give you the basis for developing a personal network of professionals in the grant-writing field.

Make every effort to attend professional workshops, seminars, and conferences.

During your job search and interviewing, you may have inquired about a budget for training. If you didn't do this before you were hired, it is wise to do so soon after so that you can draft a professional development plan for attending meetings, conferences, and workshops. If you have no budget, look to the Foundation Center affiliate library nearest you. Occasionally they sponsor workshops on all aspects of grant writing, including research for funding. Introductory sessions on the various resources available to a grant seeker are often offered free of charge. In the event that you have no travel or conference budget, advocate for one.

Visit the Council for Advancement and Support of Education (CASE) website at www.case.org.

An important conference sponsor you should definitely be looking at is the Council for the Advancement and Support of Education, known as CASE, which offers a schedule of conferences on a wide variety of topics throughout the year.

Every year CASE offers a national conference on corporate and foundation support. Most organizations in education belong to CASE, and this membership will give you a reduced rate on conferences. Even if you work for an organization in healthcare or social services, you should still attend CASE conferences. This annual CASE conference brings together the largest concentration of your professional grant-writing peers to be found anywhere. CASE regional conferences are worth considering also, especially if you will not need to travel far to attend.

There are many opportunities for continuing your education in grants research and proposal development. A search on the web will give you more than you can possibly attend.

Managing Grants Research

As you do your research on foundations, corporations, and other grant-making entities, you will want to keep track of your information and store it in a way that is easily retrievable. When you become proficient, you will also need to manage your time so that research into grant opportunities is in balance with your actual output of proposals. Initially, you might find that you spend a majority of your time on research alone. In those early days of research you may be able to keep your information on a few sheets of paper or in a single Word document. However, be prepared to be inundated with information, because if do your research systematically you will soon have more information than you can handle without a good system in place.

An organized and systematic researcher is able to maximize time available for other aspects of the grant-writing process.

As you build up a body of specialized research and begin to strategize approaches for support, the balance between research and writing will flip. More and more of your time will be needed to write proposals. Early on, it's a good idea to organize and index what you find in your research, and to develop working priorities that will make your grants research job manageable in light of the proposals you will be writing. The more efficient and organized you are at the research side of the job, the more time you will have to write.

Developing Grants Research Priorities

Early on in your grants research efforts, you should develop a method to prioritize your research in relation to other duties you will need to perform. It is important to do this for several reasons. Starting a new research program can be intensive and overwhelming. Unless research is your primary full-time duty and responsibility, you will need to devote much of your time during the work day to other activities. You want your research efforts to be effective, but not all-consuming.

Funding research priorities should be driven by the planning of your organization, which means that ultimate decisions on project or program priorities will normally be made by an executive or board. Grant writers can provide valuable information about external funding prospects for programs, projects, and other needs of an organization, and this information can be useful to officers as they determine their organizations' priorities.

> If you don't prioritize your research efforts, your productivity will suffer.

However, for a grant writer to be truly productive and successful, priorities must come from the organization's leadership. A successful grant writer will quickly become known within an organization. You may be pursued by every staff person wanting external funding. No grant writer has the time or resources to serve the interests of every staff person at an organization. You will learn to distinguish between organizational or institutional priorities and individuals' pet projects. Setting your research priorities to align with the organization's strategic plan is the place to start. Grant makers want to see that proposed projects reflect institutional priorities, so insisting on this fit before you do research is likely to make you more successful as well as more efficient.

> Research priorities should align with strategic planning.

Managing Grant Opportunity Files

As you do your research on corporate giving, you will be collecting information on grants made to other organizations that might serve as a model for your own approach for support. This may take the form of a list of grants from a website, or more detailed information such as a press release. You will also want to search for specific information about a grant making entity's areas of philanthropic interest, eligibility rules, application procedures, deadlines, contact information—any other details you can glean.

As a matter of routine, you will save the results of your web research in electronic files, but at some point it will be helpful also to set up paper files for each prospective corporate donor. You will want a place to put clippings from print journals and copies of company publications so that they are available for quick reference when you need them. You may find yourself reaching for a printed grants list from a publication or an IRS Form 990-PF to use in a strategy meeting with colleagues. Your paper files are the place to store items such as these. The place to begin organizing prospective grant-maker files is to make a simple alphabetical list for file labels. Save it and add to it as your collection of grant opportunity files expands.

Research results should be organized in both electronic files and paper files.

Using Spreadsheets and Databases to Manage Research into Grant Opportunities

Beyond these hard files, you will also need a way to organize your grant opportunity research so you can analyze the vital information that you are amassing and document your efforts. Start out with a paper checklist. Next, develop a spreadsheet that initially contains basic information about the grant maker such as name and address, key contacts, grant cycles and deadlines, special requirements such as requiring a letter of inquiry before a proposal, and program funding interests. Include categories related to eligibility, special restrictions placed on grant-seeking organizations, and organizational needs and priorities of likely interest to the grant maker. Storing all of this information in a spreadsheet will enable you to sort and filter it by category, which will be tremendously helpful as your body of research grows.

A well-organized grants research spreadsheet is a resource you will update continually and consult on a daily basis.

Soon you will develop a methodology for concisely recording vital information about grant makers. As you document the funding interests of each grant maker, you try to identify at least one project or program need of your organization that is a potential match.

If you do it right, at some point your research will become too large to handle in simple lists or even spreadsheets, and you will want to create your own database to track funding opportunities. For more information about using a database to track grant-funding opportunities, see Chapter 13, "Tracking Your Successes."

When you have too much research for a spreadsheet, it is time to think about database technology.

Presenting Grants Research Internally

From time to time you will want to present selections of your research internally within your organization. It could be something as simple as a note, memorandum, or email message to selected colleagues and staff of your organization alerting them of a new grant opportunity. It is a good idea to develop a standard memo format for presenting your research in meetings and discussions with colleagues.

Developing Internal Reports

Always consider confidentiality issues when writing a report on funding possibilities. Information on funders that you have collected externally is usually public record and presents no problem. However, information you have collected internally may not be public record. Relationships between staff of your organization and external funders are confidential, and the confidentiality of information gained through those relationships must be protected. Also, always keep in mind that the planning of projects or new programs may not yet have been formally announced within your organization, in which case you should respect the confidentiality of the planning process. In addition, consider institutional financial information to be confidential until your financial officer tells you it is for public consumption.

You will develop reports on funding resources for decision-makers and staff of your organization. Consider your readership anew each time you draft a report. Ask yourself what are the primary facts and concepts you want your readers to understand, and organize your report in a way that will make it easy for them to skim to the things they are most interested in.

> Be mindful of confidentiality concerns and the specific needs of your audience when preparing reports for internal use.

Once your research is well under way, begin to develop project-oriented reports for colleagues seeking new funding opportunities. You will also need to develop executive reports of funding prospects that need the involvement of organization executives. Again, keep your audience in mind. The ideal grants research report for executive eyes is usually one page long—no more. Aim at brevity, and be prepared to provide more details on request. Your research should always be presented to support future proposal submissions. See Figure 4.14 for a sample report that illustrates the selectivity needed for an executive report. Note that

SAMPLE FUNDING PROSPECT REPORT TO AN EXECUTIVE OFFICER

FR. MEGER
CENTER
FOR SOCIAL JUSTICE

May 15, 2012

TO: Rev. Msgr. John Doe, Executive Director
         Dr. Robert Jones, Deputy Director

FR: Tim Kachinske, Grants Office

RE: The Salvelinus Foundation - New Grant Opportunity

This past week the Salvelinus Foundation announced a new grant program for innovative social services delivery projects not exceeding $100,000. Proposed projects must either create new programs or extend current services to a new geographical area.

Deadlines: Proposals due July 15. Decisions to be made at the foundation's September 15 board meeting. Full grant payments to be made by December 31.

We may submit only one proposal. We have at least three plans worth considering for this proposal opportunity:
- Extend current autism respite program to neighboring St. Charles County
- New program: supported employment for adults with developmental disabilities
- New program: English-language instruction for Spanish-speaking parents of children with developmental disabilities.

Next steps:
1) Determine which potential project would best fit our priorities at this time;
2) Determine whether the Executive Director should visit the Salvelinus Foundation prior to proposal submission;
3) Begin developing proposal.

Past Salvelinus Foundation Grants to the Fr. Meger Center:

Year	Amount	Purpose
2009	$ 75,000	Economic Justice Initiative for Seniors
2010	25,000	Homeless In-Reach Project
2011	37,500	One Stop Senior Support Project

Note that detailed grants research is offered but not included in a report to executive officers about a new grant opportunity

I have a complete record of all Salvelinus Foundation grants over the past five years available for your review, including lists categorized by year, by program, and by recipient.

Figure 4.14 *Sample funding prospect report to executive officers.*

research conclusions are presented. Much of the information collected in the course of your research activities will inform the writing of the report but not be included in it. Note, too, that the research presented will typically be used to elicit decisions on a strategy that moves forward to presenting a proposal.

Your 90-Day Grants Research Checklist

✓ Research past grant support for your organization and create a spreadsheet that will enable you to access the information easily.

✓ Discuss the issue of confidentiality with your superiors and form a clear understanding of your organization's procedures and expectations with respect to confidentiality.

✓ Identify the organizations that are in competition with your own for funding and begin to collect research on their programs and sources of grant support.

✓ Read at least three books related to private philanthropy.

✓ Familiarize yourself with *The Foundation Directory* and the Foundation Center's website www.foundationcenter.org .

✓ Become knowledgeable about your local community foundation.

✓ Become a regular user of the 990 Finder and know how to locate significant information contained on an IRS 990-PF.

✓ Learn to analyze information contained on an IRS 990-PF and utilize it to strategize your grant seeking.

✓ Identify potential sources of foundation support for your organization and create electronic and paper files to organize your research results.

✓ Identify potential sources of corporate support for your organization and create electronic and paper files to organize your research results.

✓ Attend at least three workshops, seminars, or conferences on grant writing.

✓ Establish a network of at least five people in the grant-writing profession with whom you can share research questions and findings.

✓ Be able to respond quickly and effectively to these questions: "What are your current research priorities? Why?"

Chapter 5

Managing Relationships

- Relationships with Colleagues
- Relationships with Grant Makers
- Managing Team-Driven Proposals
- Developing a Mentoring Plan

The image of a writer scribbling away in a garret, deep in thought and isolated from human contact, does not fit the grant writer. On the contrary, grant writing is a very social activity. The successful grant writer is continually engaged with others both inside and outside her organization, pulling together people and ideas to make it possible for good things to happen. There comes a time, of course, when the grant writer must close the door and take responsibility for the actual writing of a grant. However, in the days or weeks leading up to that time a lot of interpersonal relationships need to be managed to maximize the chances for success.

Relationships with Colleagues

The relationships you establish with your colleagues are critical.

The first relationships grant writers need to cultivate are relationships with colleagues. Because the grant writer provides a service to colleagues within the organization, it follows that open lines of communication are critical. You can't serve colleagues well if you don't know them and they don't know you. Your aim is to develop collaborative professional relationships characterized by trust and respect. Productive, high-level collaboration doesn't just happen; you need to orchestrate it. Ultimately, if you manage relationships well, your collaboration will rise to the level of synergy.

The nature of collaboration varies depending on how the role of the grant writer is defined within an organization. Grant writers in development offices are usually expected to assist program officers, administrators, or faculty. Typical expectations include identifying sources of grant support, guiding the project development process, managing contacts and visits, and taking the lead in proposal development. In a small institution or nonprofit organization, you may be the only writer available and may work with just about everyone at all stages of the proposal development process.

The grant writer's network of collaborators is determined by factors such as the size of the organization and how it is structured.

Grant writers who work in administrative units of a large organization typically perform research and writing tasks exclusively with faculty or program officers of their own unit. Those who work in sponsored research offices will work almost exclusively with faculty or other research staff and may develop strong working partnerships and highly specialized subject area expertise. Close collaboration with researchers is essential for success in obtaining large foundation and government research grants.

Whatever role you may find yourself in as a grant writer, be prepared to develop cordial working relationships with the executive, administrative, teaching, and program staff in your organization. The time and effort you invest in these relationships with colleagues will pay off.

Getting Off to a Good Start

If you are new to an organization, you should develop a plan that will enable you to become familiar with the people whom you serve as quickly as possible. Begin with colleagues in your immediate circle. Make it clear that you are glad to be there and anxious to contribute to the good of the cause. Be friendly but not inquisitive. Don't neglect the support staff, because if you get off to a bad start with a support person, it may be very difficult indeed to undo the damage. On the other hand, if you get off to a good start with the support staff in your office, you stand to benefit from their good will and assistance.

> Try to make a good first impression. It is much easier to create a good first impression than it is to eradicate a misconception.

The first relationship you need to manage is the one with your immediate superior. Make certain that you clearly understand what his priorities are and what is expected of you. Written job targets can help in that respect, but you won't always find that level of formality in the nonprofit world. Often as not, you will need to come to a verbal understanding of expectations, priorities, and the criteria on which you will be evaluated. Keep in mind that in the grant-seeking business, priorities can change from one day to the next because you are operating in a dynamic environment. One week's top priority may be usurped by the next week's emergency. This makes it even more important to establish a solid relationship with the person who will do your performance evaluation. It is not unusual for grant writers to spend a great deal of time engaged in the classic last line of the job description, "Performs other duties as assigned."

> Make sure you understand your supervisor's expectations.

Next, reach out to your financial executive or her deputy. It is critical for a grant writer to have a good working relationship with someone on the financial side of the organization. You will need a finance colleague to consult about proposal budgets during the development phase and to review your budgets before submission. From time to time, you will need specific and highly technical information, and this is the person who can give it to you. Often you will find a gulf between people on the budget side and people on the program side of an organization. Bridge that gulf if at all possible.

> A partnership forged between a budget person and a grant writer is a prescription for success.

In a large institution, you may not be able to consult with the chief financial officer. Don't worry if that is the case. The finance relationship you need most is someone you can contact at relatively short notice in the course of your work on proposals and budgets. An approachable person who reports in the chain leading up to your chief financial officer is ideal.

Learn as much as you can from an experienced finance person. It will stand you in good stead no matter where your career leads you.

At a small organization, there may be only one individual to consult for financial information and advice. In that case, cultivate that relationship with great care. Learn everything you can from that person. Every successful grant writer needs a partnership with an expert budget person.

Outreach Beyond Your Immediate Circle

In a large organization, if your grant writing is primarily driven by the priorities of your organization's executive officers and board, you may at first be carrying out the vision of people you have never met. In that case, you will rely initially on documents and the advice of your supervisor. Communication with executives will be channeled through your supervisor, and you may rarely, if ever, meet or talk to board members. In a small organization, you may meet everyone from the board members down to volunteers early on and interact regularly and freely up and down the chain. The important thing for you as a new grant writer is to scope out how communication works in your organization and where you fit in the communication chain. If you find that protocol dictates who may communicate with whom, stick to the protocol.

Find out whether a communication protocol in your organization dictates whom you may and may not contact directly.

If you are free to communicate with staff at all levels in your organization, take advantage of that freedom to establish relationships at all levels.

If you are not constrained by communication protocols, consider yourself fortunate. You can construct a proactive plan to meet with all administrative office chiefs or department heads in your first few weeks on the job. These meetings will have a dual purpose: to develop a concrete sense of the organization's needs and strengths, and to begin establishing important relationships. Such meetings should go way beyond the usual meet and greet, so you should prepare carefully by learning as much as you can about the individual you are to meet and the department or unit she manages. You should not ask any questions you could look up in advance.

In your conversations with key people, you want to leave the impression that you are prepared to search aggressively for proposal opportunities to support any reasonable need of the organization. Solicit their input. You might, for example, ask them to identify their top three equipment needs, their top three program needs, and the top three accomplishments of their units. Take notes in these meetings, and transfer what you learn to a spreadsheet for future reference. See the spreadsheet example in Figure 5.1 for how you might organize and retain information collected in initial meetings with key personnel.

Let your colleagues know that you are ready to channel your energy and competencies on behalf of their needs.

Record of Needs and Accomplishments Reported in Initial Meetings

Department	# 1 Equipment Need	#2 Equipment Need	#3 Equipment Need	# 1 Program Need	# 2 Program Need	#3 Program Need	#1 Accomplishment	#2 Accomplishment	#3 Accomplishment
Anthropology									
Art									
Biology									
Chemistry									
Classics									
Economics									
English									
German									
History									
Mathematics									
Music									
Philosophy									
Physics									
Political Science									
Psychology									
Romance Langs									
Theatre									

Figure 5.1

Technology can also be used to introduce yourself, jump-start relationships, and solicit information from key people in your organization. You or your supervisor might send out an email introduction containing information about your background and what you hope to accomplish in your new role. You may want to utilize a printed form or a web form in which faculty or staff can send you new project ideas, needs, or research interests. Perhaps this might evolve into an e-newsletter that you prepare and distribute regularly as a means of keeping in touch about grant opportunities. Keep in mind that any outreach plan you put together should be reviewed by your supervisor before you implement it.

Harness technology to communicate with colleagues on their own time.

Relationships with Grant Makers

As you do your research on grant makers, you will want to develop a plan to approach each corporation, foundation, or other grant-making entity. Each approach should be tailored to a specific grant maker with the objective of submitting a successful proposal. You will want to avoid what are sometimes called blind submissions. In other words, do not look up the name and address of a grant maker and send off a generic proposal. Never, ever send out a blind proposal.

Submissions should always be preceded by careful planning. A grant maker should never be surprised to find your proposal in the mail.

Instead, whenever you send out a proposal you should ensure beforehand that it will be welcomed by the grant-making entity that receives it. A relationship between your organization and the grant maker must have been established prior to submission in order for this to happen. In addition, your proposal must be well tailored to a grant-maker's interests and perfectly tailored to its guidelines.

It is important to be strategic in your selection of a point person to represent your organization with a grant maker.

The person communicating with a grant prospect may well be you. Sometimes it may be more advantageous for someone else at your organization to make that contact. Determining who in your organization is best positioned to initiate and maintain contact with a particular grant-making entity is a strategic decision that should be made for logical, strategic reasons. Perhaps there is an existing relationship that you can capitalize on. Perhaps a mutual acquaintance can broker a relationship between someone in your organization and a key person at the grant-making organization. As a grant writer, you will want to coordinate and track every contact made between someone at your organization and any person at a grant-making entity so that approaches are not bungled due to mishandled relationships.

A seasoned grant writer will orchestrate the submission process in such a way that all stakeholders feel a genuine sense of accomplishment when it is successful.

At all stages of the submission process, from planning the approach to writing the proposal and obtaining the required signatures, you will be communicating with colleagues and others associated with your organization. The relationships you develop during the course of these communications are critical, so it is very important to do it right the first few times you go through the submission process. How you conduct yourself and manage the process will determine how you are perceived. If you do it well, everyone involved will take ownership in the final outcome. This means that when a proposal is successful, the satisfaction and sense of accomplishment will be shared by your colleagues, which is exactly what you want to happen. If you mess it up and a proposal is denied, all fingers will point directly at you. Managing and coordinating relationships between your organization and grant makers is an important part of a grant-writer's role, as illustrated in Figure 5.2.

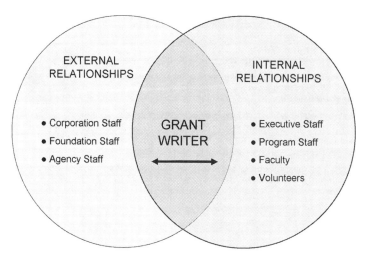

Figure 5.2

Cultivation Strategies

As a grant writer, you will want to be able to manage and coordinate relationships with a prospective grant maker to make certain that each approach for funding rolls out as planned. You may find that board members, officers, or colleagues already have relationships with a grant maker you have identified for a potential proposal submission. So long as these relationships don't require damage control, they will give you a foundation to build on. Meet with colleagues and others so that you gain an understanding of the nature and history of each existing relationship and how it might fit into your plan to submit a proposal.

A good grant writer manages and coordinates relationships so that a successful approach can be orchestrated.

It is perhaps more common for a new grant writer to find that no one in the organization has a relationship with a particular grant maker, or that the relationship has lapsed. Then it will fall to you to develop or reinvigorate a relationship.

From time to time, a one-day course called "Cultivating Grantmaker Relationships" is offered by the Foundation Center in New York or at one of its regional affiliate libraries or organizations. This course provides an excellent introduction to developing relationships with prospective foundation donors. (See Figure 5.3.)

If at all possible, try to take advantage of the professional development on managing relationships offered through the Foundation Center.

FOUNDATION CENTER
Knowledge to build on.

CULTIVATING GRANTMAKER RELATIONSHIPS
Thursday, September 17 in Washington, DC

Cultivating Grantmaker Relationships
Thursday, September 17 in Washington, DC

For every nonprofit grantseeker and board member who wants to nurture and sustain their grantmaker relationships, from the initial approach through the life of a grant and beyond.

When the demand for services escalates while funding sources diminish, a productive partnership with grantmakers is crucially important. In this course, you will learn how to make contact with new prospects, ensure the funder feels connected to your mission, nurture healthy dialogue throughout the grant process, and secure long-term commitment.

"I am so glad you added this course, it's one of the most useful training sessions I've ever attended. Relationship building and cultivation are essential skills for anyone in foundation fundraising."

– Development Associate, Washington, DC

BENEFITS

- Improve the success rate of your initial contact with grantmakers
- Make cultivation a routine part of your interaction with funders
- Develop key members of your organization to become more effective grantseekers
- Keep your organization top-of-mind with grantmakers

TOPICS

- What funders expect from their nonprofit partners
- Strategies for making a strong initial contact
- Points of contact in a grant relationship
- Developing strong talking points about your organization and project
- Effective cultivation techniques and when to use them
- Planning for grantmaker site visits and meetings
- Maintaining productive relationships after a grant decision

BONUSES

- Applicable for six CFRE^{TM} International points for initial or re-certification

REGISTER NOW!
Cultivating Grantmaker Relationships

Motivate and empower everyone on your team.

SPECIAL DISCOUNT
SAVE $25 for each additional registration made at the same time.

Figure 5.3 *Website notice of a Foundation Center course devoted to building relationships with grant makers.*

Even though Foundation Center courses such as this one are aimed specifically at foundations, the methodology for relationship building will transfer to grant-making companies and government agencies. Attendance at Foundation Center courses will give you exposure not only to the seasoned grant writers and development officers who teach them but also to other aspiring grant writers with whom you might later network for advice and counsel.

Do Your Research First

Letters, email messages, or phone calls to a prospective grant maker should be carefully thought out. Assume that foundation, corporate, or government agency staff are very busy people. Often they are fielding communications and dealing with proposals from literally hundreds of organizations. Anything that can be construed as bothering or pestering them will work to your disadvantage.

Never call a grant maker for information that can be found on a website or in a publication. If you do that, you are in essence telling the grant maker that you are not good at the research side of your job as a grant writer.

Always do research before you ask questions.

Communicating by Letter, Phone, and Email

Choose your method of initial communication carefully. For an initial contact, a formal letter requesting information is usually better than a phone call. In an initial contact letter, you can be both the author and the signer if your purpose is simply to seek general information. If you are writing to request published information about guidelines or opportunities, it is fine to use a generic letter, as shown in Figure 5.4. In subsequent correspondence, you will probably find yourself drafting letters for others in your organization. Your executive officer, for example, may be the point person for developing a relationship with a grant maker, in which case you will draft letters to be signed by her.

Initial contacts with a grant maker should be carefully planned.

If you need to make a phone call, prepare yourself for a successful contact. Write out what you expect to accomplish. Make a checklist or outline for your conversation. Have your research material ready in front of you, tabbed so you can refer to it without shuffling through paper. When you do pick the phone up, be sure that you have everything at your fingertips that you might conceivably need to have available during the call. You won't

SAMPLE LETTER REQUESTING GUIDELINES

University
of the United States

July 25, 2022

Mr. John Doe
The Doe Foundation
125 Park Avenue
New York, NY 10011

Dear Mr. Doe:

I write to ask for a copy of the current guidelines and grant application procedures of The Doe Foundation. I would also appreciate receiving the current annual report, if available, and any other current publications of the Foundation.

Thank you very much for your consideration.

Sincerely,

Timothy Kachinske
Senior Grant Writer

> Always ask for additional publications with your request for guidelines. This ensures that if they have a mailing list, your name and address will be place on it.

Figure 5.4 *Sample letter requesting guidelines.*

make a good impression if all you can do when asked a question is to say, "I'll check on that and get back to you." Sometimes that's an understandable and acceptable response, but it is a good idea to anticipate what you will be asked so that you can respond immediately. When your approach strategy involves a phone call to be made by your executive officer or another person in your organization, prepare that individual in advance as you would yourself. Provide a concise statement of the strategic purpose and a set of talking points for the phone call.

Take charge of phone contacts with grant makers by planning carefully in advance of the call.

Sometimes grant makers offer an email address for an individual or a corporate entity (such as grantsinfo@thegreatcompany.com) where grant information can be requested. Usually the grant information provided will consist of funding interests and submission guidelines. This may even be the means for requesting the formal document called the Request for Proposals or RFP. It's fine to request information this way if the grant maker invites such email requests in public communication. Always include your name, title, and mailing address in the signature of your email message. Be judicious with email messages to funders; if you don't find an email address specifically set up for initial queries or RFP requests, send a letter.

Plan your communications with grant makers carefully. Make sure that everything you might need is in front of you before you pick up the phone.

Making Personal Visits

As you move forward, you may from time to time request to visit a grant maker. In general, this should not be a generic visit but a meeting requested for a strategic purpose. In the case of new grant prospects, take time to develop a research-based strategy before you make your approach for a visit.

If you move into a situation where your organization has long-standing, close relationships with one or more grant makers, it may make sense to plan visits soon after you take your position as a means of introducing yourself. This will ensure that when you contact them about specific grant-related issues they will know who you are. Take the opportunity to provide an update on previous successful grant projects, and have something in mind to discuss about the future as well.

You may wish to visit major grantors to introduce yourself and solicit ideas for future support.

A visit planned as a strategic step in an approach will, of course, begin with research. You also will want to prepare materials to bring along. If the person you are visiting has a personal connection to your organization, you might bring a token gift branded with your logo or name. It should be something modest.

For example, if you are working for a school or college and are visiting an alumnus, the token item could be a mug, a pennant, or recent issues of the college newspaper.

You may wish to bring a selection of reading materials or a token gift when you visit a prospective grant maker.

If there is no personal connection between the person you are visiting and your organization, anything you bring should be relevant to the professional purpose of your visit. If you have not already sent a copy of your organization's annual report or other publication, bring one along. Consider bringing items relevant to proposal project ideas you might want to discuss, such as newspaper clippings, magazine articles, special reports, or news releases.

Coordinating Visits for Others

When you coordinate a visit for a colleague, go through all the preparation you would do if you were going yourself.

As a grant writer, you may not be the one to visit a grant maker; it may be more appropriate for another staff person to make the visit. Often it will be the executive officer who takes the initiative with respect to contact with funders. In colleges and universities, the president will often want to be the touch bearer whenever a prospective grant meets a relatively high dollar amount. At a research institution or nonprofit organization, it may be logical for the principal investigator or project director of a prospective grant to be the lead contact in discussing the project with outside funders. You may find that a staff person at your organization already has an established relationship with the grant maker and is therefore the best person to make a personal visit. Regardless of who the lead contact is, you as a grant writer should coordinate everything to ensure that the visit is as successful as possible.

A good grant writer will ensure that the representative of the organization has everything needed to make a visit successful.

Prepare your lead contact as you would prepare for visits you make yourself. Assemble any background information, research, and reports that will be needed. See the sample foundation visit planning document in Figure 5.5 for a simple model of how to prepare an executive for a foundation visit. It may also fall to you to draft letters, make phone calls, and brief the lead contact in advance of a visit. Whatever tasks need to be taken care of to pave the way for a good visit is the default role of a successful grant writer.

Take a minute to read through Figure 5.5. Note that the document is only one page long and does not contain a great deal of dense text. The audience in this case is the chief executive officer of the organization, who will want to be able to take in everything he needs to know at a glance. The grant maker's contact

SAMPLE FOUNDATION VISIT PLANNING DOCUMENT

Methodius College Development Office

Planning Document: The General Foundation

Time and Date of Visit: 10:00am   March 12, 2022

Place of Visit: The General Foundation
30 Rockefeller Plaza   (212) 555-4000

Foundation Official: John Doe, Executive Director

Methodius College Visitor: President John Johnson

Purpose of Visit: To continue dialogue established during President Johnson's first visit to the Foundation on March 15, 2015, and to discuss our intention to apply for a $500,000 grant for an endowed ethics program.

According to Jane Doe, Methodius Board Member, the foundation is well disposed to our ethics program and would fund its endowment. The Foundation's main concerns are our ability to attract other major grants, and our endowment growth.

Methodius College Achievements Over Past 3 Years

Major Foundation Grants:
John and Jane Doe Foundation   Jim Smith Foundation
XYZ Foundation   Great Foundation

Faculty Recipients of Fulbright Awards:
Dr. Evelyn Smith   Dr. Jane Smith

Endowment Growth
2020: $105.5 million   2021: $188.5 million

Figure 5.5 *Sample foundation visit planning document.*

information (including the address and phone number) should be clear, as your visitor will be referencing this document on the way to the grant-maker's office. Note that the purpose of the visit and talking point details are brief and tailored to your organization's existing relationship with the grant maker.

Documenting Contacts with Grant Makers

It is important to track and record information about any contact between people at your organization and a grant maker. Letters you draft yourself will easily make their way into your paper and electronic files, and your email correspondence is easily accessible so long as you maintain well-organized archives. The challenge you face is that grant-maker contact files need to contain not only your own contact history but also the contact history of all other persons in your organization who have been in touch with the grant maker via letter, telephone, email, or personal visit.

Your challenge as a grant writer is to be able to coordinate not only your own contacts with grant makers but also those of others in your organization.

In order to keep track of all of this, you will need to be systematic. Make your colleagues aware that you would like to know about any phone or personal contact they may be considering. Ideally, you would want to be part of any discussion prior to the contact, but in the case you are not, assure them that you will find it helpful to know about the contact after the fact. If they think you are being meddlesome, explain your intent is to ensure that you are all on the same page because it leaves a poor impression if it appears that you aren't communicating amongst yourselves.

It is important to capture basic information about a contact as soon as possible after it takes place.

Make it easy for your colleagues to funnel information to you. Some may happily write up an email or a short paper memo for your records. For those who won't do this without prompting, talk over what has transpired and take notes so that you can write up a file memo yourself. If you have been involved in orchestrating a visit, offer to take notes in a phone call after the meeting is over. This will take the burden off your colleague, who will be glad not to have to write up the visit while on the road. Leaving visit memos for later is not a good practice; meeting notes are best when they are recorded immediately after an event.

Sometimes teaching by example can be the most effective way to get your colleagues in the habit of taking notes on their visits or other communications with grant makers. As a grant writer, you will write up a memorandum of record for any contacts you are aware of, including those you have made yourself. See Figure 5.6

SAMPLE FILE MEMO AFTER A VISIT TO A CORPORATION

Memorandum to the file

TO: American Bath Fixtures Company file

FR: Tim Kachinske, Grants Officer

RE: Visit to the American Bath Fixtures Company corporate offices, May 23, 2012

Purpose of Visit: To update ABF Company officials on Methodius College in general, and to seek opportunities for grant support.

ABF Officials Met: Randolph Severnsen, CEO
Herb Fornier, Director of Human Resources

I met briefly with Mr. Severnsen to provide him with an update on the College. He is interested in seeing more local children attend Methodius because they are more likely to seek professional positions at ABF. The relatively isolated location of ABF has presented challenges in recruiting new management hires. Mr. Severnsen is very well disposed to Methodius, and would like to meet our President. I met at length with Mr. Fornier, who would like to support a summer internship program out of his HR budget. Mr. Fornier also recommended having our president submit a proposal for scholarship support.

Next Steps: Meet with Dan Johnson, Methodius College Director of Placement, to discuss developing a paid summer management internship program for rising sophomores and juniors. Herb Fornier will consider a training grant of up to $25,000 per year to plan the internship program. The grant can be spent on travel, materials, and stipend for training assistants. The funding would not come from the corporate foundation, but rather from ABF's corporate budget.

Discuss the possibility of offering scholarships for applicants living in the ABF corporate headquarters community. If our record of applications and acceptances show sufficient numbers, the ABF Company Foundation would consider annual grant applications up to $25,000 per year.

Review the results of this meeting with the President, and plan for his forthcoming visit to Mr. Severnsen in early fall.

Figure 5.6 *Sample file memo after a visit to a corporation.*

for an example of the type of memo you might want to use with colleagues to model the kind of note taking that will help your organization roll out a smooth, strategic, well-orchestrated approach.

Hosting Grant Makers

From time to time, you may have an opportunity to invite a grant-maker representative to visit your organization. Occasionally a representative may ask to make such a visit. This will only happen after you have developed a relationship on the basis of some program or activity that is of special interest to the grant maker.

A grant-maker's visit presents an opportunity for you to showcase your organization at its best.

A grant-maker's visit might be a straightforward affair, in which you coordinate the schedule and accompany the visitor yourself, or it could be a fairly complicated schedule of meetings involving a number of executives and program staff at your organization. It may have been set up at the invitation of someone else at your organization, in which case you should volunteer to assist that staff person in any way possible.

You can assist your colleagues by coaching them prior to the visit to ensure that the message projected is consistent and coherent from one staff member to the next. Any appearance of disagreement, discord, or confusion will diminish your prospects for a successful application. Talk briefly with colleagues afterward to learn about comments or incidents you did not witness yourself, and follow up the visit with a memo or note for your file.

The investment in time and energy you put into grant-makers' visits can be the critical ingredient in a successful proposal.

Often, you will be responsible for all of the details of a grant-maker's visit, and it can be a lot of work. However, a successful visit can make a critical difference, particularly if a grant maker is considering making a major investment in your organization.

Managing Team-Driven Proposals

All of the groundwork you do to establish good relationships within your own organization will come to fruition as you begin to manage team-driven proposals. Most proposals call for the active involvement of several people in addition to the grant writer responsible for the final draft. A complex proposal may require content contribution from many people. The individuals who will be responsible for implementing the projects a proposal will fund need to provide input along the way to ensure that the project design and timeline are realistic. Whether simple or complex, every proposal needs the advice and review of a financial expert. Most important, every proposal will need to be approved and signed by executive staff before submission. From conception to implementation and accountability, most successful grant projects are team efforts.

Team-driven proposals involve input from all levels of the organization.

Team-driven proposals often involve a half dozen or more people. It is important that the team have a leader, and it should not be the grant writer. You may coordinate the efforts and input of all these people, but if at all possible the team should be led by an executive or program person. The team leader should be a decision-maker able to take the lead in situations where a grant writer is neither qualified nor authorized to make decisions.

In an academic setting, a proposal team leader should be a person who holds an administrative appointment such as department chair or assistant dean. In a nonprofit organization, a proposal team leader should be a deputy of the executive officer or a department head. The team leader needs to have both administrative authority and the qualifications necessary to judge the substance of the proposal.

The team leader should be someone with the authority to supervise and the qualifications or experience needed to determine whether the content of a proposal is acceptable.

You will turn to the team leader for assistance in dealing with team members responsible for providing the concept, content, and data for proposals. Ideally, all participants in a team-driven proposal will meet the deadlines set for producing whatever is needed. In reality, when a team member is not responsive, you will need someone in authority who can hold the unresponsive team member accountable or replace him. As a grant writer, you will want to deflect all issues regarding a poorly performing team member to a person with authority. You will have enough to deal with pulling the project together.

Sometimes the professionals you work with may have extraordinary academic qualifications and vast experience of the subject of a proposal. In conversation they may seem brilliant. But not everyone can write well. It is not uncommon to have first draft content that is unintelligible, inchoate, incoherent, disorganized, or otherwise unacceptable. It should be the role of the team leader to deal with anyone whose writing and organization skills fail to meet the standards of a good proposal. Decisions regarding whether a content contributor should be asked for revisions, referred to a writing skills class, or replaced by someone who can write, should be up to a team leader.

When a team member submits unacceptable content, the team leader must determine how to proceed.

As a grant writer intent on getting a proposal submitted on time, you will want to help all team members to understand what is required of them. Provide copies of the grant-maker's own documents and publications to help team members understand what you need from them. If you need to have ideas fleshed out or verbiage supplied, give them enough background information so that they understand the context of the proposal.

> At the end of the day, it is up to the grant writer to pull together all of the input submitted by a team and transform it into a coherent proposal for support.

Team-driven proposals are never written by a team. Ultimately a grant writer must pull together and assemble a team's contributions into one coherent, compelling proposal for support. That proposal can only have one voice. It is up to the grant writer to determine a voice for the proposal and carry that voice from beginning to end.

Developing a Mentoring Plan

As a beginning grant writer, you will not only be concerned with relationships within your organization and between your organization and potential funders; you will also want to cultivate your own network of relationships among people who share your professional interests and can support your career aspirations.

> Remember to cultivate relationships that serve your own interests as well as the interests of your employer.

From this point forward, start thinking of people you know and meet as potential mentors. Of course it is helpful to have a mentor within your organization to teach you the ropes and put forward a positive word when you need it. You should also seek mentors outside your organization. Involvement in professional associations, conferences, and seminars is invaluable because it will put you in touch with other professionals who understand exactly what is involved with your job.

Conferences provide a collection of such people with the experience and inclination to be available when you need advice. Actually, it is a good idea to have potential mentor goals for every conference and seminar you attend. For example, when you attend a multi-day national conference devoted to grant seeking (such as the annual CASE conference on corporate and foundation relations) it would be reasonable to set a goal of meeting at least three people who might be potential mentors.

> Look for mentors both inside and outside your organization.

At a smaller regional seminar, you might have a goal of meeting just one. The point is, you must intentionally reach out and build relationships. If you do reach out, you will find your mentors.

Your 90-Day Checklist for Managing Relationships

✓ Develop and implement a plan for getting acquainted with all key people involved in securing grant support for your organization.

✓ Have a clear understanding of what your superior expects of you in terms of responsibilities, productivity, and the criteria that will be used for your annual performance evaluation.

✓ Identify your internal finance contact and establish a good working relationship with that person.

✓ Have a clear understanding of the communication protocols that apply to your organization.

✓ Initiate or orchestrate contacts between your organization and at least three potential grant makers.

✓ Reach out to your colleagues in person and by means of at least one method of technology-based communication such as an e-newsletter.

✓ Introduce yourself to all grant makers who are major contributors to the activities of your organization.

✓ Attend at least one national and two local or regional training seminars or conferences related to cultivating relationships with grant makers.

✓ Establish a systematic procedure for preparing your colleagues for successful contacts with potential grant makers.

✓ Orchestrate at least one successful visit with a grant maker, either on-site or at their headquarters.

✓ Establish a systemic procedure for documenting communications between your organization and grant makers.

✓ Develop a mentoring plan that identifies at least one internal and three external mentors from whom you can seek advice and counsel.

Chapter 6

Writing

This chapter is intended for aspiring grant writers who do not yet feel entirely confident about their writing skills. If you are a seasoned writer interested in grant writing as a way to leverage that skill set into a profitable career, you can skip this chapter. If you are an inexperienced writer deeply involved in an organization or a cause that needs grant support, this chapter is intended for you.

If you are a seasoned writer, you can skip this chapter.

Writing is a magical process, because it enables us to communicate directly with people we have never met. There are four interrelated domains of verbal communication: speaking, listening, reading, and writing. Most of us are capable of functioning automatically in all four domains so long as the setting is familiar and relatively small. Speaking to colleagues in a small meeting does not typically generate the discomfort experienced when speaking to hundreds of strangers in an auditorium or millions via television. The inexperienced public speaker feels unease and perhaps even panic because the large group setting potentially involves wide exposure to criticism. The inexperienced writer can feel similar emotions because of the potential exposure to criticism. Writing makes many people nervous. It shouldn't; if you can speak and listen and read, you should be able to write.

Writers naturally feel vulnerable because their work inevitably involves exposure to criticism.

Because writing usually needs to be understood by readers outside the speaker's immediate circle, it is governed by generally accepted rules and conventions that facilitate comprehension. The key to success for speakers of English who want to become confident writers is to master the generally accepted rules and conventions of written English. If your home language is different, those conventions can sometimes seem intimidating. They needn't. Don't worry about it. Don't look at grammar and usage conventions as a fixed indicator of educational level, ethnic identity, or social class. Instead, think of the conventions of standard written English as a code you intend to crack.

Standard written English is a code that anyone can crack.

The grant writer has a set of basic building blocks: words, sentences, and paragraphs. Utilizing these tools effectively requires paying attention to vocabulary, sentence structure and variety, and paragraph organization. It's that simple.

Words

The craft of writing is all about putting words together. Good writers tend to have big vocabularies that they don't use very much. A big vocabulary allows a writer to choose precisely the right word. Your job as a beginning grant writer will involve acquiring a good working knowledge of the vocabulary used in your institution or organization. If you are writing on behalf of a nonprofit conservation organization, you will need to familiarize yourself with the scientific and technical vocabulary used to discuss the issues important to your organization's mission. If you are seeking support for K-12 education, you will need to master the language of curriculum, instruction, and assessment. If you are working in a college or university, you may need to acquire new vocabulary each time you receive a new assignment.

Depending on the audience for your proposal, it may not be appropriate to utilize specialized vocabulary because doing so would cause you to lose your reader. Nevertheless, you will want to acquire the vocabulary needed to understand what you are writing about.

Broadly speaking, the short words are the best, and the old words best of all.
—Sir Winston Churchill

It is a good idea to maintain your own glossary of terms related to your grant-writing work. Start by making a simple electronic file of words and their definitions. As part of your regular routine, set aside five or ten minutes each day to add to your glossary. Whenever you come across an unfamiliar word, look it up and add it. Include acronyms, jargon—anything unusual you encounter in your daily work. Your writing will benefit from the cumulative effect of disciplined efforts at vocabulary building.

Keep an electronic glossary of terms that are used in your work.

Fortunately, there are many free resources available online to support your vocabulary-building efforts. (See Figures 6.1 and 6.2.) Online dictionaries are quick and simple to use. Create a Dictionaries folder in your Internet Explorer Favorites so that you can easily access the online dictionaries you find most helpful.

Microsoft Word also includes dictionary and thesaurus support accessible from the toolbar at the top of your screen. If you want to avoid repeating a word, place the cursor on the word for which you need a synonym, go to Tools, and select Language from the

Figure 6.1

Thefreedictionary.com also includes links to foreign language dictionaries and reference.

drop-down, as shown in Figure 6.3. A research window will appear on the right-hand side of your screen displaying alternatives, any one of which you can click on to see additional alternatives, as shown in Figure 6.4. If you want to check a definition, you would use the same sequence but click on the down arrow in the research window to access the *Encarta Dictionary: English (North America).*

Figure 6.2
Merriam-Webster OnLine.

Thesaurus and dictionary support are available onscreen in Microsoft Word.

Figure 6.3 **Figure 6.4**

Sentences

Learning to write well is largely a matter of mastering the craft of writing good sentences. In order to be a successful grant writer, it is essential that you master this craft. When you are the primary author of a proposal, you will need to write your own good sentences—thousands of them. When (as is very often the case) you are given a preliminary proposal draft written in ungrammatical or convoluted English and expected to transform it into acceptable English, you will need to be able to re-write other people's bad sentences.

If you can write a good sentence, you can write a good proposal.

Writing good sentences requires an understanding of two distinct issues: correctness and style. Of these, the first to address is simple correctness. Grant proposals must not contain basic errors such as sentence fragments, run-on sentences, subject-verb agreement errors, pronoun reference problems, or dangling modifiers. If you feel uneasy about basic sentence structure issues such as these, a good handbook or online resource will help you to sort yourself out quickly. An old standby that has stood the test of time is the *Harbrace College Handbook*, originally written by John C. Hodges and Mary E. Whitten and published by Harcourt Brace in 1941. Run-on sentences haven't changed much in the past 60 years, so even a well-worn copy of this handbook will serve you

First and foremost, your sentences must be correct.

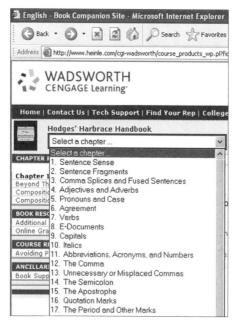

Figure 6.5
The Harbrace Handbook is now available for purchase in an online edition.

well as a source of information on grammar and usage. The current version is better still. *Hodge's Harbrace Handbook* (16th edition) by Cheryl Glenn and Loretta Gray, offers buyers of the handbook an online version that is up to date and very user-friendly.

Ask someone to critique your writing if you are unsure about your ability to construct correct, effective sentences.

If you do not feel confident in your ability to recognize basic errors in sentences, find a good writer whom you trust to read over your work and give you feedback. This person should be someone who is not connected with your workplace. If you have a former teacher who retains an interest in your professional welfare, ask for her advice and make it clear you are not fishing for compliments. (You may be surprised at how pleased teachers are to see their students after an interval of years.) This type of critique really needs to be done by a person; grammar-checking software can help, but it isn't always accurate. Your grant proposals will be read by people.

Once you are confident about the correctness of your sentences, the second issue to address is their style. Whereas sentence correctness is usually a matter of black and white—your participle is either dangling or it is tucked up where it belongs—style comes in many shades of gray. Style incorporates tone, attitude, word choice, word order, and elusive factors such as taste.

It is important that your sentences not only be correct but also that they achieve the desired effect.

For the grant writer, stylistic considerations are important because they influence whether or not your writing achieves the desired effect. If a portion of text is intended to impress the reader, does it do that? If your intention is to persuade the reader that the need you are describing is urgent and profound, do your sentences convey that? If you are trying to explain something highly complex so that it can be understood by an ordinary reader, have you succeeded in doing that? In order to fulfill intentions such as these, you need to make conscious, intentional decisions as you construct sentences.

A sentence should contain no unnecessary words, a paragraph no unnecessary sentences, for the same reason that a drawing should have no unnecessary lines and a machine no unnecessary parts.
—William Strunk, Jr.

Writing effective sentences depends in part on your ability to manipulate phrases and clauses. Practice combining two related sentences into one, or three related sentences into two. Practice combining them in several different ways and note the different effects achieved. Practice eliminating every single word that is not essential. The more you play around with your sentences, the more aware you will become of your linguistic options. Writing sentences is all about exercising linguistic options.

The most famous American style manual is *The Elements of Style* by William Strunk, Jr. and E. G. White. It sets out time-tested rules and principles for writing clear, effective American English sentences. As a grant writer, you may need at times to disregard what it says about never using the passive voice, but you will find most of the advice in this slim book relevant to your work.

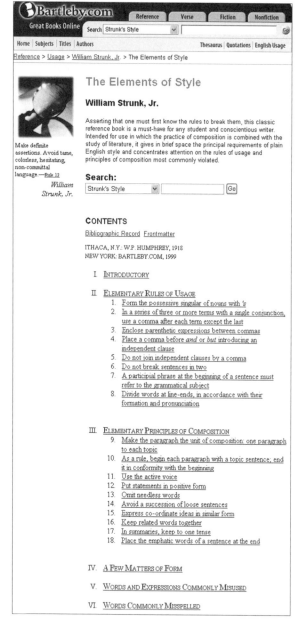

Figure 6.6
The Elements of Style *by William Strunk, Jr. (1918 edition) is available for free on Bartleby.com.*

Paragraphs

Sentences need to be organized into paragraphs in order for a sustained narrative or argument to be made comprehensible. No one will give your organization money on the basis of a bullet list of sentences. You will need to use paragraphs to subdivide and organize material so that it can be understood.

Although a great deal of creativity goes into grant writing when it is done well, grant writing is not creative writing. You will do best to organize your writing into conventional paragraphs with topic sentences that can be easily identified. A topic sentence expresses the main idea of the paragraph. Teachers usually tell their students to make the first sentence in each paragraph the topic sentence. It is fine to do that, but it is not the only way to construct an effective paragraph. Try using a transition or a lead-in sentence as your first sentence, and then put your topic sentence second. You may find that this improves the flow of ideas in your proposal. Another common placement for a topic sentence is at the very end. In this type of paragraph, you will build up momentum sentence by sentence and sum up forcefully in the last sentence. If you are making a case, this can be very effective because by the time the reader reaches the topic sentence, you will have already convinced him to agree with your contention.

Every paragraph needs a topic sentence that expresses the main idea of the paragraph.

There is no single best way to organize paragraphs. What is best is to organize your paragraphs in a variety of different ways. Just as a reader will respond positively to variety in sentence length or structure, so too will a reader respond positively to variety in paragraph organization. The important thing is that your organization must be intentional. Don't write a huge block of text and then arbitrarily separate it into chunks.

Paragraphs must be organized intentionally. Never arbitrarily chop up the text.

Before you begin to write a proposal section, draft a series of topic sentences. When you finish a piece of work, highlight the topic sentences and then read them out loud in the order in which they appear. Do they make sense? Is the sequence coherent? Can they stand alone? Are they persuasive?

A wonderful, free online resource you can turn to for advice on all your writing questions is The Purdue Online Writing Lab, known informally as the Purdue OWL. Founded in 1994, the Purdue OWL, shown in Figure 6.7, offers over 200 free resources for writers and teachers of writing. Put a link to the Purdue OWL in your Favorites folder.

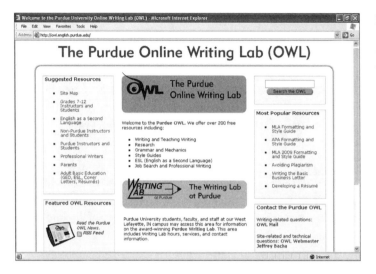

Figure 6.7
The Purdue OWL offers comprehensive support for writers.

The Writing Process

It is generally agreed that writing is a process, and there are lots of "process models" available for writers to use. Some are to be found in textbooks. Others can be purchased from companies that offer commercial seminars on writing. All represent an effort to set down the steps that good writers go through when they write. The idea behind writing process models is that if you do what good writers do, you will produce good writing. That doesn't always happen, of course, but going through a sequenced process will greatly increase the odds that you will be successful.

All of the writing process models involve variations on the following sequence of steps:

* Brainstorming
* Organizing
* Drafting
* Editing
* Proofreading
* Peer Review

It might seem as though going through all those steps will take forever—that you would be better off to just sit down, roll up your sleeves, and write the proposal. However, going through the steps or stages of the writing process actually saves time in the long run because it will prevent you from getting stuck. If you begin your

Going through all of the steps of the writing process will save you time in the long run.

grant-proposal project with "drafting," for example, you may find yourself wasting a great deal of time feeling uneasy and unproductive because you don't have a plan in place. On the other hand, if you write the first draft after you have thoroughly brainstormed the topic, identified the ideas you want to include, and organized them into a coherent case for support, you will be able to dive into the first draft confident that you know where you are going.

Brainstorming

When you brainstorm ideas, let your mind jump around and free-associate. Allow yourself to think out loud.

The initial stage of the writing process is where you will want to be as free and creative as possible. It is the time for thinking "outside the box" and letting your mind go wherever it takes you. Proposal development teams often want to engage in this process together as a group in order to have the opportunity for ideas to bounce from colleague to colleague.

Usually grant proposals lay out a problem and then propose a solution. Creative problem-solving is essential in order to develop new and innovative solutions that will appeal to funders. If you are brainstorming proposal development ideas as a group, you will want to make certain that there is a central place where everyone can see the ideas being generated. Ideally this is accomplished using interactive whiteboard technology, which puts everyone at a meeting into a multimedia environment visible to all. A facilitator using a white board is able to write over the top of projected computer images (see Figure 6.8).

The thinking processes of the average person are greatly stimulated by visual mapping and collaboration.

The efficacy of making ideas visible through visual mapping is so well established that software programs are available to facilitate the process. Mind mapping software can be utilized with interactive whiteboard technology to create a powerful tool for generating ideas in groups. Two mind mapping programs are illustrated in Figures 6.9 and 6.10.

Figure 6.8

An interactive whiteboard is ideal for group brainstorming activities.

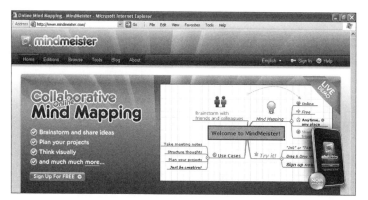

Figure 6.9
*MindMeister
software for visual
mapping.*

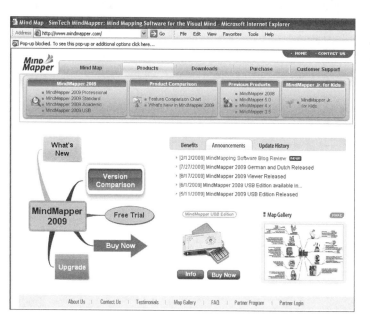

Figure 6.10
*MindMapper
software for visual
mapping.*

If resources such as whiteboards and visual mapping software are not available in your organization, you can still make ideas visible using chart paper clipped onto an easel or taped on a wall. In order to ensure that the group does not feel that you are trying to control the outcome, call on a colleague who is good at capturing ideas as they emerge and give her a marking pen to take it all down.

If you find yourself in a situation where people might not feel comfortable sharing their ideas, hand out index cards and collect anonymous responses in a basket. Do whatever you need to do to generate as many ideas as possible.

The absence of technology need not mean that your organization is unable to generate first-rate ideas. Remember, Einstein did not have a computer.

Organizing

Once you have generated as many ideas as you and your colleagues are able to come up with, you will need to take a hard look and decide which ideas to keep and which to discard or save for another project. When those decisions have been made, it is time to organize what you have decided to keep.

Outlining can be done the old-fashioned way on paper or the contemporary way on a computer. Either way works.

Organizing the ideas to be presented in a grant proposal involves prioritizing and arranging them in a manner that will persuade your potential funder to give you a grant. This can be done on a tablet or a computer, depending on your personal preference. You might enjoy using specialized software such as Webspiration that will take you from the brainstorming stage through the completion of an outline of your proposal. This can be particularly handy if you are called upon to present evidence of where you are at intervals during proposal development.

Figure 6.11
Webspiration is a visual thinking and outlining tool.

For detailed advice on organizing ideas for presentation in a grant proposal, see Chapter 7, "Organizing Information."

Drafting

When you sit down to do the first draft of a grant proposal, you will pull together everything you have learned about the project up to this point. You will have an outline that includes a list of topic sentences. You will have data and other documentation to support all of your main points. You will have a clear under-standing of what you are requesting and why your request has merit.

Write out your first draft as quickly as you can. Don't labor over every single word. Don't run a grammar or spell check. This is not the stage for second thoughts. Forge straight through it, being as expressive and emphatic as you would be if you were talking to a small receptive audience. The important thing is to get it all down.

First drafts should be written quickly. They are called "rough" for a reason.

Writing a first draft is intense. Especially at the very beginning, you might find that you are filled with nervous energy and want to walk around. If so, get up and walk around. It is hard to get revved up sitting in a chair staring at a screen. If formulating that first sentence is causing you to freeze, try a few old writers' tricks. Rehearse what you intend to say with a friend or a trusted col-league. Record the first paragraph and then transcribe it onto the computer, or ask someone to enter text onto the computer as you talk. Write on a legal pad while standing up. Do a few jumping jacks. Play your favorite music. Everyone is different. With expe-rience, you will learn what tricks motivate you to kick start that initial draft and get it moving forward. Once your momentum is established, you will probably be able to sit down quietly at your computer and finish it. First, however, you have to get started. Do whatever it takes to make that happen. Grant writers can't be pro-crastinators.

Every writer finds ways to get the ini-tial process going. Experiment and find what works for you.

Editing

Editing or revision is the heart of the writing process. It is the stage where you will determine where your draft achieves the desired effect and where it does not. It is often best to begin edit-ing by reading the text out loud because your ear will register sen-tence structure problems your eye misses. Hearing the text will also give you a sense of whether it is logical, complete, consistent, and convincing.

Novice writers tend to dislike revision because it feels like "doing it over." Many of us have suffered the experience of having an essay returned covered in red marks with a note from the teacher demanding that it be redone. This unpleasant association is rea-son enough to use the more professional word, editing, to describe what good writers do at this stage in the writing process. Good writers re-write and re-write until they get it right.

Editing is the stage where your skills as a writer will truly make a difference.

It is helpful to think of editing in terms of the simple ways you can manipulate the text to make it more effective:

- Add text
- Cut text
- Move text
- Change text

Adding, cutting, and moving are easy operations. Where you see that your case would be strengthened by additional explanation or information, add what is needed. Where you see that you have been redundant or have gone off on a tangent, cut the offending text. Where you see that the reader would better be able to follow your reasoning if facts or ideas were presented in a different sequence, move things around.

Editing involves adding, deleting, moving, and changing text.

Changing text is more challenging because it potentially involves so many types of editing—from changing the content to improving the sentence and paragraph structure. The more you do this type of editing, the more comfortable you will feel about doing it. Mastering this stage of the writing process will turn you from an amateur into a professional. As you gain confidence as a writer, it will probably become your favorite part of the process because it is the stage where your writing comes alive.

Proofreading

Edit and then proofread.

Proofreading comes after editing because there is no point in tidying up sentences that may be re-written or eliminated. It is the stage in the writing process where you take one last look to make certain there are no misspelled words or errors in punctuation or capitalization. Although it comes last, it is not an unimportant stage in the writing process. If you do not proofread carefully and miss glaring errors, some readers will see nothing else but the glaring errors.

Reliance on spell-checking software can get you into trouble.

Software checks can help you with proofreading, especially spelling, but it is unwise to rely on solely software because it has limitations. You still should proofread for spelling because computer-based spell checks don't always find 100% of errors. For example, "principal" and "principle" have different meanings, but each will pass a spell check. "The man" can be incorrectly typed as "them an" without alerting spell check. Sometimes you may have to review a proposal in a PDF or printed format.

A good way to catch spelling errors in print is to read the text backwards. It is boring, but it works as long as you are a good speller.

There are a number of tricks you can use to proofread your work for other types of errors. The first is to let it sit awhile. If you have just written a piece, it will simply look familiar and you will find it difficult to view it with a critical eye. Even a few hours away from the text will help you to distance yourself from what you have written. Reading the text aloud is a helpful technique because it will enable you to hear problems in punctuation; poorly punctuated sentences usually cause the reader to stumble. Circling each comma and then explaining the grammatical reason for its presence is another helpful exercise.

Know your weaknesses, and figure out a strategy for checking them. If you know you have a tendency to confuse "its" with "it's," then do an electronic search and check each one to make sure you have used it correctly. If you have trouble with pronouns, find each one and identify its referent.

> Writing is like bread dough. You need to let it rest awhile before you attack it again.

Peer Review

Peer review comes last because every writer must be responsible for her own proofreading. Peer review should give you an honest reaction to the content and organization of what you have written. If you give out a piece of writing that is full of errors, the reviewers won't see anything but the errors.

Because your grant proposals will be judged or scored by outside readers, it makes sense to get feedback from outside readers prior to submission. Your colleagues are the ideal preliminary outside readers. Sometimes the feedback you get from colleagues will surprise you. Sometimes it will annoy you. Often it will send you back to the editing stage of the writing process. When that happens, editing and peer review can loop round and round until all stakeholders are satisfied with the proposal.

> Feedback from peers is invaluable because it gives you an insight into how reviewers will react to your writing.

Don't allow yourself to become angry or frustrated if you find yourself in the editing/peer review loop. Remember that what you write represents the organization or institution you work for. Soliciting feedback and incorporating good suggestions can protect you from negative consequences in the event that a proposal is not successful.

Writing Purposes

You don't need to take a class in composition theory to become a good grant writer. However, it is helpful to be conscious of the purpose of the text you are composing. Each mode of discourse has its own conventions, and being aware of them can help you to communicate with readers who have internalized these conventions through their reading. The primary purposes of grant writing are to inform (or describe or explain) through expository writing and to persuade.

Writing to Inform

Although the ultimate purpose of your grant proposals will be to persuade those who receive them to support your organization, a good grant proposal always sets forth a certain amount of information. Grant makers do not make decisions based solely on persuasive arguments. You will need to be able to organize expository text, which may involve explanation, description, and the presentation of information. Sometimes a paragraph or section of a proposal may be dominated by just one of these types of writing. More often than not, your exposition will involve a combination of all three.

Most grant proposals involve explanatory, descriptive, and informative writing.

Informative writing communicates best when it conforms to familiar patterns and employs familiar devices. Paragraphs should be structured so that the reader can easily identify your main idea and supporting details. The logic behind the order in which you sequence information (e.g., chronological or categorical) should be obvious. Descriptions should be accompanied by examples or analogies to enable the reader to relate what is unfamiliar with something that is familiar. Similarities and differences should be explained. Cause and effect relationships should be made clear. Comparisons and contrasts should be drawn where appropriate.

Informative writing should employ patterns routinely used for thinking.

All of these devices align with basic patterns of thought and reasoning. Informative writing is most effective when it is consistent with our patterns of thinking.

Writing to Persuade

Aristotle identified three modes of persuasion that are just as effective today as they were 2,000+ years ago. These are:

- *Logos*—the appeal to reason
- *Ethos*—the appeal to character
- *Pathos*—the appeal to emotion

As a grant writer, you will employ all three, but your primary mode should always be the appeal to reason.

Whereas informative writing is usually organized around main ideas and details, persuasive writing is organized around claims (sometimes called arguments) and supports. A persuasive paragraph might be organized this way:

- Claim
  - Support #1
    - Explanation or elaboration of Support #1
  - Support #2
    - Explanation or elaboration of Support #2
  - Support #3
    - Explanation or elaboration of Support #3
- Conclusion

> Persuasive writing is organized around claims, supports, and conclusions.

If this type of paragraph is done well, by the time a reasonable person reaches the concluding sentence she should be in agreement with the claim made in the first sentence.

Connecting with Your Audience

No matter how well done a piece of writing is, it will fall flat if it doesn't connect with the audience for which it is intended. Writing is communication. If you aren't aware of your audience, it is unlikely that you will communicate effectively. To be successful at grant writing, you need to be very clear about who you are writing for and what they need.

Who Will Read Your Grant Proposal?

Grant makers don't always publicize how their grants are reviewed and by whom.

Sometimes grant makers will publish information about how funding decisions are made. More often than not, they don't. Networking is a great way to learn about who is involved in the proposal review process and how the process is conducted. This information is helpful not so that you can try to influence reviewers (which would be a catastrophic mistake) but so that you can pitch your proposal to what you know about their interests and level of expertise.

Grants written for an audience of experts must be written on their level.

If your proposal is to be reviewed by a panel of experts, you will need to write for a panel of experts. This means that no attempt should be made to simplify the content or to define specialized vocabulary. Your proposal will assume that the reader already knows a great deal about the subject area.

Grants written for a general audience must be written to account for what might not be understood without explanation.

A proposal written for a general audience assumes that the reader does not know a great deal about the subject area. If the subject is technical or highly specialized, you will need to simplify. You may need to define terms or substitute less technical terms to avoid confusion and misunderstanding. You may need to furnish extensive background information. This can be accomplished by providing detailed explanations that include comparisons, examples, and analogies. You might even consider including a story or two to illustrate the impact of your organization's work. Stories can serve to engage the general reader on an emotional level.

Always try to find out whatever you can about who will read your proposal and adjust the level of language and level of detail accordingly.

References

Style manuals provide guidance for attribution, documentation, and lists of references.

Grant proposals in academic, scientific, and technical fields need to meet the same standards for attribution and documentation that are expected of papers prepared for publication. If you are a grant writer in this type of setting, you will need to be familiar with the style manual used in the discipline you are writing about.

The "default" option for education and the social sciences is the *Publication Manual of the American Psychological Association*, known informally as *APA Style*.

> **NOTE**
>
> The "style manuals" discussed here are not the same type of "style manual" as Strunk and White's *The Elements of Style*. The phrase "style manual" is also routinely used to identify books dealing with documentation of research sources and preparation of manuscripts for publication.

Figure 6.12
APA Style *is a good choice if you are in doubt as to how to document references.*

The Modern Language Association (MLA) publishes another standard work, the *MLA Style Manual and Guide to Scholarly Publishing*, which is used in many academic disciplines.

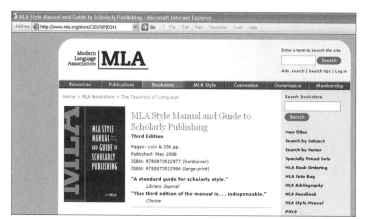

Figure 6.13
The MLA Style Manual *is widely used to document references in a variety of academic disciplines.*

The *Chicago Manual of Style*, published by the University of Chicago Press, is another standard work used for manuscript preparation. It is available online by subscription.

Figure 6.14
The Chicago Manual of Style *is available online.*

Kate Turabian's *A Manual for Writers of Research Papers, Theses, and Dissertations* also represents "Chicago style." Turabian was the graduate school dissertation secretary at the University of Chicago for 30 years.

Your 90-Day Writing Skills Checklist

✓ Create an electronic glossary of terms related to your grant-writing work, and update this glossary on a daily basis.

✓ Create an Internet Explorer Favorites folder for storing links to online dictionary, encyclopedia, and thesaurus resources.

✓ Purchase either a vintage Harbrace Handbook or the current version with online access.

✓ Identify a writing mentor who is willing to read your work and give you honest feedback.

✓ Engage in regular critical reviews and revisions of your own writing.

✓ Purchase a current version of Strunk and White or put the 1918 Strunk version available on Bartleby.com in an Internet Explorer Favorites folder.

✓ Add the Purdue OWL to your Favorites folder and use it on a daily basis.

✓ Become familiar with what an interactive whiteboard can do to bring your organization up to speed.

✓ Become familiar with the ways in which visual mapping software can assist your organization's grant-seeking efforts.

✓ Exercise the following four editing operations: adding text, deleting text, moving text, and changing text.

✓ Develop a set of proofreading strategies that protect you from the embarrassment of misspelled words and grammatical errors.

✓ Competently use the conventions for writing to inform and writing to persuade.

✓ Identify the documentation or style manual appropriate for your organization and purchase it or subscribe to an online version.

✓ Complete all steps of the writing process each time you produce a finished piece of writing for submission or review.

Chapter 7

Organizing Information

- Organizing Information to Make a Case
- Introductory and Summary Sections
- The Body of the Proposal
- Organizing the Submission Process

After you have completed your preliminary research and coordinated contacts with all of the key people involved in your grant project, it is time to close the door and begin the process of developing the grant proposal. What you do not under any circumstances want to do is start at the top of a blank screen or piece of paper and work your way down. What you want to do is to carefully and systematically organize all of the information you have assembled.

Organizing Information to Make a Case

Before you actually begin to write, you will make an outline. Your outline will be informed by your research, expertise, strategy decisions, and communication with colleagues and grant makers. Once you have an outline, even a proposal that promises to be 100 pages long will begin to feel manageable. A good outline will transform a large, overwhelming writing task into a series of smaller, achievable chunks of work.

Always outline your proposal before you begin to write.

Developing a Proposal Outline

The first thing to do as you begin your proposal outline is to review once again your grant-maker's guidelines. It could be that these guidelines will structure the main elements of your outline for you. If the grant maker has requested that proposals be of a certain length and contain prescribed sections presented in a certain order, construct an outline that exactly mirrors what the guidelines stipulate.

Before beginning your outline, refer to the grant-maker's guidelines.

Guidelines can ask for information that will comprise whole sections of your proposal, such as the purpose, goals and objectives, budget summary, and key personnel involved. Sometimes guidelines require specific attachments such as evidence of your tax-exempt status, letters of support, and resumes of principal investigators or key program people. Often proposals require attached institutional documentation, such as a list of board members or your organization's annual budget.

The hard and fast rule of proposal organization is that your proposal should follow the format of the grant-maker's guidelines. If it doesn't, it will appear to be an unsuccessful proposal written for a different grant maker that you have recycled in the hope that it might meet with better luck the second or third time around.

If there are no published guidelines, you must be creative and organize the proposal in a logical sequence. Fortunately, there are some proposal conventions that will help you to present your case in a coherent and compelling way.

When outlining a proposal, always follow a grant-maker's proposal guidelines exactly. Don't take any liberties with published guidelines.

Thinking in Sections

It's helpful to conceive a proposal outline in components that will become sections of your first draft. After you have some experience in grant writing, you will actually begin to think in proposal sections. During the pre-writing stages, you will organize and file your information section by section so that it will be easy to pull out when the time comes to draft each section.

The convention of formatting proposals in sections with headings has evolved as a means of assisting the reader. Just as a textbook will have chapter titles, chapter headings, and chapter subheadings to help a reader navigate the text, so too should a well-organized grant proposal. A proposal without headings would require the reader to plough through dense text to locate specific information. You can anticipate that any reader evaluating your proposal for funding will be looking for specific things. An important part of your job as a grant writer is to make it as easy as possible for an evaluator to find them.

Dividing your proposal into sections will help the reader to understand how you have organized the material you are presenting.

In this chapter, you will find a discussion of typical proposal sections. Take a look at the sample proposal outline in Figure 7.1 to get a sense of the various sections you might include in a proposal outline.

A few standard proposal components, such as an executive summary or abstract, are of necessity always placed at the very beginning of a proposal. Other components, such as tax-exempt documentation, board lists, and institutional budgets will normally be included at the end of a proposal as attachments. Most of the information you will need to organize will be placed in sections that will fall somewhere in between and will constitute the body of a well-developed proposal.

An executive summary or abstract will always appear at the beginning of a proposal, whereas documentation that supports the body of the proposal will usually appear at the very end.

SAMPLE PROPOSAL OUTLINE

1. Executive Summary

2. Background

4. Statement of Need

4. Project Description

5. Goals and Objectives

6. Project Narrative/Implementation

7. Dissemination Plan

8. Sustainability Plan

9. Replication Plan

10. Evaluation Plan

11. Budgetary Information

12. Appendices

    A. Project staff biographies and qualifications
    B. Copy of IRS letter 501 (c) (3)
    C. Most recent annual budget
    D. List of governing board members and their affiliations

Figure 7.1 *Basic outline for a proposal.*

Introductory and Summary Sections

What is placed at the very front of a proposal is important. These are the first words the reader will see, so they need to capture that reader's attention. Beyond the obvious need to make a positive first impression, other considerations call for a carefully drafted beginning. The writer of prefatory information needs to bear in mind that there are readers who will look at nothing else. For example, a proposal summary may be reproduced for decision makers who do not receive a copy of the full proposal for review. In such cases, the summary has to function as a stand-alone document.

> It is important to make a good first impression with a strong beginning.

Even when full proposals have been read at an earlier stage in the decision process, final decisions may be made on a review of proposal summaries. Sometimes the summary will reach audiences beyond the circle of reviewers. If a proposal receives a favorable review and a grant is awarded, the grant maker may extract the executive summary for external documentation or press information about grant awards. Thus, an executive summary can be expected to have a life beyond a proposal in print publications and web pages.

> Proposal summaries often have a life of their own independent of the rest of the grant proposal.

Executive Summary

The executive summary always appears at the beginning of a grant proposal. However, it is usually the last section you will write. It is very hard to summarize and introduce something that hasn't yet been written. However, once the rest of the proposal is finished, the task of summarizing is simple.

Even if your colleagues voice stylistic objections to placing the word "executive" before the word "summary," you should use it. The first sentence of the executive summary should be something like, "_____ (your organization) requests support in the amount of $_____ from the X Foundation for _____." What follows will be a distillation of the proposal.

> The executive summary should summarize what follows in the grant proposal.

If you have written your proposal in sections, you will be able to craft a sentence or phrase for each section to describe the purpose, need, scope, goals and objectives, timeline, method of evaluation, sustainability plan, and so on. The key is to be brief. Ideally, you are shooting for a third of a page of text or less.

> The executive summary must be cogent and complete. Write it last.

A summary that covers a full page of text is no longer an executive summary. Every word must be carefully selected because the executive summary could be the only portion of your proposal that some people will read in the decision-making process.

Abstract

Sometimes a grant maker will require an abstract. The primary difference between an executive summary and an abstract is its length. Abstracts have more generous length requirements or limits, and sometimes they can fill the entire first page of a proposal. Whereas an executive summary would always be a single paragraph, an abstract will be comprised of a series of paragraphs. Abstracts are required by many federal agency grant programs for which the proposals are very long and distributed for peer review. Foundations that fund research grants also tend to require abstracts.

Abstracts tend to have longer length requirements or limits than an executive summary.

A grant maker might require an abstract but not specify what is to be in it, in which case you can summarize the entire proposal as you see fit. Sometimes the grant maker will specify that the abstract contain information from designated sections of the proposal. If guidance is given for the contents of the abstract, follow it closely. An abstract will not necessarily condense every single section or major item in your proposal. Like an executive summary, it should be written after the rest of the proposal has been completed.

Think of the abstract as a one-page proposal. It should include all of the high points.

The reader of an abstract should come away with a sense of having read a one-page proposal, when actually there could be several hundred pages of highly detailed information and support to follow in the proposal itself. The sample abstract in Figure 7.2 shows six short paragraphs in a logical sequence. The first paragraph is a single sentence that summarizes the proposed request for support. This is followed by a paragraph containing a statement of need. The next paragraph summarizes the organization's background as highly appropriate for the proposed project. Two short paragraphs follow that describe the project, and the final paragraph demonstrates the financial commitment of the organization to complete the project successfully.

Abstracts are very important in the decision review process. Your proposal could be in a stack of dozens of competing proposals. Your abstract must read well. A poorly written abstract sends a signal to a busy reviewer that there is no need to read further.

SAMPLE PROPOSAL ABSTRACT

The University of the United States Press is seeking a challenge grant of $500,000 from the National Endowment of the Humanities to stimulate giving to fund a new endowment for the permanent establishment of the Library of Polish Literature, a new series of original texts accompanied by facing-page English translations of major literary works in the Polish language.

The need for this new series was confirmed by the results of a survey of membership of US and foreign members of the National Academy as well as extensive survey of Polish-American fraternal, social, and political associations and groups in the United States. Among the respondents were scholars and students from all major academic centers of Slavic languages and East European studies in North America. The respondents also included professionals outside academe who are influential in their communities. The results of the survey indicated that the vast majority would recommend that their libraries subscribe to the series, and would themselves subscribe as individuals.

The University of the United States Press is the best press to initiate and publish the new series because of the resources that are available to it among the faculty and staff of constituent schools and libraries of the university. The University has academic units that specialize in Polish language study in the departments of political science, European literature, and area studies. The Department of Slavic Studies houses the greatest number of tenured faculty teaching Polish of any university in the western hemisphere. Library and archival materials in the University's library draw scholars in Polish language, literature and culture from throughout the world.

Each volume in the Library of Polish Literature will include the best available edition of the original text with a fresh, modern translation presented on a facing page. The new volumes will be published in affordable yet sturdy cloth and paperback editions on the model of the Harvard Classics Library. When a sufficient number of printed editions is available, provision will be made for publication in electronic form.

To ensure that the individual volumes of the series are affordable, The Press will need funding that cannot come from book sales income alone. Such funding would be used to meet modest editorial expenses and some expenses related to manufacturing costs. We propose to raise $1 million dollars in addition to the challenge grant to result in a $1.5 million permanent restricted endowment for the Library of Polish Literature.

The University of the United State has previous successful experience in matching NEH challenge grants. The University is in the planning stage for a $1 billion capital campaign, and a plan is underway to seek matching funds from alumni, friends and foundations that are particularly interested in the Press. The University's Board of Governors has agreed to view the needs of the University Press as a priority and personally seek to meet this challenge.

Figure 7.2 *Sample abstract.*

Background

Following your executive summary, you may choose to include a section introducing your organization. You might entitle this section "Background," or you might simply use the name of your organization as the section title. This is the area of the proposal where you can convince the reader that your organization is solid, effective, and worthy of support. In addition, you will want to make it very clear that your organization is capable of carrying out the project you are proposing.

The background section should be structured to give the reader confidence in your organization's track record and fitness to undertake the proposed project.

As you develop a repertoire of grant proposals, you will undoubtedly amass a certain amount of standard language used to describe your organization and its activities. Sometimes there may be text that has been vetted by your legal department that is required to be used in certain circumstances. Used judiciously, standard descriptions are a timesaver and can be a safeguard against unintentional errors or omissions. However, your background section must nevertheless be tailored to each proposal if it is to be effective. Never simply cut and paste canned verbiage about your organization. Each time you write a proposal you will need to consider the audience receiving it and the project or program you are proposing to undertake.

Standard language used to describe your organization can be helpful, but it is important not to disregard the specific needs of your audience.

Every proposal presents a unique set of circumstances. For example, in a proposal for a university applying for a high energy nuclear physics research grant, the background section would emphasize the university's history and reputation as a leader in physics research. If the same university were to seek support for an undergraduate teacher training program, the background section would highlight the accomplishments and strengths of its school of education. A grant writer in charge of both proposals might begin with a generic description of the university that is identical in both proposals and then branch out in succeeding paragraphs with information specific to the proposed grant project. If you want to include extensive information, consider breaking it up with subheadings to help the reader.

Subheadings help the reader to navigate the text.

The background section of a proposal presents you with an opportunity to "sell" your organization. Don't hold back. Make it as impressive and persuasive as possible. If your organization is uniquely poised to carry out the proposed project, explain the reasons why in some detail. Be sure to include recent awards and public distinctions. If your organization ranks high in relevant comparative lists, include this information. For example, a nonprofit social service organization given an excellent efficiency rating by *Forbes* for spending a high percentage of funds raised on direct services for clients would showcase that rating. A college that places high on *U.S. News and World Report's* "Best Colleges" list would mention that ranking if it is relevant to the proposal.

> When describing your organization and its accomplishments in a grant proposal, make sure you highlight successes that relate to your request.

The Body of the Proposal

The body of your proposal will be comprised of various separate sections. As explained previously, if the grant maker has prescribed these sections, you will follow submission guidelines. If not, you can follow or adapt conventions in standard use. Samples of standard proposal sections are discussed here to get you started.

> Standard proposal conventions will help you to organize proposal information in a meaningful way.

Statement of Need

The needs section is critical because it drives both your project and the grant-maker's motivation to support it. It is the reason you are writing the proposal. It describes the status quo and defines the problem you are proposing to address or solve.

For example, if you work for a social service agency and are proposing to develop a new program for people with disabilities, you would want to present facts, statistics, and perhaps vignettes or testimonials to substantiate the pressing social and humanitarian need for your project. For a proposal dealing with an environmental issue, you would include expert opinions and all the factual information needed to persuade a reasonable person that the problem you want to address is real and urgent.

The statement of need must be compelling but accurate and truthful. Assume that your reader is well-informed but not necessarily an expert in the field.

> The statement of need is the reason you are writing the proposal.

Project Description

The project description flows naturally from the needs section because it describes the solution you are proposing to the problem defined in your statement of need. It too must be compelling, accurate, and truthful. You will need to present a logical, convincing case for your project as a promising course of action likely to solve or mitigate the problem you have described. In most cases, you will also need to show how your proposed solution is new and innovative.

> The project description must convince the reader that your need is genuine and that your project will address the need effectively.

Federal agencies will often mandate that solutions or interventions be selected from a list of programs shown through research to be effective. Corporations tend to take a pragmatic approach and fund any solution to a problem that appears likely to work as long as it aligns with corporate objectives. Foundations, however, are usually committed to supporting new and innovative programming. In order to secure foundation support, even if you are proposing to apply strategies shown through research to have been successful elsewhere, it will be essential to demonstrate that what you are proposing to do has not been done before in quite the way you are proposing to do it.

Foundations tend to favor projects they perceive as new and innovative.

Goals and Objectives

The goals and objectives section of a proposal should likewise link directly to the statement of need. This section lays out how you anticipate your proposed project will bring about the change that is needed. This section describes what you intend to accomplish, expressed in measurable terms. Measurability is essential because it establishes the quantitative framework for program evaluation. Sometimes you will see the two words used almost interchangeably, but in the grant-writing world, "goals" tend to be more general than "objectives."

Goals and objectives need to be measurable. They express the terms you will use to judge whether or not your project is successful.

For example, if your overall goal is reduction in the dropout rate for high school students, you would need baseline data (to show what the dropout rate is currently) and objectives that express the expected improvement in quantitative terms. For example: By December 31, 2022, the dropout rate will have decreased from 15.2% to 8.0%.

Program objectives must be clear, measurable, reasonable, and attainable. A reader should be able to see a direct correlation between your project and the improvement you are trying to bring about.

Project objectives must be measurable and reasonable.

You should study grant-maker guidelines for any measurement requirements or recommendations when formulating goals. You will find that guidance in this area will vary considerably. Some foundations and government agencies that fund research grants require elaborate empirical methods for evaluation. For these grants, proposal goals and objectives are developed carefully and precisely by the person directing the research project. A grant writer might review the goals and objectives for such a project, but would not develop them.

Other grant makers will have more general requirements about measurability in evaluation, in which case you will have some flexibility in developing goals. Grant makers supporting human services delivery tend to look for increases in the numbers of persons served or quantifiable results that demonstrate positive outcomes for the persons served.

Remember, goals and objectives are closely linked to a proposal's evaluation plan. The evaluation section of a proposal tends to be placed toward the end. Make certain that the link between the two sections is clear, even though they are not consecutive.

Goals and objectives are always linked closely to the evaluation plan.

Project Narrative or Implementation

The project narrative section calls for greater descriptive detail than would be given in a project description. The section title might include the name of your project. For example, if you are proposing a new scholarship program for minority students at a college or university, you might call this section "Project Narrative: Methodius College Minority Scholarship Initiative." If you work for an environmental organization proposing a project to save an endangered species, you might entitle the section "Project Narrative: Saving the Lepidarius Butterfly."

A project narrative is best organized chronologically, and sometimes you may actually want to include a timeline, calendar, or Gantt Chart. See Figure 7.3 for an example of a Gantt Chart. Begin by outlining the beginning, middle, and end of the project. Then develop paragraphs of the narrative based on the chronological sequence of events. If you are requesting multi-year support, it is best to organize the narrative year by year, providing subheadings for "Year 1," Year 2," "Year 3," and so on. Subheadings will help the reader to visualize the way the project will unfold and to absorb or locate information within the narrative.

Chronological organization is best for a project narrative.

Be mindful of the project's goals and objectives as you develop the project narrative or implementation plan.

Dissemination Plan

You may find it to your advantage to include a section on dissemination in a proposal. Some corporations and foundations give preference to projects and programs that result in publicity of substance. Some agency programs likewise look favorably on publicity, especially if it links to a generally positive story. You

Basic Gantt Chart

VIEW PDF ⊕

Security and Access Control System												Created Using Milestones Software www.kidasa.com

P-R-O-J-E-C-T	2000			2001									R-E-S-P
	Oct	Nov	Dec	Jan	Feb	Mar	Apr	May	Jun	Jul	Aug	Sep	
ENGINEERING													ENGINEERING
Site Survey	18 △▱▱▱▼15												Marwell Engineering
Draft Survey Results	18 △▱▱▱▱▱▼4												Marwell Engineering
GMBH Review			4 △▱▱▱▼29										Lost Creek Point Mgmt
Survey RPT (Final)				1 △▱▱▼22									Electrical Contractor
GMBH RFV Approval				3 △▱▱▱▼6									Lost Creek Point Mgmt
System Design					14 △▱▱▱▼20								Marwell Engineering
HMBC Review					20 △▱▼4								Electrical Contractor
Bid and Award						4 △▱▱▱▱▱▱▼4							Marwell Engineering
Construction Support						27 △▱▱▱▱▱▱▱▱▱▱▱▱▱▱▼5							Marwell Engineering
CONSTRUCTION													CONSTRUCTION
Buy Cable Conduit						24 △▱▱▼16							Electrical Contractor
Install Cable						2 △▱▱▱▼7							Electrical Contractor
Procure Hardware						24 △▱▱▼21							A & J Security
Install Hardware						21 △▱▱▱▼20							A & J Security
Deliver Console						3 △▱▱▱▼11							A & J Security
Load Data							13 △▱▱▼11						Lost Creek Point Mgmt.
Configure Software						1 △▱▱▼26							A & J Security

This is a Basic Gantt chart example. It shows tasks in a Security and Access Control project. Tasks are outlined in two sections. Each task uses a yellow triangle to indicate the start date of the task and a green down triangle to indicate the finish date of the task. Also shown on this schedule are the responsible sub-contractors for the project (in the column labeled R-E-S-P).

All schedules used in this web site were created using Milestones software. Learn More

Corporate Home | Contact Us

Figure 7.3 *Sample Gantt Chart on KIDASA Software website.*

might, for example, kick off the project with a press conference and issue news releases or video news releases regularly during the course of the project.

Consider the possibilities for dissemination in an academic or professional context as well. Colleagues who will be directing and managing the project or program you are proposing often will have the capability and willingness to promote a grant-funded project within their professional circles. This type of dissemination could include presenting professional papers or conducting seminars on the project at professional meetings or conferences. You might even structure a win-win for everyone by building the cost of conference participation into the project budget. Similarly, any dissemination of project results that is published in academic publications will add credibility to your project. Make sure that your colleagues understand that any activity proposed for dissemination in professional circles should have the review and approval of the grant maker. Your proposal should clearly indicate the grant-maker's right of review.

A good dissemination plan can give your project credibility.

If your dissemination plan includes public relations activity, see the discussion "Publicizing Grant Awards" in Chapter 12 for ideas on venues to consider for a dissemination section of your proposal. Keep in mind that any dissemination activities you propose should mesh with the grant-maker's guidelines and wishes.

Foundations tend to favor projects that promise to result in publicity of substance.

Sustainability

Generally speaking, corporations, foundations, and other grant-making organizations support projects only for a specified period of time. They do not enter into support with the assumption that they will continue to fund your project as long as it is successful and needed. However, they do not want to support change that does not endure after the project has ended. Hence the need for a sustainability plan or a "future funding" plan.

Funders usually want to support positive change that will endure after the conclusion of a grant project.

Often funders will require that one section of your proposal address sustainability. Even if this is not an explicit requirement, your grant proposal will be greatly strengthened if you can demonstrate in a reasonable way the steps your organization will take to sustain positive change after the initial project is completed. For example, a proposal requesting support for training to increase your organization's capacity to provide a particular service might include plans for follow-up training and monitoring

Many grant makers see themselves as investors in society, and they generally view the projects they fund as seed projects.

for fidelity of implementation after the conclusion of the training. Such a sustainability plan might require a formal budget commitment on the part of your organization, which of course would need to have the appropriate approval.

If you are working for an educational institution, and your project has the capability of being incorporated into your organization's curricular or co-curricular budget after successful completion, you might want to develop a sustainability section in your proposal to demonstrate precisely how your organization can maintain the program. For example, if you are requesting funding to develop a new science curriculum, and project expenses are primarily for faculty release time and new laboratory equipment, the sustainability plan might be comprised of laboratory maintenance costs to be borne by your organization's operating budget after completion of the grant. Other streams of revenue that could contribute to maintaining the project in the long term, such as income from student laboratory fees, should be identified and included in the sustainability plan.

A sustainability plan should be creative but believable.

A proposal requesting funding for the expansion of a social service might include a plan for revenue generation to sustain the expansion of those services found through data analysis to be effective. Often local or state jurisdictions can be brought in to help maintain innovative services, and client fees can also be used to sustain a new project after initial grant seed funding.

Sustainability plans sometimes invoke the creation of an endowment to provide long-term funding for a project that has been granted seed money. Be very careful when doing this. Your organization will need to demonstrate that it has the capacity to raise funds and maintain a restricted endowment for the project. Your organization will also need a record of endowment fundraising and management for your plan to have any credibility. You should assume that the grant maker would have the knowledge and methodology to determine whether your plan is feasible without even consulting your organization's financial officials and financial records. Raising an endowment would represent a significant complication to your proposal project involving top officers of your organization and your governing board. See Chapter 10, "Proposals for Endowment Support," for more information.

Creation of an endowment is perhaps the most difficult type of sustainability plan to implement successfully.

Developing a sustainability plan requires careful thought and consultation with colleagues beyond the program area for assistance and advice. A finance officer can often bring a valuable perspective on ways to sustain a successful pilot project in the long term. The finance officers at a nonprofit organization are likely to know whether charging for services or seeking local authority support are feasible options. They are also the most likely people at any nonprofit to know of previously successful sustainability activities following seed funding from a grant. Sustainability plans need to be realistic. Always assume that grant makers are able to evaluate a plan for its feasibility.

Grant makers are experts at evaluating sustainability plans.

Some strategies are unlikely ever to be viewed as feasible. For example, don't present a sustainability plan that calls for returning to the grant maker for future support in the event that the project is successful. Similarly, to state that you would seek funding from other grant makers for a renewal of support in future years is weak, because the reader of your proposal will know that other grant makers are unlikely to want to pick up where they leave off. Grant makers typically are interested in projects or programs that can develop their own intrinsic worth and garner future support from individuals, groups, or audiences that are stakeholders to some extent in the proposed project.

Don't present a sustainability plan that depends on seeking additional grant support for the same project.

Replication

Many foundations consider themselves catalysts for change, and the projects and causes they support are aimed at changing society in some way for the common good. Some corporations and government agencies may also offer grant programs that fund projects intended to serve as models for application in other locations or organizations. You will find in your research that some grant makers see a distinct advantage in funding projects or new programs that have potential to be duplicated elsewhere.

You will know the specific kinds of social changes favored by a grant maker through careful study and research of past grants and other information. See Figure 7.4 for an example of the "Replication Strategies" page on the website of The Wellmark Foundation. The motto on this page is, "There is no need to reinvent the wheel." Nonprofits in health and human services delivery are directed to descriptions and contact information about projects the Foundation has funded and deemed worthy of replicating.

Many grant makers favor projects that have the potential to be successfully replicated elsewhere.

Figure 7.4

"Replication Strategies" page from The Wellmark Foundation website.

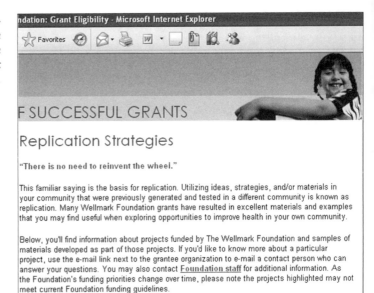

If you have identified a match between a new project at your institution and a grant maker that aims for expanded change, consider developing a replication plan included as a separate section for your proposal. Done well, a detailed plan for replication of a project can strengthen your proposal. Consult your colleagues to design the model and method of replication and the conditions under which replication would be undertaken. Determining whether or not to replicate is a decision that will need to be substantiated by data, so your plan should include details of data to be collected and how the data will be analyzed and evaluated. Qualitative data alone is rarely considered sufficient evidence for program replication.

If your project director or principal investigator is a local, regional, or national leader in his field, his coordinated efforts at dissemination will add strength to the case of your proposal. Your plan will be even stronger if your organization has a regional or national presence and an established network that has been used in the past to promote project replication. The project replication section of a proposal is no place for creative writing. It is crucial that project directors and the leadership of your organization support and contribute to a replication plan if it is to be credible and eventually effective.

Projects proposing replicability must be credible.

Evaluation

An evaluation section can serve several useful purposes. First, of course, it will structure how you will determine whether your project is a success or a failure. In addition, it presents an opportunity for you to demonstrate that you know what you are doing and have the ability to analyze and present project results in a professional manner. Beyond that, project evaluation yields information that can be used to provide an occasion for continued communication with the foundation after the grant cycle has ended.

The evaluation section of a proposal shows how you will define success. It also enables you to showcase your expertise.

The method of evaluation outlined in a proposal should be designed and written with the grant-maker's guidelines in mind. If the guidelines suggest nothing specifically related to project evaluation, check your files on the grant maker and review their reporting requirements. Often grant reporting requirements will give you a roadmap for developing a credible evaluation method that will appeal to a specific grant maker. See Figure 7.5 for an example of The McGowan Fund's reporting requirements, which note their expectation of measurable outcomes. A link on this page leads to this foundation's detailed "Grant Evaluation Rubrics." Needless, to say, you would study this information carefully before submitting a proposal to The McGowan Fund.

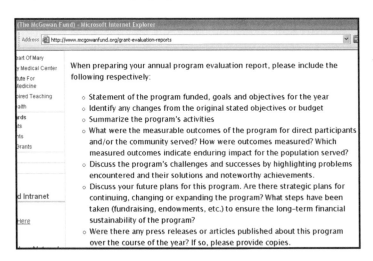

Figure 7.5

Evaluation guidelines for evaluation on The McGowan Fund's website.

Assume that every grant maker requires different evaluation methods. Some, like the Cailloux Foundation, may accept both quantitative and qualitative data and review in an evaluation, as shown in Figure 7.6.

Figure 7.6

Grant evaluation guidelines from The Cailloux Foundation website.

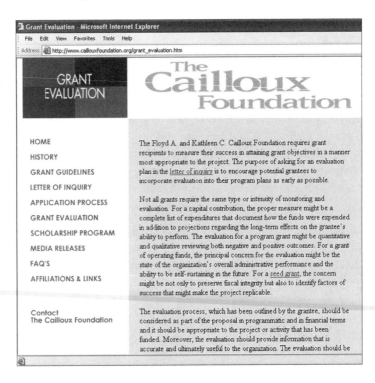

Grant-proposal evaluation should always be designed with a grant-maker's guidelines in mind.

Similar research should be done prior to preparing an evaluation plan for any proposal. Ideally, you should share any information you find with your colleagues who are designing the project and work with them as they design evaluation so that you can write about it effectively and accurately in a proposal. Evaluation design is an area of proposal writing that requires very close collaboration with colleagues who will be implementing the project.

Budgetary Information

Comprehensive, detailed budget information for projects or programs will usually be provided to you by program people after approval by the financial officer of your organization. In an ideal situation, you will not be expected to cost out exactly what your organization needs in order to undertake a program.

What you will be expected to do is communicate that budget information concisely and effectively. Your budget summary, like the executive summary, is a brief paragraph that will tell the reader exactly how much money you are requesting and how it will be spent. If it is an extensive project, you may need several paragraphs to describe the expenses, in which case you will write a budget narrative.

The proposal budget must lay out how much money your organization is requesting and exactly how it will be spent.

When writing a budget summary or budget narrative, make sure it links closely to your executive summary. The busy person who only reads the executive summary of each proposal will probably turn next to the budget section if impressed with the executive summary. Therefore, plan your proposal to satisfy a reader who looks at these two sections and nothing else.

The proposal budget should link directly to the executive summary or abstract.

If your organization is small or new to the grant-seeking process, you may find that you need to develop your own budget expertise quickly. Establishing a good working partnership with your finance person is critical. It may by default fall to you to do grant proposal estimations, calculations, projections, and any number of other financial tasks you weren't counting on. Embrace the opportunity to learn this aspect of grant preparation, because it is critical. Grants are money, after all. If you can become more or less self-sufficient with respect to drafting budgets, you will have a skill set that will be truly valued by the program people in your organization. The grant writer who can, for example, calculate fringe benefits accurately with the click of a mouse is in a stronger position for success than one who has no idea how to do that and must depend on other people to "figure out the money piece." Search for opportunities to attend seminars and conferences on grant proposal budgeting, and take advantage of those opportunities whenever you are able to do so.

A good relationship with your organization's budget person is priceless.

Appendices and Attachments

Some of the detailed information that a grant maker seriously interested in funding your project would need to have available is best included in appendices. Examples of information you might attach to a proposal as appendices include:

- Documentation of 501(c)(3) status
- Documentation of recognized accreditation or membership in a credentialing organization
- Board members and their affiliations
- Organization budget information
- Relevant audit information

- Resumes of project director, principal investigator, and other key personnel
- Data tables that show the source of data critical to establishing your case for support

Always review the grant-maker's proposal guidelines to make certain that you provide the required attachments or appendices.

Grant applications frequently include attached materials that directly relate to the project or program proposed for support. Sometimes attached materials may be institutional information or documentation that the grant maker requires for any proposal under consideration. The first and most important rule about proposal attachments is to follow the grant-maker's guidelines and provide any appended information required in a proposal application.

Corporations and foundations routinely require that any proposal requesting financial support be accompanied with a copy of the official Internal Revenue Service letter confirming your organization's nonprofit status under IRS Code 501(c)(3). This is one of the first documents you should obtain when you start your job; make copies of this letter so that you will have them handy for future grant submissions. Your organization's 501(c)(3) letter will occupy the first of several hard files you set up for routinely requested documentation.

An IRS Code 501(c)(3) letter is routinely required as an attachment to any proposal for corporation or foundation support.

Another frequently required proposal attachment is a list of your governing board members. It is a good idea to develop several formats of this list. Keep them as Word files so you can easily update and print them as needed. See Figure 7.7 for an example. One board list format you will need is a simple alphabetical list with notations for the chairperson and any ex-officio members such as your chief executive officer or other staff. Sometimes guidelines require that the board list include committee assignments or outside affiliations. As you begin submitting proposals, you will become familiar with this aspect of proposal preparation. Each time you create a board list with new criteria, save it to be adapted for later use.

Consult your organization's financial officer about preparing an organizational budget summary that provides an appropriate level of detail.

Be prepared also to submit attachments about your organization's annual budget. It's advisable to talk to your chief financial officer about how to present budget information in proposals in advance of needing it. Otherwise, you may be given a document that is too long to reasonably fit in a proposal. Your financial office professionals can help you produce a neat and tidy annual budget summary that will be exact and still look good in a proposal. Whether it's a scanned page or a printed spreadsheet, you

FR. MEGER
CENTER
FOR SOCIAL JUSTICE

Board of Trustees

Ron Arone
CEO, AR Industries

Lewis Atwater
Retired, General Pipe Co.

Herbert Berman
Vice President, M&A Bank

Jane Carr, *Chairperson*
President, Cooper Wire, Inc.

Randolph A. Coleman, S.J.
Rector, St. Cyril Monastery

Harriet Dusenburg
Owner, Branston Stables

John Enmen, *Ex Officio*
President, Methodius College

William Earhart
Pomeranian Resorts

Rudolph Gerstweiler
Professor, Methodius College

Anne Hoffman, *Vice-Chair*
Vice President, Hoffman Cos.

Robert M. Johnson, Esq.
Partner, Johnson and Stein

Raymond Lazarus, Secretary
Director, Cool Industries

Carl Robeson
Partner, Cooke Accounting

Francis X. Wakowski
Vice President, Wak Company

Barry Yount
CFO, Hedman Industries

George Zebron
Director, National Web Co.

Figure 7.7 *Sample proposal attachment: List of board members.*

will want to reserve good hard copies or scanned electronic files for proposal preparation.

Your organization's annual report is another document you can assume will sometimes be required with a grant application. Tuck away a good supply of this publication, because you will also need copies for grant-maker cultivation purposes outlined in Chapter 5.

Make sure that proposal collaborators understand how to decide what information belongs in the proposal itself and what should be appended.

If you are collaborating with colleagues on a grant, make sure they understand the distinction between what should be contained in the body of a proposal and what can appropriately be included in an appendix or attachment. Review guidelines regarding attachments with all collaborators who might be responsible for their content. It is not unusual for a grant writer to receive a first draft in which vital information about the case is relegated to an attachment. Explain to your colleagues that while appendices and attachments may be important, they are not where you will make your case for support.

Appendices contain information that supports what is presented in the body of the proposal.

Always remember that appendices are only consulted by proposal reviewers who are seriously interested in your proposal. Never force the reader to consult an appendix in order to make sense of your project narrative. Instead, include in your appendices the types of information and evidentiary support that will effectively support the case presented in your project narrative. The proposal reviewer should be able to turn to an appendix, review the information presented, and say, "Yes, this is solid evidence supporting what it says in the proposal narrative."

Organizing the Submission Process

You may come to your new role as a grant writer and find that a clear and well-documented proposal submission process is already in place. If you find yourself in this situation, you simply need to study the process and work within the rules that have been set down for you to follow.

It is important to know who in your organization needs to sign off on grant proposals prior to submission.

However, more often than not, a beginning grant writer fills a newly-created position or replaces a predecessor who leaves little behind with respect to the submission protocol of the organization. If you find yourself in such an unstructured situation, you will need to ferret out the steps your organization requires to get a proposal approved for preparation and cleared for submission after it is written.

Every grant writer needs access to a written set of steps for internal approval of proposals. If this does not yet exist in your organization, you will need to develop a working document (see Figure 7.8). Consult with the person you report to before you plan this document, and apprise that person of any discussions you might want to have with others in your organization's management hierarchy during the course of its development. Your supervisor might want to do some of the work herself. Every grant proposal represents a potential commitment, so it is vital to have approval from the top on down before commencing work.

Pre-Proposal Stage Clearance

Staff time equates to money, so a grant writer needs to have some means of getting a proposal idea approved before spending time outlining and writing a proposal. You should not assume institutional priorities, nor should you take on the responsibility of determining your organization's priorities. Those priorities need to be identified by your board and management.

Institutional priorities are defined at the highest level of an organization.

You have been hired to produce proposals that result in external funding. You will be judged primarily on the results of your proposals. This means that you will need a way to prioritize your proposal writing and allocate your research and writing activities to advance your priorities. Those priorities must be determined by the executive officers of your organization. If an approval procedure is not already in place, you should suggest that an executive of your organization approve all proposal ideas put forth before you begin work on drafting a proposal.

At a college or university, many proposal ideas will come directly from the executives of the institution, and these of course would therefore be automatically approved as priorities. However, you might find that mid-level administrators and faculty members bring forward proposal ideas for you to work on that do not mesh with your organization's priorities. You should not be the person to tell a faculty member or staff person that a project is not a priority for you. That message should be conveyed by an organization executive or chief academic officer.

Before you begin working on a proposal idea, make certain that it is an organizational priority.

If you are a new grant writer at a nonprofit organization, you will want your proposal-writing priorities to be approved by either the chief executive officer or her deputy.

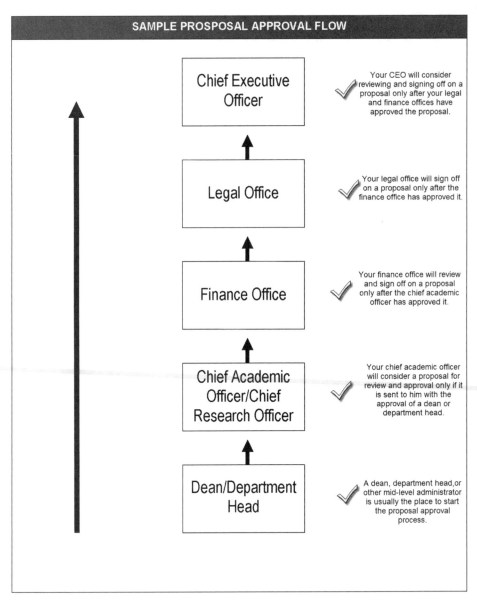

Figure 7.8 *Sample proposal approval flow.*

Clearing Submissions Internally

At most universities, colleges, and nonprofit organizations, the chief executive officer must "sign off" on any proposal submitted for external funding. Usually there are also governing provisions for someone else to sign off in a chief executive officer's absence. This may be a deputy of the chief executive, or in an educational institution, it could be the chief academic officer. Some federal forms accompanying a proposal call for the signature of the institutional grant administrator. This form can be signed off by the chief executive officer or his deputy.

Proposal signature authority is usually restricted to the chief executive officer.

You may find that faculty or professional staff are under the impression that they can sign off on a proposal that is ready for submission. It is not unusual for people who are responsible for the substance of a proposal to think that they have sign-off authority. In fact, you may find that professionals in education and the nonprofit world do not necessarily understand nonprofit governance. Proposals for grant funding and acceptance of external funding are subject to the approval of an organization's governing board, and only your CEO can speak on behalf of the board. Gently inform any colleagues who think that they have signatory responsibilities that they do not. Foundations in particular will expect that the cover letter for a proposal will be signed by your organization's chief executive officer.

Grant proposals usually require board approval.

Developing a Proposal Submission Calendar

It is the task of a grant writer to project grant proposal completion within a timeframe that incorporates both internal approval deadlines and the external deadlines of a grant maker. In your first days as a grant writer, you will be able to set this up using a simple blank calendar.

Some grant writers maintain a large erasable wall calendar of forthcoming deadlines and related proposal project tasks. This is a useful visual device, especially if you are working with other grant writers or administrators who need to be involved in the submission process. Others use Outlook to manage grant tasks. Although proposal deadlines are very important dates, they are not the only critical dates that a grant writer must keep in mind. Timely submission often is contingent upon activities related to

A grant activities calendar will help you to organize the sequence of events leading up to proposal signoff and submission.

research, proposal development, and securing approval to submit. It is a good idea to develop a calendar that incorporates as many grant-related activities as possible. For a discussion of using a database and calendar to track all grant-related activities, see Chapter 13.

Outlining the Proposal Submission Process

Knowing your CEO's schedule is vital when you approach the time for signoff and submission.

When setting up internal clearing procedures, it is important to have a good handle on the calendar and availability of your chief executive officer. This becomes acutely important when you are working with a tight proposal deadline. Cover letters or accompanying forms that need a signature should be presented to your CEO when a proposal is in final draft and ready for transmittal by post, fax, or electronic means. You will want to plan your final draft to be ready at a time that your CEO is available.

It's important early on in your career as a grant writer to establish a relationship with support and other staff who assist your CEO with her calendar. Having access to your CEO, even for a short time for a final look at a proposal and a signature, is not always easy given the demands on an executive's time. Treat the support people whose assistance you need for CEO access as important members of your proposal team. At larger institutions, it is common for a CEO to designate a deputy to scrutinize all proposal-related documents before she is asked for a final review and signature. You will need to establish a good working relationship with that person and her support staff as well.

Staff surrounding the CEO will be able to give you invaluable assistance obtaining signatures when time is of the essence.

At a smaller nonprofit organization or a liberal arts college, you may be able to walk down the floor for a review of a draft or a signature. At a large research organization you may have to drive to a CEO's office. Whatever the case, it's important to keep executives and their staff people aware that a proposal is nearing completion and that you will need final approval and signatures. The better you can plan your proposal submission timing, the better cooperation you will receive.

Working backward from the final signoff, you will need to factor in several other steps of clearance before a proposal is ready for your CEO. Your financial officer or his designated deputy should review all budgetary information in a proposal final draft. If your project is related to the educational mission of your organization, the chief academic officer should review the final draft of a proposal. In the case of research institutions, there are complex rules and regulations set by the federal government, including special clearances for any research that involves human subjects.

Most compliance issues are resolved well before a proposal nears a final draft. A beginning grant writer would never get involved in the development of such clearance. Sponsored research offices at research institutions often have several people dedicated to reviewing research proposals solely from the perspective of compliance with federal regulations. There may also be special reviews related to intellectual property rights. Many research institutions try to capture patents from all research performed by their staff. Just be aware that if you are assisting with the writing of research proposals, you will be relying on professionals who will provide assistance with compliance and other institutional issues.

90-Day Proposal Organization Checklist

✓ Develop a proposal outline format that can be adapted for the types of proposals you will be writing for your organization.

✓ Read a selection of successful grant proposals submitted by your organization and comparable organizations.

✓ Assemble standard, vetted text to describe your organization that can be used when appropriate in executive summaries, abstracts, and background sections of proposals.

✓ Assemble critical statistical and qualitative data to support basic needs and interests of your organization.

✓ Have conversations with key staff in your organization to gain a sense of what types of sustainability plans are realistic and feasible.

✓ Prepare yourself to explain to colleagues how a project's goals and objectives should relate to the evaluation section of a grant proposal.

✓ Consult with your finance officer to develop an organizational budget summary suitable for appending to proposals when required.

✓ Create a chart that clearly lays out the approval process required for proposal submission in your organization.

✓ Create a proposal calendar that shows not only due dates for submission but also all internal deadlines leading up to final sign-off and submission.

✓ Collaborate with colleagues to produce at least three proposals for support and submit them on time without any last-minute timeline drama.

Chapter 8

Queries and Short Proposals

- Query Letters
- Other Letters Seeking Support
- Concept Papers

Many writing tasks fall to the grant writer that are not full grant proposals containing detailed discussions of needs, budgets, and program development. In fact, many of the writing tasks you will engage in will produce relatively short documents. Examples of some of these writing tasks have already been mentioned, for example, internal research reports (Chapter 4) and correspondence and reports related to visits with grant makers (Chapter 5). It is to be hoped that you will also frequently be asked to draft grant acknowledgement letters (see Chapter 12).

Query Letters

Query letters are yet another writing task grant writers are called upon to do. Strictly speaking, query letters are not proposals, but they are very important because when done well they pave the way for successful proposal submission.

Many corporations and foundations explicitly require that any initial request for support be done with a query letter rather than a proposal.

Some corporations and foundations explicitly require that any initial request for support be done with a query letter rather than a proposal. Some agencies require a pre-proposal letter, which may be called a "letter of inquiry." See Figure 8.1 for an example of foundation online guidelines that require a letter of inquiry well in advance of any proposal submission that would be welcomed by the foundation.

Unless a grant maker has special requirements for its query letters, you should submit a one-page letter. Basically, you are writing to inquire about the grant-maker's interest in supporting whatever your research and strategy indicate to be an appropriate purpose and amount for a request. Follow any guidelines given for queries. If demonstration of eligibility is required, be sure to include this information in your letter.

Query letters allow you to get a sense of whether or not you're on target without risking a formal rejection.

Whatever you write in a query letter must be done succinctly. If your organization has elaborate letterhead, you may need to make some adjustments so that your query letters can fit on one page.

When a grant maker does not explicitly require a query letter prior to proposal submission, sometimes it can be to your advantage to send one nevertheless. Typically, when you submit a fully developed proposal to a corporation or foundation, your request goes into a hopper together with many other organizations' proposals to await a decision that will be made at a designated time.

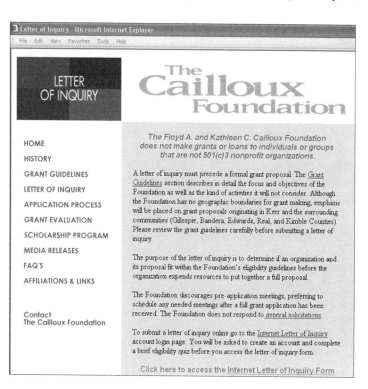

Figure 8.1
Foundation guidelines explicitly requiring a letter of inquiry before submitting a proposal.

All foundations make proposal decisions based on their funding cycle, so normally they make these decisions by a specific date on their working calendar. This may be once or twice a year. In most instances, a foundation will entertain only one proposal at a time from an organization and will expect that the single proposal submitted reflects the organization's priority need. You should never submit multiple proposals during a grant cycle unless there is clear exception to this rule.

Query letters are advantageous because they can get you timely feedback that will tell you whether or not you are moving in the right direction. Unlike proposal submissions, query letters are usually answered as they are received, rather than at a fixed time on the grant-maker's calendar. A positive query response can provide helpful information that can make your final proposal more competitive. A negative query response can give you additional time within a grant cycle to develop another funding request. Disappointing as a negative response may be, having written a query letter will prevent you from wasting time and effort developing an elaborate but unsuccessful proposal.

Query letters save time that would be lost writing a proposal that has no chance of acceptance.

Some corporations and foundations provide explicit instructions about what you should (or should not) include in a query letter. Often, if instructions require more information than would reasonably fit on one page, the page length may be two or three pages. Follow the length requirement strictly. See Figure 8.2 for an example of letter of inquiry guidelines. Always keep guidelines next to you as you outline and draft your query letter.

Figure 8.2
Sample letter of inquiry guidelines from a foundation website.

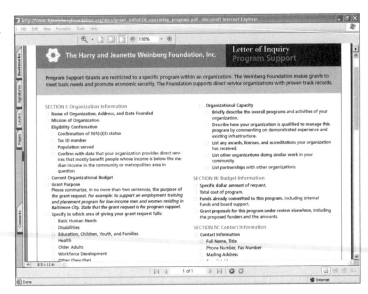

Determining the Author and Recipient

A query letter is similar to a proposal in that it is a request for support. Therefore, it should be signed by the CEO of your organization. It should be addressed to a person, not "to whom it may concern."

In the unlikely case that you can't determine the precise person who should receive your query letter, you can address it to the executive director, who will forward it to the appropriate person for a response. In most cases, you will be writing either to the executive director or to a staff person who is responsible for a particular program area.

Try to make sure your query letter is addressed to the appropriate individual at the foundation. The query letter should not come from you; your CEO should sign it.

If you have a board member who has a significant connection to the grant maker, you may want that person to co-sign the letter or you may want to orchestrate a follow-up letter from that board member to be sent immediately after your query letter is sent.

Elements of a Query Letter

The first sentence of a query letter should make your inquiry clear. It should read something like, "I am writing to inquire whether Foundation X would be interested in supporting a program for ……..at…….."

It should not begin with a general statement about your organization, or several paragraphs leading toward the point you are trying to make. If you do send a dense, multi-page query letter that requires the reader to scour it simply to determine the purpose of your inquiry, the cost of the project, and the key personnel involved, you have defeated the purpose of a query letter. Make an outline of these elements, and discipline yourself to write concisely.

It may be helpful to attach a page or two to the query letter in order to provide details, photographs, or graphics. Some foundations are systematic in their requests for query letters and may ask for specific things in an attachment. However, the query letter must be able to stand alone. See Figure 8.3 for a sample query letter.

> Query letters, sometimes called letters of inquiry, must be concise.

Potential Next Steps

As soon as your query letter goes out, you must be prepared to react to it. Since the letter did not come directly from you and does not have your telephone number on it, you must make sure that whoever signed the query letter is aware that it is "out there." Let the executive and her staff know that inquiries need to be dealt with immediately, and that you need to be informed about any phone calls or correspondence resulting from a foundation query letter. Prompt interoffice communication is critical, because if your organization receives a positive response, you will need to follow it up by producing a detailed proposal. While a query letter might contain relatively little in the way of budgetary details, program description details, or supporting data, you will want to have most of the information needed for a detailed proposal collected before the query letter is sent out. Then, if you do get a positive response, you will be able to prepare the full proposal immediately.

> Be prepared to go into action if your query letter generates an encouraging response.

SAMPLE ONE PAGE LETTER OF INQUIRY

Civil Policy
Association

April 15, 2012

Johnetta Doe, Ph.D
Executive Director
Esox Foundation for a Global Society
125 New Avenue, NW
New York, 10011

> Get straight to the point in the opening sentence of your letter of inquiry.

Dear Dr. Doe:

I am writing to inquire whether the Esox Foundation for a Global Society would be interested in supporting an Ethics in Politics conference to be held in Washington, DC early next year.

Because the Esox Foundation for a Global Society has been a supporter of ethical inquiry into public service in recent years, I believe this conference will be of interest to the Foundation.

Our present budget for the conference is $65,000. The majority of these costs involve travel and lodging expenses for a host of national figures in politics, academe, and the non-profit sector.

We intend to publish the presentations of this conference and have a contract with a major publisher in New York to release the book two months before the next presidential election.

I would be pleased to provide your with any details that you might wish to review as you consider this inquiry about support.

Thanks you for your consideration.

Sincerely,

> Your letter of inquiry should come from the chief executive officer of your organization.

Timothy Kachinske
Executive Director

Figure 8.3 *Sample letter of inquiry.*

Other Letters Seeking Support

Aside from query letters, a grant writer will frequently need to draft other short pieces. You will probably draft all correspondence related to grants, regardless of who signs it. As a matter of routine, every proposal that is submitted will be accompanied by a one-page cover letter drafted by a grant writer. Some of the short pieces you draft will actually serve as proposals for grant support. Not all proposals need to be long; sometimes grant makers actually prefer a one-page proposal. When a relationship with a grant maker has been secure and reliable over a period of years, a brief request for support may suffice and be appreciated. Depending on the circumstances of the request, a one-page proposal may generate a grant award much larger than a long, fully developed proposal.

Drafting short correspondence is a routine task for grant writers.

Cover Letters

The practice of submitting proposals accompanied by a cover letter that has been signed by the CEO of the requesting organization is more than a formality. Authorized cover letters are an element of routine practice because every grant must be approved by your organization's board. You might find colleagues in your organization who tell you that they can sign the cover letter. Gently inform them that it is not done that way because authorization to sign on behalf of the organization is required. Your CEO may formally designate someone to sign off on grant proposals in his place. At academic institutions, the chief academic officer (or provost, vice president of faculty, or dean of faculty) sometimes has this designation. At a nonprofit organization, the executive vice president may be formally designated to sign off in the place of the chief executive officer.

Grant proposal cover letters are nearly always signed by the CEO of the organization requesting support.

There may be another exception to having a CEO sign a cover letter. If a board member has a particular interest in the project, perhaps as a volunteer, or has some special credibility or influence with the grant maker, special circumstances might call for placing the board member's name on the cover letter. Even in this case, you would ideally have the CEO's signature appear on the letter as well.

If you want the cover letter to be reviewed by those who review the proposal draft before submission, you will need to draft it early on. Otherwise, it may be fine to leave the cover letter until after the final draft is complete. However, by the time a proposal is reviewed by the CEO, the cover letter must accompany it.

You do not need a complex outline when you sit down to draft a cover letter. Begin with a simple statement such as, "On behalf of The University of The United States, I write to submit a proposal to The General Foundation requesting support in the amount of $100,000 for a new program to increase women and minorities in engineering." Note that this sample first sentence introduces the amount of your proposal and its purpose. These are essential details. Never begin a cover letter with general or flowery statements about your own organization.

What follows in the letter can be a general statement about the program or need you are proposing for support. You might add a sentence or two explaining why your organization is uniquely positioned to address this need or carry out the proposed project. Do not go into dense detail, however.

Cover letters accompanying proposals should always express gratitude for any past grants.

If the grant maker has supported your organization in the past, you should create a new paragraph to take advantage of the opportunity to thank the organization again. By doing so, you will be reminding the grant maker that they have previously invested in your nonprofit or institution.

Cover letters should be brief and uncluttered.

Personal comments are best left out of a cover letter, even if your CEO has a personal relationship with someone at the grant-making corporation, foundation, or agency. Cover letters should be brief and uncluttered.

When you draft correspondence for someone else's signature, you need to capture that person's voice.

Finding a voice for a CEO's cover letters and other correspondence is something that a grant maker must learn. The quickest and easiest way to find the right voice is to listen to the CEO carefully when she is speaking to the public. Reviewing any correspondence that you may be privy to helps as well. The secret to being successful at drafting letters for someone else's signature is to speak in the right voice. The person who signs should be able to read over what you have written and say, "That sounds just like me." If you can hit that note, the person you are writing for will be very pleased indeed.

One-Page Letter Proposals

In some respects, one page is the ideal length for a proposal. It is brief enough that you know it will be read in its entirety. Of necessity, it must be clear and to the point. You can craft it quickly because it will not contain a lot of detailed information that needs to be organized and presented in a cogent way.

Small family foundations that have no particular guidelines will typically accept a one-page proposal. Grant renewal letters are another very common type of one-page proposal. If your organization has been receiving consistent support from a corporation or foundation, one page might be all that is needed to extend support for another year. Private colleges, universities, and schools often are the beneficiaries of long-term, annual scholarship support from corporations and foundations. These educational institutions are often able to renew annual grants with a grant-renewal letter that also functions as a report on the previous year's support. See Figures 8.4 and 8.5 for an example of a one-page grant renewal letter that includes an attached one-page report. Similarly, nonprofit social service organizations may enjoy consistent annual grant support for specific kinds of service delivery programs. Ideally, renewing these grants will require minimal proposal development because of the longstanding relationship that exists between the grantor and the grantee.

One-page proposals are ideal for grant makers that will accept them.

As you begin your new grant-writing position, review current and previous grants for long-term relationships. If your organization is fortunate to have such relationships with funders, take note of the calendar of past correspondence related to renewal of support, and put alerts on your own calendar to show when future grant renewal letters should be sent out. Follow the style and format of the one-page proposal letters sent in previous years, and do not introduce longer proposals unless you know that the grant maker wants a change.

SAMPLE GRANT RENEWAL LETTER

Methodius College

January 1, 2022

Ms. Jane Doe
Executive Director
The Jim and Jane Johnson Foundation
125 Park Avenue
New York, NY 10011

> Acknowledgement of your previous grant and request for continued support should be in the first paragraph.

Dear Ms. Doe:

I am writing to thank The Jim and Jane Johnson Foundation for its grant of $30,000 to Methodius College. I ask that the Foundation consider making another scholarship grant for the 2022-2023 academic year.

I would also like to report on how The Jim and Jane Johnson Foundation's grant this past year has benefited the young men and women who have been selected as recipients of the Johnson Scholarships at Methodius College. In my request last year, I proposed that Johnson Scholarships be awarded to undergraduate physics students of high academic promise. The attached report provides some basic information about this year's Johnson Scholarship students.

Once again, please extend my thanks to all trustees of The Jim and Jane Johnson Foundation for their support of Methodius College.

Sincerely,

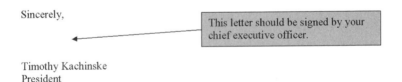

> This letter should be signed by your chief executive officer.

Timothy Kachinske
President

Figure 8.4 *Sample grant renewal letter.*

SAMPLE REPORT ATTACHED TO ONE-PAGE GRANT RENEWAL LETTER

Methodius College

> Ideally, this report should be a one-page attachment to your letter.

TO: Timothy Kachinske, President

FR: Dr. John Smith, Dean

RE: Johnson Scholarships at Methodius College

DATE: January 1, 2022

It is my pleasure to provide you with information about students who have been awarded Johnson Scholarships for the 2021-2022 academic year. All of these students are presently enrolled in Methodius College's undergraduate program.

As you know, this is a highly competitive program, and the grade point averages noted in the table below attest to the high academic quality of these students. I am also pleased to note that all of them intend to pursue careers in business and industry.

As you know, this grant has been awarded to Methodius College to develop special programs that will promote the entry into business and industry. All of the scholarship recipients will have participated in an industrial internship by the end of next year. Should you require further information about the recipients of the Johnson Scholarships, please let me know.

I would like to extend gratitude to the Jim and Jane Johnson Foundation on behalf of the young men and women who have received this scholarship support.

Student Name	Grade Average	Class Year
Jane Gates	A	Freshman
Jim Biltmore	A-	Sophomore
Robyn Goodall	B+	Sophomore
Anastasia Jivkov	A-	Sophomore
Mita Roberts	B	Freshman

Figure 8.5 *Sample report attached to one-page grant renewal letter.*

Concept Papers

A concept paper can allow you to get a sense of whether you are on target without risking a formal rejection.

Concept papers are not used very often. However, in those situations where a concept paper can be used strategically, it can be very helpful to your case. A concept paper is more elaborate than a one-page query and may at first glance look like a short proposal. However, it will not state that you are requesting a specific amount of money for a specific purpose. In other words, you won't be asking the grant maker to make a decision on funding; you are simply asking the grant maker to review an idea for support. Your introductory wording for a concept paper would be something like, "The University of The United States requests that The General Foundation review this proposed project idea."

When and When Not to Use a Concept Paper

Concept papers are typically used only after you and others at your organization have developed a relationship with foundation or corporation staff. You would never submit a concept paper without knowing that the recipient was interested in reviewing it. Occasionally a foundation program officer might ask you for one in the course of discussions.

A concept paper can be useful to a foundation or corporation that is considering moving into a new funding area but has not yet publicized that interest, in which case your ideas can help them to develop their ideas. There again, you might propose the idea of a concept paper in the context of a discussion with a foundation staff person, if for example your organization is developing a new program that you are not yet ready to flesh out into a full proposal.

Used strategically, concept papers can strengthen the relationship between your organization and a grant maker.

A concept paper extends discussions between foundation staff and your organization and has the potential to strengthen your relationship. You are giving the foundation a chance to consider and circulate an idea without having to commit to a formal decision.

SAMPLE CONCEPT PAPER, Page 1

Civil Policy Association

A Concept Paper

Presented to the General Foundation of New York

by

The Civil Policy Association

> The summary of your concept paper should be similar to a proposal in that the reader can get a quick gist of the entire document from the summary alone.

> Unlike a proposal, a concept paper most likely will not contain a request for support in a specific dollar amount. That will come later if you are invited to submit a proposal.

The Civil Policy Association requests that the General Foundation of New York consider for review a young adult leadership exchange between emerging policy leaders of Canada and the United States. The US-Canada Emerging Law Leaders Exchange is planned for the first two weeks in November, 2015 and will take place in the city of Stratford, Ontario. For twelve days, emerging leaders in law and public policy from both countries will discuss an agenda set on trade, security, foreign policy, and environmental issues of policy concern to both Canada and the United States. The purpose of the exchange will be to develop working goals and conclusions in a private sector context that will contribute to national discussions of public policy in both countries. One year following the exchange a planned follow-up mini-conference in Washington, DC will analyze progress to the 2015 goals and disseminate discussion of progress.

The Civil Policy Association

The Civil Policy Association is a nonprofit organization dedicated to inspiring American public policy leaders to learn more about their profession and the world. Founded in 1859, on the eve of our nation's Civil War, the CPA has for more than 150 years served as a catalyst for developing informed opinions on local, regional and national issues. Through balanced nonpartisan programs, the CPA encourages all persons involved in public policy discussion to engage in dialogue and mutual understanding.

Figure 8.6 *Sample concept paper, p.1.*

SAMPLE CONCEPT PAPER, Page 2

Exchange Goals

Briefly, the Civil Policy Association would like to accomplish the following goals with the young adult leadership exchange between emerging policy leaders of Canada and the United States:

- Develop a broad interchange between emerging leaders in the US and Canada.

- Increase cooperation on a bi-national level.

- Lay a foundation for lasting relationships in US-Canadian relations.

Exchange Participants

The next generation of US and Canadian policy leaders face enormous challenges, and at the same time have tremendous potential to improve mutual relations. Participants in this emerging leaders exchange will be drawn from nominations proposed by members of the American Policy Academy, the most prestigious leadership group in the United States.

> You have provided detail on dissemination because you know this to be the Foundation's greatest interest in your program.

Dissemination

The CPA has developed a newsletter entitled *Emerging Canadian-US Leadership* to be published quarterly in print and electronic media that will serve as the publication of record for all activities before and after the exchange in 2015. CPA estimates total distribution of this newsletter will be 13,000 in the US and 1,800 in Canada. Distribution lists are highly selective and drawn from active national or international CAP members.

CPA's international monthly magazine *Policy* will devote the January, 2016 issue to this exchange. The magazine will include a summary of the exchange, an analysis of working goals, and profiles of various US and Canadian participants.

The Civil Policy Association's publishing house Policy Publications will produce a hard-cover book of no less than 280 pages entitled *Emerging Leadership in US and Canadian Public Policy*. No fewer than 4,000 copies of this book will be published in June, 2015. We anticipate demand from CPA membership and public policy circles to exceed these numbers. CPA will contract for a second printing if needed.

Figure 8.7 *Sample concept paper, p.2.*

90-Day Checklist for Writing Queries, Letters, and Concept Papers

✓ Regularly review your research into grant opportunities for grant makers that prefer or require a letter of inquiry.

✓ Draft at least one letter of inquiry.

✓ Listen to your CEO speak in at least five public settings paying close attention to her diction and voice.

✓ Read a sampling of your CEO's correspondence to learn her voice and tone.

✓ Draft at least three pieces of general grant-related correspondence for your CEO.

✓ Draft at least one proposal cover letter in the voice of your CEO.

✓ Systematically review grants given to your organization over the past three years, looking for opportunities where you might write and submit a grant-renewal letter in the voice of your CEO.

✓ Tag your calendar for the next 12 months to show upcoming grant-renewal dates.

✓ Review all grant opportunities for potential concept paper development.

Chapter 9

Proposals for Projects, Programs, or Bricks and Mortar

- Proposals for Projects or Programs
- Project Proposal Scenario: Human Services Staff Development
- Project Proposal Scenario: Education Program Development
- Project Proposal Scenario: Library
- Bricks and Mortar Proposals
- Bricks and Mortar Proposal Scenario: Renovation of an Athletic Training Facility
- Bricks and Mortar Proposal Scenario: Renovation of the College Union

Most grant proposals are requests for funding to support projects or programs. The request for a project is always for a limited term. In order for the results of a project to be measurable, it must have a clearly defined beginning and end. A grant proposal may request support for the duration of a project, or it may focus on a particular phase such as start-up. Even if a proposed project has the potential or goal to become permanent, the support requested will be for a specific term. Foundations, corporations, and federal agencies sometimes make multi-year commitments to funding a project, but the majority of grants awarded are for funds that are to be expended within one year's time.

Grant projects have a start date and an end date.

Proposals for Projects or Programs

Proposals for program support are a bit different in that they request support for a program that is ongoing. Scholarships come to mind here. Scholarship support often is the largest need at an educational institution, so most educational institutions are continuously seeking support for scholarship funds. Proposals for program support are often written for corporate grant makers because of their interest in funding established worthy programs in the areas where they have a corporate presence. Many nonprofit organizations depend on program support for survival. Even then, support is typically sought and granted for a specific period of time. A corporate foundation that supports a theater, for example, may sponsor a play or provide support for a season.

Most grant proposals are for projects or programs with a single year term for funding.

Every Proposal Has a Story

Every grant proposal has its own story. Sometimes it is a long, complicated story that involves overcoming multiple obstacles on the way to a happy and successful ending. You may need to communicate intensively with colleagues and do extensive prospect research. Cultivation of the grant maker may take place over a period of months, involving correspondence, phone calls, and meetings that require travel. Project development may shift and change, sometimes right up until the time of writing the first draft. You may experience setbacks and frustration before everything comes together.

The purpose of this chapter is to introduce you to the events and activities that precede a grant proposal in its final draft. Sample scenarios present some of the grant-writing situations you may encounter. Each scenario is set in a specific type of educational institution or nonprofit organization. Although more than one person is typically involved in the preliminary stages of grant proposal development, at the end there is usually just one person who puts all of the pieces together. Each scenario presents the perspective of the person responsible for writing proposals, and each is accompanied by a sample proposal in final draft form.

> The grant-writing scenarios in this chapter will put grant projects into a context to illustrate how the work moves forward from the research stage to submission.

Project Proposal Scenario: Human Services Staff Development

As a grant writer at a private human services delivery agency, you have had some discussions with representatives of the Noble Foundation about the crisis unfolding in your state with respect to the care of disabled people who live in group homes. Sensational newspaper articles have appeared exposing poor living conditions, some of which have been life-threatening. Your organization has not been touched by this scandal. In fact, yours is regarded as a model agency. Some of the newspaper articles have singled out the group homes administered by your organization as exemplary programs.

> Sometimes external factors affect your prospects for support.

Cultivating a Grant Opportunity

In recent months, you've met with Noble Foundation representatives to discuss the crisis in care for the disabled, and you've also arranged for your Executive Director to meet with the Noble Foundation President to discuss possible solutions. The Foundation has a history of supporting innovative programs in private social services. It restricts its grant making to your state, which works to your benefit.

Your organization has identified professional development of direct care staff as a means of improving care for the disabled and has worked out a plan for a pilot project with a local university. Noble Foundation representatives are interested in the project. They have told you and your Executive Director that they would welcome a proposal for their board meeting next month. This proposal has quickly become your top priority.

> If your organization has a solution for a problem that is perceived to be urgent, timing is critical.

Your next step is to review your research. Noble Foundation guidelines show three basic requirements for a proposal:

- Description of the project
- Information about key personnel who will implement the project
- Budget for the project

When searching for a prospective donor to match a specific need, always scrutinize the grant guidelines carefully.

You know from your research that the Noble Foundation does not fund current operations or make unrestricted grants. Reviewing their recent grants, you have concluded that they tend to fund new projects and that "innovation" is a word they use frequently. The contact you and other staff have had with the Foundation confirms their interest in supporting a pilot project as long as it could be sustained in the future with funding from other sources.

Outlining and Drafting the Proposal

Now you need to outline the proposal. The aim of your outline is to make the proposal as brief as possible and still convey enough information that the Noble Foundation can make a positive decision on funding.

You prepare a basic outline as follows:

1. Executive Summary
2. Background (on your organization)
3. Demonstration of Need
4. Project Plan
5. Project Director
6. Current and Future Funding
7. Budget Summary

Always ask the person who will implement the project to review a grant proposal requesting support for it.

You will write a draft proposal organized by the sections in your outline. As the project director has designed the plan for the pilot project and is the person most intimately aware of details, you will want to share the first draft with her. She is the person who will carry out the project, so her review and revision are critical. You will need to ask your financial officer to review the budgetary information. Although you may think that the expenses are straightforward, you still need the review and approval of your financial officer.

The final review of your draft proposal should be done by your Executive Director. (See Figures 9.1, 9.2, 9.3, and 9.4.) When she

SAMPLE PROPOSAL (Direct Care Staff Development), P. 1

FR. MEGER
CENTER
FOR SOCIAL JUSTICE

A Proposal to the
Noble Foundation
from the
the Fr. Meger Center for Social Justice

Executive Summary

> Your first sentence sets out the purpose and amount of your grant request.

The Fr. Meger Center for Social Justice requests a grant of $32,000 from the Noble Foundation for a two-year pilot training project for direct-care workers in group homes that serve people with developmental disabilities. This proposed pilot training project will offer career opportunity growth to low income direct-care workers and also benefit the lives of the disabled people these workers serve. The aim of the pilot project is to develop an education program that will grow in student participation and community support long after initial funding from the Noble Foundation has been expended.

Background: The Fr. Meger Center

> Your first background paragraph establishes your organization's history and financial stability.

Since 1952, the Fr. Meger Center for Social Justice has provided services to the developmentally disabled in a six-county region. Working out of an abandoned storefront, Monsignor Stanley Meger established the first private organization in the state to support the educational and social need of the developmentally disabled. Within 20 years Fr. Meger had built a respected nonprofit organization from the ground up. Today the Center employs 200 full-time staff in 14 offices and group homes. When Fr. Meger died in 1997, the trustees and greater community contributed funds to establish a $5 million endowment in his name to help carry on his work in perpetuity.

Figure 9.1 *Sample Project Proposal (Direct Care Staff Development), p. 1.*

SAMPLE PROPOSAL (Direct Care Staff Development), P. 2

In a multi-page proposal, use headings that paginate. Also, be sure to identify both the prospective donor and your organization.

Proposal to the Noble Foundation, p. 2 of 4
From the Fr. Meger Center

Your second background paragraph develops background related to your proposed project.

Today, the Father Meger Center is the region's largest provider of services for people with developmental disabilities and is looked to as a leader in the training of direct-care workers. In connection with its core mission to serve people with developmental disabilities, the Fr. Meger Center cooperates with the School of Social Service of The University of the United States to offer fully-accredited undergraduate and certificate programs for social service paraprofessionals who have not traditionally had access to higher education.

Demonstration of Need

Develop a compelling need that positions your organization as a solution to a problem.

The six-county region is experiencing a crisis in community-based group home care for individuals with developmental disabilities. This past year the crisis received national exposure in a series of Pulitzer Prize winning articles in the *Daily News*. Among the many revelations was evidence that the health of many residents of group homes had deteriorated to a point where they became incapacitated. Some even died. The Fr. Meger Center was not involved in any of the group homes cited in these articles and is in a position to provide a solution. That solution lies in education and training for the direct-care workers who are the primary caregivers for group home residents.

Direct-care workers in group homes in the six-county region tend to have at most a high school education. They have little formal training in disability or health care issues, and they earn approximately $9 an hour. Because wages are so low, furthering their education is beyond the reach of most. Turnover is extremely high among direct-care workers primarily because of the lack of opportunities for career advancement. These realities affect the quality of care provided.

Figure 9.2 *Sample Project Proposal (Direct Care Staff Development), p. 2.*

SAMPLE PROPOSAL (Direct Care Staff Development), P. 3

Proposal to the Noble Fondation, p. 3 of 4
from the Fr. Meger Center

Project Plan

The Fr. Meger Center, in partnership with The University of the United States, will offer a four semester, 12 credit course of instruction to provide college credit toward a baccalaureate degree and a Certificate in Disability Studies. Eight motivated direct-care workers have successfully applied for Cohort 1 of the pilot program. This first cohort will commence their studies upon receiving grant support. The pilot will consist of four semesters of study that will extend over two academic years.

Distill info about your project director to the most relevant and impressive details.

Project Director

The curriculum coordinator of this pilot project is Jane Smith (B.Sc., M.S., Ph.D.), Director of Training at the Fr. Meger Center. A veteran training specialist and researcher with more than 12 years experience in staff development for direct-support caregivers, Dr. Smith previously served as Director of Training at the Center for Social Services Research and Training at St. Methodius University. Smith previously served as supervisor of group homes in a Chicago agency.

Strengthen your future funding plan with details about future sources of support or revenue.

Current and Future Funding

Without substantial scholarship assistance, it is difficult if not impossible for direct-care workers to pursue higher education opportunities. The Fr. Meger Institute seeks Noble Foundation support to complete funding of the pilot program. In the longer term, the Fr. Meger Institute will train future participants to take advantage of income-based financial aid opportunities, for which almost all will qualify. Training in securing grants and scholarships will be developed specifically for these students. Several fraternal or social organizations, such as the Knights of St. Martin and the Business Roundtable, have committed to providing additional scholarship funds once the pilot project is established and successful.

Figure 9.3 *Sample Project Proposal (Direct Care Staff Development), p. 3.*

SAMPLE PROPOSAL (Direct Care Staff Development), P. 4

Proposal to the Noble Foundation, p. 4 of 4
from the Fr. Meger Center

Budget Summary

The Fr. Meger Center requests scholarship aid for 8 students over the course of two years to complete this pilot project. Tuition amounts to $2,000 per student per year, totaling $4,000 per student over the two-year period. The total scholarship need for the pilot training project amounts to $32,000.

> Your budgetary information need not be unnecessarily complicated. This is especially true in cases where your grant maker is satisfied with a descriptive summary that clearly outlines all expenses under the grant. For such a brief budget narrative, all expenses must be easily understood by a layperson.

Figure 9.4 *Sample Project Proposal (Direct Care Staff Development), p. 4.*

is satisfied with the proposal, draft a cover letter for her consideration. You may want to include information about her last meeting with the President of the Noble Foundation if their discussion involved this project. Once she approves a final draft of the proposal and cover letter, and they are sent off in the mail, note the details in your proposal log.

All proposals should go to your CEO for a final review.

Project Proposal Scenario: Education Program Development

You are the new Education Director of the Civil Policy Association (CPA), the nation's largest membership organization of local, state, and national public policy practitioners and educators. Your interest in policy goes back to your high school years, when you took an AP course in government and politics. After completing your undergraduate degree in political science, you began teaching, first as a middle school civics teacher, and later as a high school teacher of AP Government and Politics.

While working as a teacher, you began graduate studies in Political Science, obtaining your M.A. in Political Science at Methodius College, followed by enrollment in the Ph.D. program in politics at the University of The United States. Upon completing your doctorate, you successfully applied for a position as instructor in political science at Methodius College.

Midway through your first year teaching at Methodius, you attended the annual meeting of the Civil Policy Association. During an education section panel discussion, you learned from your co-panelist that he was planning to retire as education director of the CPA. Having always wanted to have an impact on the way public policy is taught at the secondary level, you set your sights on this position. Your co-panelist appreciated your years as a volunteer for the CPA education department, and he was instrumental in the success of your application for the position. Your ideas about new high school curricular materials perked the interest of everyone who had a voice in the decision to hire you at the CPA. You are fully and completely prepared to develop curriculum. You have done a great deal of writing in the pursuit of your three degrees, but you have never written a grant proposal.

Often a passion for the subject matter or cause leads people into grant writing.

A Need for External Funding

Shortly after you moved to Washington, D.C., to take your new position, the executive director informed you that membership revenues are significantly down due to the current recession and that as a consequence, you cannot access CPA funds to develop any new programs. You are told that if you want a budget for new program development, you will need to obtain grant funding to support it. This leaves you with little choice but to seek external funding so that you can develop the programs you envision.

Grant support is sometimes the only way a desired change can be brought about.

Since you have never written a grant proposal, your first step in seeking external funding is to educate yourself as quickly as possible. You attend Foundation Center grant research and grant writing workshops. You join a local grant seekers luncheon series. You even tap into personal funds to attend a national workshop on grant writing.

Networking is vital not only in terms of contacts but also in terms of knowledge you will gain that may come in handy when you least expect it.

During your early days at the CPA, you meet executives from a number of companies that benefit directly from public policy. Your training tells you to look at companies that have an intrinsic interest in policy and policy education.

Cultivating an Opportunity for a Proposal

One company in particular has caught your attention. The Wonk Corporation has a corporate foundation that supports education. You note from your grants research that they tend to be interested in model programs and that they tend to favor projects that can be duplicated. You think you've found a match, and you write the executive director of the Wonk Corporate Foundation to request a meeting. Your executive director supports your efforts, and when you do get your meeting, he agrees to fund your travel expenses.

Research into a grant maker's past record of support can help you to predict your chances for success.

Prior to meeting with the Foundation, you touch base with three acquaintances of yours who work at the Wonk Corporation. They are interested to learn of your upcoming meeting, and one of them asks you to lunch after your visit.

When you meet with the executive director, you discuss the new high school curriculum supplements you would like to develop but cannot because of the downturn in the economy. He tells you that they, too, are experiencing some cuts, but he is interested to learn of your contacts at the Wonk Corporation and your planned luncheon. You relate that the lunch isn't just social, as you will be sharing a draft curriculum document that the Wonk employee has been reviewing for you. As you leave the meeting, the foundation director suggests that a modest grant would probably be funded if the project can sustain itself after funding. He tells you to submit a proposal soon for the next board meeting in two months.

> A successful face-to-face meeting can increase the likelihood that your grant proposal will be well received.

You leave for Washington, D.C., feeling good that you have an opportunity to get some new funding for your program. At the airport while you are waiting to catch your flight home, you outline your proposal, and you send your executive director an email message summarizing the situation. He is out of town, but responds to your message saying that this looks like a great opportunity for the CPA education program and he hopes that a proposal can go out right away.

> Prompt communication within your own organization is important as you develop an approach for support.

During your visit, you obtained a current copy of the Wonk Corporate Foundation Grant Guidelines. You note that all proposals need a detailed budget of expenditures and proof of tax exemption. You review the latest list of grants in the annual report given to you and see that several grants were awarded for pilot programs that clearly aim at self-sufficiency. You outline your proposal as follows:

1. Executive Summary
2. Background on the Civil Policy Association
3. Background on the Education Department of the CPA
4. Need for Policy Curriculum Supplements
5. Timeline for Project
6. Dissemination of Pilot Policy Curriculum
7. Sustaining Curriculum Development
8. Project Budget
9. Copy of 501 (c) (3) letter

While still traveling, you begin drafting sections of the proposal on your laptop. When you return to your office the next day, you meet with the financial officer to review a budget that you have roughed out. She makes some changes. As you finish the draft of the proposal, you send it via email to your executive director, who is still on the road. (See Figures 9.5, 9.6, 9.7, and 9.8.) He responds that he approves the proposal, and you reply that a draft cover letter and final draft will be waiting for his signature when he returns to the office tomorrow.

> Once you receive the go-ahead, it is a good idea to begin drafting as quickly as possible. If you have done a good job with research and outlining, you will be ready to write.

SAMPLE PROJECT PROPOSAL (Citizenship Education), P. 1

Civil Policy
Association

A Proposal to the

Wonk Corporate Foundation

from the Civil Policy Association

to Develop an Innovative Citizenship Curriculum Supplement

for Use in US High Schools.

> The first sentence establishes the purpose and amount of your grant request.

Executive Summary

The Civil Policy Association requests a grant of $32,500 from the Wonk Corporate Foundation to support the development of a new citizenship curriculum project that will supplement high school course materials in civics and government. Recent surveys conducted by the Civil Policy Association Education Department reveal that an overwhelming majority of high school students have little knowledge of the rights and duties of citizens and that social studies teachers are sorely lacking in supplementary materials to enliven and enrich the curriculum. The Civil Policy Association proposes to remedy this situation by developing supplementary citizenship curriculum materials.

> Make your institution as impressive as possible in the background section.

The Civil Policy Association

The Civil Policy is the oldest and largest membership organization in the United States devoted to the interests of public policy practitioners. The CPA also holds the largest membership of teachers and scholars of policy in the US. Today, more than 100,000 professionals across various disciplines are members of the CPA. Headquartered in the nation's capital, the CPA serves its members with annual national meetings and quarterly regional meetings. As the country's largest publisher of books and periodicals on policy, the CPA is a recognized center for research and theory in the area of public policy.

Figure 9.5 *Sample Project Proposal (Policy Education), p. 1.*

SAMPLE PROJECT PROPOSAL (Citizenship Education), P. 2

In a multi-page proposal, use headings that include pagination. Also, be sure to identify both the prospective donor and your organization.

Proposal to the Wonk Corporate Foundation, p. 2 of 4
from the Civil Policy Association

Be specific about the particular organizational unit and relate background information to the project.

The CPA Education Department

The CPA Education Department was formed in 1999 to support the teaching and study of citizenship in grades K-12. Early efforts were highly successful. CPA's Education Department was able to stem the decline of civics education in middle and high schools with the introduction of new teaching materials. The Department also coordinates a standing committee on education comprised of policy practitioners from across the country. This standing committee advises the Secretary of Education on all aspects of teaching citizenship in grades K-12, and members frequently appear before committees of the US Congress when issues of citizenship education are on the table.

Use facts, surveys and figures to help make your case for support.

The Need for Supplementary Citizenship Curriculum Materials

While citizenship is a domain of social studies that is covered in most middle schools, a crisis has arisen concerning citizenship instruction at the high school level. A recent *New York Times* article noted that enrollment in Advanced Placement courses in government and politics, which had enjoyed a rising trend in the 1990's, has declined sharply in recent years. Surveys conducted by the Department of Education this past year revealed that less than five percent of high school students could explain how laws are passed by the US Congress.

Present your case for a solution in the context of the need.

While the situation appears alarming, CPA leadership contends that education can bring about positive change. The Board of Directors of the CPA has formally moved to support the standing committee on education as a highest priority. A plan is ready to develop a new high school curriculum initiative focusing on citizenship.

Figure 9.6 *Sample Project Proposal (Policy Education), p. 2.*

SAMPLE PROJECT PROPOSAL (Citizenship Education), P. 3

Proposal to the Wonk Corporate Foundation, p. 3 of 4
from the Civil Policy Association

Plan and Timeline

Assuming a June 1 beginning date, the CPA high school curriculum project will be completed on within one year. The project will be implemented according to the following timeline and milestones:

June 1	Begin research on Case Study 1: National Citizenship Study
July 1	Begin research on Case Study 2: State Citizenship Study
August 1	Begin research on Case Study 3: Local Citizenship Study
September 1	Develop Case Study 1 Draft: National Citizenship Study
October 1	Develop Case Study 2 Draft: State Citizenship Study
November 1	Develop Case Study 3 Draft: Local Citizenship Study
December 1	External Review of Case Study 1: National Citizenship Study
January 1	External Review of Case Study 2: State Citizenship Study
February 1	External Review of Case Study 3: Local Citizenship Study
March 1	Publish Case Study 1: National Citizenship Study
April 1	Publish Case Study 2: State Citizenship Study
May 1	Publish Case Study 3: Local Citizenship Study
May 15	Present Inaugural Edition at Annual Meeting of Civil Policy Association
June 1	Begin National Distribution of Case Studies

Future Funding

> Strengthen your case with a plan for future funding following the completion of the grant.

The Civil Policy Association seeks funding only for the development of this curriculum program and commits to supporting the project following completion of the grant. Several sources of revenue are anticipated in support of the program once the initial materials are developed. Curriculum materials will be priced modestly in order to attract a large audience, but income from school sales is expected to cover the cost of printing future-year editions. The CPA is committed to funding future shipping costs for the distribution of classroom materials, and the CPA Education Committee has committed to raise an education fund endowment, the income of which will be restricted to developing curriculum materials for high school students studying government and politics.

Figure 9.7 *Sample Project Proposal (Policy Education), p. 3.*

SAMPLE PROJECT PROPOSAL (Citizenship Education), P. 4

Be sure to paginate and identify your organization and the grant maker in headings of your attachments.

Civil Policy
Association

Showing your organization's contribution will strengthen your case for support.

Project Budget: Citizenship Education Module for US High Schools

Seek help from a financial officer when developing a proposal budget.

	Requested Funding	CPA Contribution
Salaries and Wages		
Project Director – Fred Grant		
10% x 12 months` @ $60,000/yr		$6,000
Project Coordinator – Grant Johnson		
33.3% time @ $30,000/yr		$9,990
Intern		
20 hrs/week @ $10.00/hr x 10 weeks	$2,000	
Consulting Team		
Historian – Prof. Kate Whitney		
10 days @ $200/day	$2,000	
Practitioner – Fmr. Gov. Sara Tucker		
10 days @ $200/day	$2,000	
Practitioner – Fmr. Mayor E. Carlson		
10 days @ $200/day	$2,000	
H.S. Instructor – Sue Peterson		
10 days @ $200/day	$2,000	
Travel		
Project Director – 10 site visits	$5,000	
Consultant travel – 10 site visits	$5,000	
Printing and Mailing		
Publishing curriculum materials	$12,500	
Postage and distribution		$1,000
Totals	**$32,500**	**$16,990**

Figure 9.8 *Sample Project Proposal (Policy Education), p. 4.*

You send off the signed cover letter and proposal, and update your proposal log.

Project Proposal Scenario: Library

As the head librarian at the American Liberal Arts College of the Middle East, you have worked since the institution's founding five years ago to build a college library from the ground up. Previously you had served as a deputy librarian at a liberal arts college on the west coast of the U.S., and you enjoyed your work at this institution. However, because you did graduate studies in the Arabic language, and Arabic was not in the college's curriculum, you were never able to take advantage of your significant scholarly background in that position. When the opportunity appeared to create a college library and use your language and area studies skills, you seized it.

The America Liberal Arts College of the Middle East is an undergraduate institution based on the American model. In its first years, it has attracted bright students from many countries in the Middle East as well as semester-abroad students from liberal arts colleges in the United States. It enjoys provisional accreditation status from several U.S. organizations. The college is set to graduate its first class this year.

For more than four years, you have been working at this college as the founding Director of the Library. In general, you have found your job satisfying. In a short space of time, you have been able to amass a reasonable collection of books in a building that was empty at your arrival. A majority of these books were donated by U.S. and other western agencies in the region.

Donations and evidence of volunteer involvement in your organization will strengthen your case for grant support.

You have also received help from college librarians in the United States who have organized campus book drives on your behalf. Over the past few years, several containers of books have been shipped to your campus as a result of book drives mounted by people in the United States. This has helped greatly to build your collection. Small contributions from oil companies have also helped out. You have a very modest acquisitions budget, and have been able to purchase some books, but there are still large gaps in the collection.

Matching Need with Grant Opportunity

You do not have a fundraising background, but after your first two years as director, you realized that the library needs someone with this skill set. Your president and his fundraising staff, while friendly and generally supportive, have been given other priorities by the governing board. You cannot expect them to devote much time to help you build your library over the next few years. Your staff is local, and while they are competent in administering your library, you cannot expect them to assume fundraising responsibilities. You conclude that it if your library is to reach the ambitious goals you have set, you will need to become your own grant writer.

Grant writing skills can make all the difference for professionals whose goals and aspirations greatly exceed their operating budget.

This past year several U.S. accrediting organizations have sent groups of academics from the United States to your college for a review of curricular and co-curricular issues. By and large, the visits went well. The few disparaging remarks that were made all concerned the library collection. While student, faculty, and sports programs received stunning progress evaluations, and were determined to be comparable to those at U.S. institutions, reviewers agreed that the library has significant gaps in many areas of liberal arts study.

From the beginning, your institution has been supportive in funding your attendance at professional conferences in the U.S. This past year, you began attending the annual CASE Conference on Corporation and Foundation Support, which librarians at other colleges had recommended to you. You found the CASE conference useful not only for grant research and writing skills, but also because it enabled you to establish a network of professionals in the U.S. who are interested in giving advice as you build your library. You have established a "Friends of the ALACME Library" group to solicit modest donations in the region. You have done some groundwork in researching U.S. corporations and foundations that have an intrinsic interest in the Middle East and higher education.

Conference attendance is a great way to get started as a grant writer.

At the CASE conference, you attended a panel presentation by representatives from several national foundations. One panelist in particular interested you. Ms. Jane Noble from the General National Foundation noted that her foundation is developing a new program to support democracy initiatives in the Middle East. You make a point of introducing yourself to Ms. Noble and find that she expects to travel in your area this year. She is interested in your college and would like to visit your library.

Conferences are helpful not only for the information you receive but also for the people you meet.

When you return to the Middle East, you correspond via email with Ms. Noble. You arrange for her to visit the college and provide her with a tour of the library. She visits your campus, and during her tour of the library, she is able to recognize some of the gaps in your collection. Just before she leaves, she tells you to submit a proposal based on the gaps noted in accreditation reports. You consult with the president of the college, who recommends putting the proposal together immediately.

Drafting and Sending the Proposal

Before you begin an outline for the proposal, you pull together everything you have been able to find about the General National Foundation. You have their published current guidelines, which you obtained at the CASE conference last year. You turn to the foundation's website to see whether there have been any changes in guidelines, and note there have been no changes.

The General National Foundation requires that proposals contain information in these categories:

- Background on the organization
- Description of the request
- Brief information about the project director
- Budget of any purchases or services related to the grant request

You set out to organize your proposal sections as follows:

1. Executive Summary
2. Background on the American Liberal Arts College of the Middle East
3. Background on the Library of ALACME
4. Project Director
5. Budget Summary
6. Budget (full page)

Always do your best to follow grant guidelines and best practices, even when those who outrank you suggest doing otherwise.

You draft the proposal and present it to your president for review. (See Figures 9.9, 9.10, 9.11, 9.12, and 9.13.) The two of you discuss the background section in detail. He suggests adding additional text, perhaps even a page, to describe in detail the progress of the organization over the past five years. You say that the background of the college in general should occupy as much space as the background material on the library, according to the

---

SAMPLE PROJECT PROPOSAL (Library), P. 1

The American Liberal Arts College of the Middle East
Founded in 2007

A Proposal Submitted to the

General National Foundation

From The American Liberal Arts College of the Middle East

December 12, 2012

Executive Summary

> The first sentence establishes the purpose and amount of your grant request.

The American Liberal Arts College of the Middle East requests a grant of $80,000 from the General National Foundation for the purchase of library acquisitions needed for full accreditation. These library purchases have been identified as an urgent need by several US accrediting delegations. Successful library holdings augmentation will enhance the College's case to move from provisional accreditation to full accreditation. The Board of Trustees has given this library need a high priority among the school's other capital needs and has committed funding for shelving space and cataloguing services, should the General National Foundation fund this request for support.

The American Liberal Arts College of the Middle East

> Begin your background section with general information that will introduce your institution.

Founded in 2007 with grants from the U.S. Agency for International Development and the Global Oil Company, the American Liberal Arts College in the Middle East (ALCME) serves as a major undergraduate institution educating young men and women in the region. Grounded in the American liberal arts theory of knowledge that no single discipline or approach monopolizes the search for truth, ALCME is structured on the four-year residential liberal arts college model that has enjoyed success in the United States for two centuries.

> Be prepared to develop your background section from the general to the particular.

Figure 9.9 *Sample Project Proposal (Library), p. 1.*

SAMPLE PROJECT PROPOSAL (Library), P. 2

Proposal to the General National Foundation, p.2 of 5
from The American Liberal Arts College of the Middle East

> Use the most impressive facts about your institution when presenting background information.

The American Liberal Arts College of the Middle East (continued)

The American Liberal Arts College of the Middle East has within five years been able to draw a student body that would be the envy of many liberal arts colleges in the United States. The average SAT score for incoming freshmen is in the 88th percentile (Combined Reasoning Math and Verbal 1,380; with Writing Test 1,899). Freshmen who take the ACT average a score of 29. All students whose native language is not English are required to perform satisfactorily on the EPE (English Proficiency Examination), and ALCME applicants typically score in the 70th percentile or higher. Students favor the traditional liberal arts curriculum: the three most popular majors are English, history and classical languages. All students participate in athletics, either in as members of an inter-mural team or in varsity and junior varsity sports.

The Library

> Present background to a unit of your institution if your request addresses a need of that unit.

The Library of the American Liberal Arts College of the Middle East began in 2007 with a grant for the purchase of books from Lake Superior Oil Company. Early acquisitions focused on introductory texts to support general education course offerings to freshmen and sophomore students. For several years various colleges and universities in the USA have assisted with book drives in liberal arts subjects, and today the ALCME Library holds 67,000 books in English, the largest collection of books in English in the entire Middle East region. The library is housed in a purpose-built four storey building at the center of the college quadrangle, constructed with funds from the US agency ASHA (American Schools and Hospitals Abroad) and a grant from the Lake Superior Oil Company.

Figure 9.10 *Sample Project Proposal (Library), p. 2.*

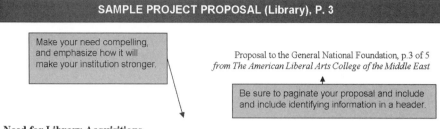

SAMPLE PROJECT PROPOSAL (Library), P. 3

Make your need compelling, and emphasize how it will make your institution stronger.

Proposal to the General National Foundation, p.3 of 5
from The American Liberal Arts College of the Middle East

Be sure to paginate your proposal and include and include identifying information in a header.

Need for Library Acquisitions

While library holdings are impressive, given the short history of the college, there remains much work to be done to further excellence at the American Liberal Arts College of the Middle East. In the past two years, visiting scholars from the United States under the auspices of the North East Association of Colleges and Schools (NEACS) have evaluated the curricular and co-curricular foundations of ALCME. Currently the college enjoys provisional accreditation from NEACS, which allows students from the United States to spend a semester abroad at the college and receive credit at their home institutions. Also, students from the Middle East have entered the college assuming provisional accreditation will evolve into permanent status.

Evaluation visits have been positive in all respects but one: the library is lacking sufficient holdings to support junior and senior courses in the liberal arts. While colleges in the United States can supplement holdings by membership in local library consortia and thereby augment insufficiencies through interlibrary loan agreements, this option is not available to students at ALCME. In collaboration with the accrediting teams, resident faculty have compiled a list of more than 2,000 books needed to support advanced coursework in the liberal arts. Funds needed for these acquisitions total $80,000.

The college has placed library acquisition needs at the top of college priorities. Members of the Board of Trustees have committed to fund new shelving and cataloguing costs, which amount to more than $50,000 if book purchases are made this year.

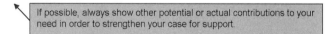

If possible, always show other potential or actual contributions to your need in order to strengthen your case for support.

Figure 9.11 *Sample Project Proposal (Library), p. 3.*

SAMPLE PROJECT PROPOSAL (Library), P. 4

Be sure to paginate your proposal and include and include identifying information in a header.

Proposal to the General National Foundation, p.4 of 5
from The American Liberal Arts College of the Middle East

Project Director

Should the National General Foundation look favorably on this request, the proposed library acquisitions project will be directed by Robert Jones, Director of the Library of The American College in the Middle East. As founding librarian at ALCME, Jones has overseen the library from its first book purchases and gifts to the present day. He has coordinated all meetings and correspondence related to the evaluation of the library, and he has hosted visiting scholars and delegations from accrediting committees. Jones is responsible for the documentation of all accrediting reports related to the library, and he maintains the master priority title list for which this proposal seeks funding.

Establish the role of the project director before documenting academic background and professional activities.

Robert Jones received his A.B. from Carleton College and his M.L.S. from the University of California at Los Angeles. He also holds an M.A. in Arabic Literature from UCLA. He is fluent in Pashtun, and he speaks and reads Farsi. Jones is a Fellow of the American Library Association, and he sits on the ALA Standing Committee on International Affairs. He is also a member of the ALA Study Group on Arabic.

When providing information about a project director or other key personnel, always relate professional activities to your proposed project.

Budget Summary

Should the General International Foundation award this grant, the American Liberal Arts College in the Middle East is prepared to purchase all needed books within a period of six months. Funds requested amount to $80,000 for 1,600 books that will support the liberal arts mission of ALCME. Books needed include 500 reference works related to the study of English by Arabic-speaking students, as well as 1,100 books related to specific liberal arts disciplines. An itemized list of these categories is detailed in the attached budget.

Figure 9.12 *Sample Project Proposal (Library), p. 4.*

SAMPLE PROPOSAL (Library), p. 5

On budgets and other items appended to a proposal, be sure to paginate your proposal and include identifying information in a header.

Proposal to the General National Foundation, p.5 of 5
from The American Liberal Arts College of the Middle East

Budget

Needed Library Acquistions

	# Volumes	Cost
Arabic-English Reference Works	250	$12,500
English-Arabic Reference Works	250	12,500
Applied Science	100	5,000
Arts	100	5,000
Literature	200	10,000
Geography	150	7,500
History	100	5,000
Natural Sciences	150	7,500
Language and Linguistics	100	5,000
Social Sciences	200	10,000
Totals	**1600**	**$80,000**

Draw up a budget for your proposal with the help of your financial officer. Make sure that he reviews all items and sums.

Figure 9.13 *Sample Project Proposal (Library), p. 5.*

grant-writing experts you have talked to. He agrees, and the proposal is put into final draft and submitted via email with a cover letter from the president.

Bricks and Mortar Proposals

Grant writers typically refer to proposals for construction projects as "bricks and mortar" proposals.

Bricks and mortar proposals are like project proposals in that they always have a beginning, middle, and end. Buildings and building renovations are planned, executed, and completed. The people you will depend on for information and details about a bricks and mortar need are likely to be not only the executives of your organization but also its building and grounds professionals.

Writing a successful bricks and mortar proposal involves close collaboration with your finance officer, buildings and grounds (or operations) managers, and whoever is in charge of the project.

Financial officers are also important, as they are in all proposals. However, if a bricks and mortar project is extensive your organization may hire a professional project manager to oversee its planning and management. This person would be another good source for budgetary and descriptive knowledge that will lend substance to your conversations and proposals about bricks and mortar needs. Of course, you will want your chief financial officer to review any budgetary information that you have received from a project manager, buildings and grounds director, or any other staff.

Budgets for bricks are mortar projects need to be highly detailed.

You do not need a background in construction or engineering to write successful bricks and mortar grant proposals. However, you will need to develop relationships with colleagues who do have this expertise so that you can effectively articulate needs and present accurate budgetary information.

DIALOGUE WITH A PROFESSIONAL: ANTHONY MALLERDINO

For nearly 30 years, Anthony Mallerdino has worked in a variety of fundraising positions in education and the arts. He is expert at seeking support from individuals, corporations, and foundations, including the management of grant proposals from the research phase to writing and submission. Mallerdino is currently consulting with small and mid-sized Chicago-area nonprofits. He offers a variety of services to his clients, including prospect research and grant writing.

Between 2006 and 2009, Mallerdino served as Senior Advancement Officer for Department Operations at the Chicago Shakespeare Theater, where he led a team responsible for a wide variety of back-of-house activities including database management and reporting, gift acknowledgements, donor stewardship and special events, departmental budget oversight, and human resources. Mallerdino's group supported the Theater's two grant writers with donor prospecting and research, development of support materials and reports, and assistance in tracking grant-related activities.

Mallerdino began his career in 1981 at the University of Chicago Medical Center. In the course of six years, he rose to the position of Assistant Director of Medical Center Development, where he was responsible for writing general, research, and capital campaign grant proposals. He went on to serve as Director of Corporate and Foundation Relations at Lake Forest College, a selective, private liberal arts college in Lake Forest, Illinois. He served as the chief proposal writer for the college during a capital campaign. In this capacity, he wrote his first successful Kresge Foundation Capital Campaign Challenge Grant request.

In 1990, Mallerdino joined the Chicago Symphony Orchestra, where he served as the Orchestra's Director of Foundation Relations and Director of Development for its training orchestra, the Civic Orchestra of Chicago. In 1995, he was recruited to Chicago's Lincoln Park Zoo to write his second successful Kresge Foundation Challenge Grant request. Later that year, he moved to the Chicago Academy for the Arts, serving as Director of Development for this private arts high school. In 2001, he left the Academy to start his own consulting practice and to further his education.

Mallerdino earned a B.A. in history and theology at Georgetown University in Washington, D.C., an M.A. in the History of Christianity from The University of Chicago Divinity School, and a second M.A. in Higher Education Administration from Northeastern Illinois University.

So, how did you get into fundraising, and what was your first grant-writing job?

Like so many other young people fresh out of school with a liberal arts degree, I had no idea what I wanted to be when I "grew up." Well that wasn't entirely the case—I actually wanted to teach medieval history at a college or university. Even 30 years ago, however, the competition for teaching jobs at that level was very strong. And although I was enrolled in a very prestigious graduate program at the University of Chicago, the thought of completing my studies seemed a daunting and possibly unrewarding task based on the number of well-qualified Ph.D.s who were driving cabs at the time.

While looking for on-campus employment, I got what turned out to be a lucky break. I applied for and was hired to work in the Alumni Office of The University of Chicago Pritzker School of Medicine. It wasn't long before my research and writing talents were "discovered," and I began doing grant writing for the Medical Center. Although biological and medical research weren't my areas of expertise, I was soon writing successful grant proposals and the rest is, as they say, history.

You then went on to work for Lake Forest College where you served as the chief proposal writer for the development effort. How did you get that position, and what do you think made you competitive?

I believe that I was competitive in my job search for two reasons. First and foremost, I had almost five years of grant-writing experience in relatively complex areas—biomedical research and capital campaign funding—at a prestigious research university. Second, I was relatively young for one with such a level of expertise and I couldn't demand or expect a salary commensurate with that experience.

What kind of educational background is best-suited for someone who is interested in a job that involves grant proposal writing?

Obviously, I am biased towards those having a liberal arts degree. But my bias shouldn't stop anyone from getting into grant writing.

I think that there are two things—a skill and a personality trait—that a person needs to have to be a successful proposal writer. The skill that is most important is the ability to write in coherent, grammatically correct sentences. The personality trait that is most important is a sense of inquisitiveness. I don't think that I could have shifted gears from my interest in history, to doing research and writing in biology and medicine, if I wasn't fascinated by and drawn to learning a completely new area of interest.

Now, I'm going to say something that is going to make me sound like an old fogy. I really believe that many young people I meet today have a very narrow focus of interest and can't be bothered to learn about anything else. I think that a lot of this has to do with the current state of American education. In the guise of relevance, education has become a smorgasbord at which students are not expected to try a little bit of everything.

It's a shame that today fewer and fewer colleges expect their students to take two years of training in a core curriculum before deciding to focus on a major. While I may not have earned the best grades or recall everything learned from the core curriculum of my undergraduate years, I can still look back fondly on my college experiences in a chemistry lab or in a class on Kant. You'll never know if something might interest you unless you move beyond your comfort zone.

Are there special skills that a grant writer needs, beyond basic good writing skills?

Very few of us grant writers have the luxury of writing about the things that we personally love. As I mentioned before I think that it's important to be inquisitive or, to put it in a more up-to-date way, to be open to life-long learning opportunities. Don't be afraid to fail or to betray your ignorance. I know it's a cliché, but there really are no "dumb" questions for a grant writer doing background research for a proposal.

Can you give an example of life-long learning in your own career?

I am reminded of when I started working at Lake Forest College. The College was in the middle of its first major capital campaign in many years. The College leadership knew it had to renovate and modernize almost every building on campus. One of the first projects I was assigned to tackle was the College's suite of physics laboratories.

At that time, I hadn't been exposed to physics in more than a decade. Because the College was a small but relatively comprehensive liberal arts college, they knew that the only way their physics students could compete was by offering these students "hands-on" research experience with their professor/mentors. In order for me to write credibly and convincingly, I had to take a crash course in some fairly cutting-edge physics.

How did you approach your project in physics?

I approached the project initially as if I were a journalist. I asked simple and naïve questions. As I became more comfortable with the professors, I began to gain in understanding and to identify the areas that I needed to focus on to prepare a successful proposal.

This is how a successful grant writer needs to be able to relate to people. One of the many things that I have learned in almost 30 years of grant writing is that professionals don't like to work with writers who don't share their enthusiasm and understanding of their projects. It's important for a grant writer, as he or she gains in understanding, to mirror the enthusiasm of their "professional" partners. You can't be successful if the professionals that you work with and for don't think you get at the very least at a minimal level what it is they're trying to accomplish.

What other tips do you have for a new grant writer working with professionals?

You need to be in constant communication with your "professionals." Make sure you build in enough time so that they can read drafts and make comments and suggestions as you write. You should never assume that you understand the nuances of what it is that they are trying to accomplish.

Your relationship and communication with the people you work with has an impact on your ability to get your projects funded. If the funding agency professionals who are evaluating your request think that your proposal betrays a basic lack of understanding of the subject, your proposal will be rejected, your professionals' abilities will be questioned, and your organization's future funding will quite possibly be jeopardized.

Resources on the internet didn't exist when you began grant writing. How have the web and the internet helped grant writers?

The web has had an incredible impact. Most important are funding agency websites. Here you can find funding guidelines, grant forms, annual reports, and lists of past grantees. I don't know how many times I've met with funding agencies' representatives who have said, "Do your homework. Please know as much about us as possible. The more you know about us, the more likely you are to getting funding from us."

And don't rule out looking at the websites of your competitors. By looking at their annual reports, you can find agencies that are funding their programs, and who have a better likelihood of funding your projects.

You should really consider paying for online access to the *New York Times* and the *Wall Street Journal*. For example, your *Times* subscription will give you access to some but not all of their archives, and it's relatively inexpensive to add on the ability to get information all the way back to 1851.

I also wouldn't rule out using a general search engine, such as Microsoft's Bing. With any web-based information, I do recommend that you verify what you discover against other sources. Although Wikipedia is considered by many to be the worst offender because anybody can edit an article, every search engine pulls in thousands of other dubious web entries from so-called legitimate sources. As they say, if it sounds too good to be true, it's probably not worth trusting.

Is it possible to get volunteer experience at grant writing?

Yes, you can get experience as a volunteer. There are nonprofit organizations everywhere in this country that could benefit from a volunteer grant writer. There is a distinct probability that you could offer your services to a small or medium-sized group in need of funding. Most of these organizations don't have professional fundraising staff members, let alone professional grant writers.

As a volunteer grant writer, I would suggest that you consider working for an organization for which you have some affinity. I think it might be helpful at the earliest stages of your efforts to work with a group for which you have some passion. As you grow in confidence, gain some experience, and get some requests funded, you'll be able to branch out into freelance work, or even a paid position with a larger organization.

What kind of training might be available for someone who aspires to a job that involves grant writing?

Many major metropolitan areas have organizations that represent local area nonprofits. In the Chicago-area we have the Donors Forum, which represents both funding agencies and grant seekers. The Donors Forum is a great group because it offers low-cost training for nonprofits in a number of areas, including grant writing. So I would check to see if such an organization exists in your area or state.

Another organization that offers training is the Council for the Advancement and Support of Education (CASE). Although the costs of their programs may seem expensive, their courses are taught by fundraising professionals who are among the most successful practitioners in their fields of expertise.

Dealing with budgets and budget summaries is an important part of the grant-writing process. What would you say or recommend to a new or aspiring grant writer who might feel a bit intimidated by budgets?

Take a class or two in accounting at your local community college. The cost is relatively minimal and you'll be able to find your way around a budget and a corporate balance sheet. You'll get a broad understanding of budget concepts such as general operating expenses, overhead costs, capital outlays, and depreciation.

Over the years, I've found that agencies don't always classify general operating expenses in exactly the same way. For example, some may treat lab techs as research personnel and others as support personnel. By having a little accounting training, you'll be able to pick your way through your organization's budget and be able to build a budget that answers the funding agency's financial questions.

What was your most challenging proposal project, and what did you do to meet that challenge?

I've worked on a number of challenging grant requests. Some of the most daunting have been requests to federal agencies and to the Kresge Foundation for one of its challenge grants.

To be successful, it is most important to read the guidelines and instructions, the questions that need to be answered, and any other materials that you receive with the Request for Proposal (RFP). As you read through these materials, write down what the agency is looking for. Think through the project, break it into many smaller tasks, and determine which of your colleagues you should ask for advice, counsel, and information.

Often you won't have the expertise to answer the questions in as sophisticated a manner as possible. You may have to delegate some of the proposal contents to a colleague. For example, when I worked at the Chicago Symphony Orchestra I was charged with writing the proposals to the National Endowment for the Arts (NEA). The NEA required that you submit a tape of live performances that showed the range and artistry of the Orchestra. I had neither the expertise to determine which performances best showcased the Orchestra's artistry nor the access to the live performance recordings. Instead, I had to turn to the staff of the Artistic Administration who worked with the conductor to determine the best performances and they then put the submission tape together.

As you do this background work, you should begin to map out a timeline for completing the project and determining to whom you will delegate tasks. When you give tasks to colleagues, give them enough time to complete a project, but also give them a deadline well in advance of the submission deadline. Often they won't complete a project on time. Then you will have to use your charm to get them to complete the task. Sometimes you will have to appeal to their boss to get them moving on the project. Maybe you will have to step up the pressure by having your boss talk to their boss. When you get the materials thank them profusely.

With large-scale projects, you will ask your colleagues to read and edit your materials a number of times. Build in time for this as well. Remember there is no pride of authorship in the grant-writing profession. Take advice and criticism happily. Make sure that you understand exactly what needs to be changed and how it needs to be said.

In the case of these large-scale projects, you will not be able to complete the project straight through. Be able to switch gears and move on to another project. However, keep your eyes on the goal, and make sure you remind the colleagues on whom you are depending to keep their eyes also on the goal.

You've worked on challenge grants. How do these proposals differ from most other proposals?

The aspect that sets challenge grant proposals apart from other proposals is putting together a convincing plan to meet the challenge. As you know, funding agencies that entertain challenge grant requests want to know how your organization will use their grant to leverage additional funds from other sources.

Most challenge grants require increasing the giving level of current donors, securing new or lapsed donors, or both.

As you develop your proposal, it is necessary to work with other members of the advancement team, particularly those working with low to mid-level individual donors, because most challenge grants are generally aimed at increasing the number and giving level of individual donors. You should involve these colleagues in the writing of the plan to meet the challenge. With their input, you will have a better sense of how much you can expect from these donors.

They will help you to understand why these donors support your organization, their level of connection to your organization, and their capacity to increase their giving. With their help, you will be able to set a reasonable goal so that you can successfully meet the challenge in the time frame. There are few things worse for an institution than an unsuccessful challenge grant program.

What about challenge grants in a capital campaign?

In the case of a capital campaign challenge, individual giving officers are concerned that your organization's annual fund (general operating support) won't be "cannibalized" by the challenge grant. That is, much needed general operating support will be diverted to capital programs for some period of time.

If you find yourself in this situation, it's important that every stakeholder from the highest institutional levels on down to your professional colleagues in the development office have input into the challenge grant plan. Annual fund revenue projections and annual operating expenses might have to be adjusted downward to take into account the effect of the diversion of funds to the capital campaign for the challenge grant period.

You mentioned the Kresge Foundation earlier.

Yes, Kresge Challenge Grants are very time-consuming, but they are also very rewarding. The Kresge Foundation will want to know every detail of your plan to meet the challenge. For example, they will want to know the amount of increased revenue you will secure, how many new and recaptured donors will support the challenge, what is your time frame for meeting the challenge, what will be your strategy—that is, the marketing plan—to get donors to support the program, and countless other details.

The good thing about the Kresge Foundation is that they really work with you on every step of the proposal process to ensure your ultimate success. If your organization doesn't exhibit the necessary level of planning to meet the challenge, they'll tell you so and ask you to come back at a later date with another project. It is in everyone's best interest to meet the challenge successfully.

Bricks and Mortar Proposal Scenario: Renovation of an Athletic Training Facility

You have several responsibilities in the administration of a private school called The Meger Academy. One of your responsibilities is to write grant proposals for your school's annual fund and any capital gift and grant fundraising. No one at your school has the title "grant writer," but because your institution is dependent on private support, you are in effect the chief proposal writer for the school whenever a prospective private donor requires a proposal.

Sometimes grant-writing responsibilities are incorporated by default into a job description that encompasses many other duties.

A New Proposal Opportunity

Your headmaster briefs you on the previous evening's meeting of the Board of Trustees at which he presented a progress report on efforts to raise funds to create a new athletic training center. The project involves no new construction, but instead calls for renovating existing space and purchasing new equipment. The total costs amount to nearly $500,000, and the school has had some success already with more than $250,000 in individual gifts and grants committed to the project. You have been involved in developing the plans for the project and have extensive notes on both the need and the costs of the project.

The headmaster tells you that Mr. Harold Noble, an alumnus and trustee, approached him after the board meeting and told him his company had done very well with federal contracts this past year. Mr. Noble said that he expects his company foundation to have "a banner year for grants." He suggested sending a proposal. Mr. Noble stipulated that the proposal should include the names of other trustees and the amounts each has contributed to the project. He said that if this information is included in the proposal, the foundation would probably consider a grant for $100,000.

> Board involvement and commitment can be a critical factor in persuading a donor that a project is worthy of support.

The headmaster finishes his debriefing by telling you that this grant would push the project close to completion. You, of course, have already made this conclusion, but you are glad to see he considers this a very significant step in completing the fundraising for the school's new athletic training center.

Outlining Your Proposal

Your top priority now is to prepare a proposal for the headmaster to send to the Noble Foundation. You will first review the guidelines again to make certain they are current. You see that no specific format is required when submitting a proposal. However, the foundation requires that proof of tax-exempt status be attached to any proposal submitted for funding. You prepare a basic outline of proposal sections based on your knowledge of the project and what the foundation might need to make a decision to fund your request:

> Sometimes a foundation will not have proposal guidelines, in which case you must organize your proposal in a way that will make sense to the intended readers.

1. Executive Summary
2. Background on The Meger Academy
3. Need
4. Description
5. Budget Summary
6. Board of Trustees Contributions to Project
7. Attached Copy: 501 (c) (3) letter

From First Draft to Final Draft

Now you review your notes on the project, consult with your financial officer to ensure you have accurate and understandable dollar figures and summary notes, and perhaps even consult again with the Director of Athletics who is leading the project plan. He might have some useful insights, and he can update you on the project.

You will also need to consult with the person at your school who tracks contributions from board members. You need to develop a list of contributors to the athletic training facility project, and the amounts of the contributions. You assure this person that the information will be kept in strict confidentiality and will only be shared with the Noble Foundation board. You prepare a draft proposal as shown in Figures 9.14, 9.15, and 9.16.

Always make certain that confidential information is only seen by those who need to see it.

Next, you will have your school's financial officer review the draft budget summary. He may want to read the entire proposal, so you might need to finish the full draft before asking for his approval on the budget summary.

After you prepare a draft of the proposal, you will draft a cover letter for the headmaster's signature as well, and present both drafts to him for consideration. You know from experience that the headmaster will make some changes in the letter draft. He will also catch any typos that escape your eye, although you carefully proofread everything you present to him. Once the letter and proposal are revised to the headmaster's satisfaction, you prepare final copies for signature and send off the proposal. You then note details of the submission in your proposal log.

Always enter submission information into your proposal log promptly while the details are fresh in your mind.

SAMPLE BRICKS & MORTAR PROPOSAL (Training Facility), P. 1

The Meger Academy

A Proposal to the
Noble Foundation
from
The Meger Academy

Executive Summary

> The first sentence establishes the purpose and amount of your grant request.

The Meger Academy requests a grant of $100,000 toward the completion of a new athletic training facility. This training facility has been identified as a high priority among the school's current capital needs. The Meger Academy currently has more than $250,000 in commitments toward a $420,000 goal for the project. Facilities for fitness and athletic training will be expanded by renovating and reconfiguring current facilities in Presumption Hall, the school's main athletic building. Additional upgrades will be accomplished with the purchase of modern training equipment, sports medicine equipment, and new lockers.

> Present your institution's best factoids in the background section.

The Meger Academy: A Boy's School of Excellence

Founded by The Very Reverend Stanley Meger in 1896, the Roman Catholic boys school known today as The Meger Academy began with the humble name of First Street School. With the help of generous business leaders, Fr. Meger opened the school to "all boys of character regardless of need," and for more than 110 years disadvantaged boys from the city center have received a college preparatory education at the school named for Fr. Meger after his death. Today, The Meger Academy is considered a top area school where excellence in academics and athletics are the norm. 96% of students in each graduating class are accepted to the college of their choice. Most graduate with passing scores in at least two AP courses. All boys participate in athletics as members of one of the school's 32 sports teams.

> Be sure to link your background section directly to the project.

Figure 9.14 *Sample Bricks and Mortar Proposal (Training Facility), p. 1.*

SAMPLE BRICKS MORTAR PROPOSAL (Training Facility), P. 2

In a multi-page proposal, use headings that include pagination. Also, be sure to identify the prospective donor and your organization.

Proposal to the Noble Foundation, p. 2 of 3
from The Meger Academy

Need

Current athletic training facilities do not meet the needs of Meger Academy boys. The weight room is small and can handle a maximum of 12 boys safely, whereas demand frequently exceeds three times that number for classes and team training. The equipment dates from an era before the design of aerobic exercise machines. The school needs modern fitness and training equipment such as stair climbers, cycles, and rowing machines for individual fitness or team training. Much of the weight equipment is worn or broken after more than four decades of use. The lockers are more than forty years old, and they are worn and in need of replacement.

Description of Proposed Renovation

Use your description section to set forth the plan of your renovation project.

Over the past two academics years, the Director of Athletics, coaches, and training staff have observed modern fitness and training facilities at comparable schools. Staff have researched renovation and equipment costs associated with improving school facilities. The Meger Academy Board of Trustees has accepted a plan submitted by athletics staff and have resolved to make this plan a priority:

- **New Fitness and Training Space**: Reconfiguration would increase training space, and replacing lockers with half-lockers will deliver an additional 2,400 square feet for new training space.

- **New Lockers**: Existing large lockers dating to 1956 were intended for large equipment and are well-worn. Some are dysfunctional. Presently many lockers go unused.

- **Remodeled Weight Room and Trainer's Office**: More than 40 years old, the Weight Room would receive a shock-absorbing floor. Worn equipment would be replaced, and equipment with contemporary design would be added. A Trainer's Office would be added with adjacent space for equipment. Computer equipment would be added to maintain health records as well as rehabilitation resources.

Figure 9.15 *Sample Bricks and Mortar Proposal (Training Facility), p. 2.*

SAMPLE BRICKS MORTAR PROPOSAL (Training Facility), P. 3

Proposal to the Noble Foundation, p. 3 of 3
from The Meger Academy

Financial Summary

> Work with your financial officer to present accurate and easily understandable costs in a budget summary.

Gifts and grants totaling more than $480,000 are needed to create a new training center at The Meger Academy. As the school cannot fund this need out of current operating expenses, renovation will not be able to proceed until sufficient funds are in hand. Should gifts and grants for this capital need exceed the amount of renovation and equipment costs, such excess gifts and grants would be applied to a restricted endowment fund to maintain the training center at The Meger Academy. The exact remodeling and equipment expenses are as follows:

Stage One	Locker Replacement	$200,000
	Remodeling	$110,000
Stage Two	Shock-Absorbing Floor	$40,000
Stage Three	Fitness & Training Equipment	$130,000
	Total Need	**$480,000**

Contributions to date from members of the Board of Trustees in support of this project:

Dr. William Arnowski '59	$25,000
Mrs. Jane Bartleby, *Parent* '12	5,000
Mr. Richard Hurley	1,000
Ms. Alice Sunderland, *Parent* '12	12,563
Mr. David Turnbuckle, '62	25,000

> Keep in mind that this information requested by the Noble Foundation is highly confidential.

Figure 9.16 *Sample Bricks and Mortar Proposal (Training Facility), p. 3.*

Bricks and Mortar Proposal Scenario: Renovation of the College Union

As the Director of Corporate and Foundation Relations at Methodius College, a selective liberal arts institution in the Midwest, you are the chief proposal writer for all annual and capital requests for private grant support. Your college is currently engaged in a capital campaign called "Restoring the Heritage," in which there are several $1 million+ building restoration projects. Others at the college are engaged in seeking major gifts from individuals to support these bricks and mortar projects. You are expected to develop a plan to add corporate and foundation grants to the sum total of these capital needs.

Sometimes a grant writer is called upon to solicit grant support to make up the difference between funds raised and funds needed for a project.

In the course of your review of all past corporate donors to the college, you have identified the Lake Superior Oil Company as a prime proposal prospect for the College Union project. Three years ago, the company made a $50,000 grant toward the renovation of the main college administration building. The company has done exceedingly well over the past three years, delivering consistently large dividends to stockholders.

Past support usually indicates a willingness to consider current support.

Cultivating a Grant Opportunity

Lake Superior Oil Company recruits rising seniors as management interns on your campus. You arranged a successful visit to Lake Superior Oil with your campus career development director. Both of you met with the Vice President of Human Resources, who is also the administrator of the Lake Superior Oil Corporate Giving Program.

Corporate giving tends to reflect corporate interests. It is not unusual to find a corporate-giving program housed in Human Resources.

Following the visit, you further communicated by phone with this company official and arranged for him to visit the campus during a recruiting session. Since you are well aware of his interest in environmental issues, you also arranged for him to meet with a professor of biology who manages a prairie restoration project adjacent to the campus. The professor, with whom you've established a good relationship, gave the Lake Superior Oil official a tour of the project.

A site visit to your organization or institution will give a potential grant maker firsthand experience of the work you are doing.

A short while after the campus visit, you contacted this company official regarding the submission of a proposal for capital support. You know from your research that the company's giving guidelines restrict capital grants to institutions of higher education. You asked the official whether this would be an opportune time to submit a proposal for capital support of the college union restoration project. He said this would be a fine time, and that since your college hasn't received a grant for several years there is a good chance it would be funded.

It is important to research a grant-maker's giving history to determine how big a request is reasonable.

You know from your research that other colleges and universities have received capital grants averaging $100,000 for building construction or renovation projects. As you finish your conversation, you know the time has come to submit a proposal.

Outlining Your Proposal

You need to develop a proposal outline, but first you must review proposal guidelines and make sure they are current. Lake Superior Oil Company has clear guidelines for proposals seeking funds for building construction or renovation. Most important in the guidelines is a statement in bold letters that a budget of the overall project needs to accompany any proposal. The company also requires that the proposal include a description of the project as well as some information about the need for the project.

Specific grant-maker guidelines must be followed to the letter.

You also know something that isn't in the guidelines. At conferences you have learned from your counterparts at other colleges that Lake Superior Oil is a strong supporter of undergraduate institutions not only in your state but also in the neighboring three states. You have been able to talk to a few individuals who have submitted successful bricks and mortar grant proposals over the past year, and you have learned that these colleges have hosted company officials for a campus visit during the dedication ceremonies.

Grant writers tend to be collegial, and they often share helpful information. Having a professional network is important for this reason.

During your last conversation with the Lake Superior Oil official, you asked whether it would be okay to note in the proposal that you would recognize the company's support in traditional ways such as publications, but that you would also invite company officials to participate in the re-dedication of the college union. You were told that this would be fine and would be looked at favorably and seriously.

The outline for this proposal needs to include the following sections:

1. Summary
2. Background on Methodius College
3. The Need to Restore the College Union
4. Description of Renovation
5. Budget Summary (in prose)
6. Donor Recognition
7. Project Budget

From First Draft to Final Draft

As you set out to write the proposal, you alert your supervisor about the opportunity. He immediately tells the president, and the two of them drop in as you are composing a draft of the proposal. They ask whether the college request can be raised to $250,000. This sum would complete fundraising on the project and relieve pressure that many people are feeling at the college. You reply that if it were likely to be looked at favorably, you would agree.

You note respectfully that you have done some research on the grants given by Lake Superior Oil over the past two years. Colleges have typically received between $75,000 and $125,000 for capital project grants during this period. You state that asking for double the amount of the largest grant they made last year might result in a decline to support the project. Your view is that the request should be in the range of the average comparable grant. You note that $100,000 is that average, and it is twice the amount of the grant that Lake Superior awarded to Methodius College three years ago. They accept your explanation and reasoning. The amount requested in the proposal is to be $100,000.

Requesting more than a grant maker typically awards can result in a turndown.

You complete a first draft of the proposal and draft a cover letter from the president. (See Figures 9.17, 9.18, 9.19, and 9.20.) The draft proposal is approved, and the president has made several changes to the cover letter. You prepare final drafts for his approval and signature, send out the proposal, and note it in your proposal log.

SAMPLE BRICKS & MORTAR PROPOSAL (College Union), P. 1

Methodius College

A Proposal to

the Lake Superior Oil Company
from

Methodius College

April 27, 2010

> The first sentence establishes the purpose and amount of your bricks & mortar request.

Summary

Methodius College seeks a grant of $100,000 for renovation of the college union from the Lake Superior Oil Company. This request is part of the College's capital campaign *Restoring the Heritage*, a multi-year effort at renovating all campus buildings built more than 100 years ago. If awarded, this grant would be used toward a $1 million restoration and modernization project of the Methodius College union, an important campus building erected in 1859. The General Communications Corporation has committed a $100,000 challenge grant to the college union restoration, and Methodius College now requests that the Lake Superior Oil Company help to meet this challenge.

> Showing that you've already garnered some support for your bricks & mortar project can help strengthen your case.

Methodius College

Founded in 1855, Methodius College is a traditional four-year selective liberal arts college dedicated to excellence in education. The College's educational program is built on the premise that has always characterized liberal arts learning. This premise holds that no single approach or no single discipline monopolizes the search for truth or the methodology for teaching and learning.

Figure 9.17 *Sample Bricks and Mortar Proposal (College Union), p. 1.*

SAMPLE BRICKS & MORTAR PROPSAL (College Union), p. 2.

Continue to emphasize your organization's highpoints and achievements in your background section.

Proposal p. 2 of 4 to the Lake Superior Oil Company

from Methodius College

Methodius is selective in its admissions. As one of only 9 percent of the nation's colleges to host a chapter of Phi Beta Kappa, Methodius College can boast an above-average student body by any national measurement. Typically students at Methodius rank in the upper 10 percent of their high school graduating class, and in college entrance test scores they typically rank in the top 20 percent. It is significant to note that more than 50 percent of Methodius graduates go on to do graduate professional or academic studies and receive post-graduate degrees.

Need

Set out your case for bricks & mortar support in the need section.

Deferred maintenance is one of the greatest challenges facing older American colleges and universities. Methodius College, like most other historic institutions that are more than 100 years old, has campus buildings erected before modern conveniences and safety features existed. A systematic study of Methodius' physical plant revealed that an update of the college union's interior and exterior was needed. Surveys of prospective and current parents and students overwhelmingly expressed appreciation for the union's architecture but concern for the well-worn condition of the interior. Access for the disabled is inadequate.

Description

Make sure your description agrees with information in your need section and in the project budget.

Extensive work needs to be done on remodeling the interior of the college union. Interior walls and wood work need refurbishing, and a new plumbing system must be installed. Extensive interior renovation includes important safety and convenience projects, as well as modifications to make the building accessible to students and staff with disabilities. A fire-safety sprinkler system must be installed. Exterior renovation needed includes refurbishment of the walls and roof. Energy-conserving windows will replace all existing windows, but the design will match the historical look of the college union, and no renovation will disrupt the pre-civil war design.

Figure 9.18 *Sample Bricks and Mortar Proposal (College Union), p. 2.*

SAMPLE BRICKS & MORTAR PROPSAL (College Union), p. 3.

Proposal p. 3 of 4 to the Midwest Oil Company
from Methodius College

Be prepared to discuss the budget in layman's terms.

Budget Summary

The total cost for renovation of the college union is $1,000,971. Exterior and interior remodeling costs amount to $672,971 and construction costs amount to $293,000. An additional $89,000 is needed for site work. A detailed budget for the college union renovation is attached to this proposal.

Make sure your grant maker finds your proposed donor recognition acceptable.

Donor Recognition

Should the Lake Superior Oil Company award this grant to Methodius College, the company will be recognized as a major contributor to the college union renovation project. Following completion of the renovation, all major contributors will be listed on a plaque at the college union entrance. A "grand re-opening" in the fall of 2011 will offer public tours. Representatives of the Lake Superior Oil Company will be invited to all events, including the anticipated visit of a reporter from Architectural History, who plans to use the college union project as the subject for a story on campus historical preservation. Major donors to the college union renovation project will be recognized in Methodius College publications, including the magazine *Methodius Monthly.*

Figure 9.19 *Sample Bricks and Mortar Proposal (College Union), p. 3.*

SAMPLE BRICKS & MORTAR PROPSAL (College Union), p. 4.

Seek guidance from your financial officer on a bricks & mortar budget. Ask her to explain anything you do not understand in layman's terms so you can explain items.   If your prospective grant maker wants to discuss details, your financial offer should be involved in the discussion.

Proposal to, p. 4 of 4 to the Midwest Oil Company
from Methodius College

M Methodius College

Don't forget to include headers on budgets and other proposal attachments.

College Union Renovation Budget

Renovation Costs

Remodeling	$ 402,318	
Mechanical and Plumbing	80,000	
Electrical	43,000	
Sprinkler, Three Floors	21,000	
New Roof and Flashing	44,653	
Tuckpoint Exterior Walls	32,000	
Window Replacement	36,000	
Asbestos Removal	14,000	$672,971

New Construction Costs

Builder's Risk Insurance	$ 5,000		
Architect's Reimbursables	8,000		
Startup	4,000		
Furnishings	160,000		
Owner's Contingency	62,000	$293,000	$911,971

Construction & Renovation	$911,971
Site Work	89,000
TOTAL	$1,000,971

Figure 9.20 *Sample Bricks and Mortar Proposal (College Union), p. 4.*

DIALOGUE WITH A PROFESSIONAL: BINH Q. TRAN

Binh Q. Tran is one of the nation's rising stars in biomedical research, and he is an accomplished grant proposal writer for educational and research programs. Tran is chairman and associate professor in the Department of Biomedical Engineering and Assistant Dean of the School of Engineering at The Catholic University of America in Washington, D.C.

Tran has served as chair of the Biomedical Engineering Department for seven of the ten years he has served on the faculty of Catholic University. He has written many proposals for educational programs and research projects that have been funded by various federal agencies, including the National Institutes of Health, the National Science Foundation, the Department of Commerce, the Department of Education, and the Food and Drug Administration. Tran has also written numerous successful proposals for projects supported by grants from foundations and nonprofit organizations.

Tran has significant experience in private industry, where he has worked in research and development, design, manufacturing, and process engineering. He serves as a grant review panelist for the National Institutes of Health and the Department of Commerce programs on research funding for small businesses. Tran has received national and institutional honors and awards for teaching and research excellence. He is president of the Washington Academy of Biomedical Engineering, and is a member of the Academic Council of the American Institute of Biomedical Engineering. Tran also serves on the Council of Chairs of the Biomedical Engineering Society.

A graduate of the University of California, San Diego, Tran earned an M.S. in Mechanical Engineering from San Diego State University and a Ph.D. in Biomedical Engineering at the University of Iowa. Binh Q. Tran is a veteran of the U.S. Navy and served as a corpsman in Naval Hospital emergency rooms.

So, you have a background in engineering and medical care. How did you first get involved in grant writing?

Yes, my academic and research background is in biomedical engineering. I was first involved in grant writing as a graduate student at the University of Iowa. In several of my courses, the major project was to develop a written mock grant proposal to NIH, NSF, and other grant agencies on pertinent research projects for the course. These efforts trained us as future researchers in the art of grant writing. This required us to go beyond the technical skills we were developing in our courses. Then, as an upper-level doctoral student, my research mentor encouraged me to submit grants for doctoral fellowships. I was fortunate to receive several fellowships.

As a unique part of my training, I was involved in an entrepreneurship program at the University of Iowa in which engineering students were encouraged to complete a certificate program in conjunction with the business school. As a part of the program, I had the opportunity to write a business plan that was formally reviewed for funding. The plan was for a start-up internet business that was launched with several colleagues back in 1997. Overall, this graduate school training prepared me for grant writing for both technical and non-technical audiences.

During your years in graduate school and afterward, you were successful in applying for fellowships. How similar are fellowship applications to writing proposals for research or educational program support?

In principle, fellowship applications are almost identical to proposals submitted for research funding for independent investigators. In practice, however, as graduate students do not yet have a significant track record of research accomplishment, reviewers tend to put a great deal of consideration into the research environment. Things like "who is your research mentor" or "what are your laboratory resources" count for a lot in fellowship applications. When you later develop a research track record, that becomes more important in grant proposals.

Usually graduate fellowships in the science arena focus predominantly on the scientific aspects of a proposal. This is very different from grant writing to develop educational programs, where things like educational outcomes or educational methodology take prime importance.

What was your most challenging grant-writing situation, and how did you approach the challenge so that you were successful?

I'm currently working on an interdisciplinary grant proposal to improve science education. The project is a collaboration among several disciplines: engineering, biology, chemistry, physics, and education. The biggest challenge on this project is that everyone communicates in a slightly different manner. While the common ties that bind the team are education and science, we all approach these topics from a different perspective. It's just like several people looking at a prism. People do not perceive colors in exact similarity.

Physicists are trained to be theoretical in nature, while engineers are practical and focus on applied work. Biologists and chemists are experimentalists. It takes quite a skilled manager to ensure that no one person or group dominates the discussion and to facilitate involvement of the entire team. Also, on large projects such as this one, being organized is essential. You need to have a detailed timeline showing when pieces need to come together. This is vital. I've observed first-hand, too many times unfortunately, where grants come together in the 11th hour, without even a good proofread of the final product. As a reviewer on several grant panels, it's easy to identify these submissions.

What in your educational background do you think best prepared you for grant writing?

I attribute my success in grant writing to my scientific and engineering training. As engineers, we are taught to solve problems systematically. Project management and meeting deadlines, budgeting and finance, and organization is part of what we do innately. We're Type A people.

Do you involve your undergraduate or graduate students in grant writing?

Occasionally, I will involve graduate students in preparation of literature review and scientific portions of a grant proposal. In my mind, this is part of the academic training of the next generation of researchers. This was instrumental in my own training as I supported my mentor in his grant efforts, and I believe this will develop and prepare my own students for their future careers. Grant-writing experience and success is an important part of the hiring process for academia. Students with demonstrated success in this regard have a leg up when applying for their first faculty position.

Besides your own experience in grant writing, you've also hired grant writers to work on academic and research projects. What are the qualities you look for in a person applying for a grant-writing position?

Yes, I've worked with several grant writers over the years. Most grant writers I've worked with have not had technical training. The most successful ones have been able to understand the topic matter at a cursory level and they've been able to translate that knowledge into a compelling proposal. Also, grant writers can be very helpful in assisting the researcher in identifying key gaps in the project. Sometimes, a researcher or faculty member knows subject matter so well that they forget that not all reviewers are domain experts, especially on interdisciplinary projects. On my current inter-disciplinary project, our grant writer on the project is able to listen to all the different perspectives and pull the thoughts together into a seamless message.

What would you consider the major challenges for a person who is new to a position in grant writing?

I assume you're talking about a new "grant writer" as opposed to a new faculty member who would be required to write grant proposals as part of the tenure process. Grant writers often are dropped into a team of academics who are domain experts. This can be a very intimidating experience. An assertive, tactful grant writer who is an integral part of the team can be a major asset and contributor to any grant project. My advice to this person is not to be afraid ask questions, to challenge questionable approaches whenever necessary, and to help the team to see the overall picture and not get lost in any particular detail.

When you look at the educational and work background of someone applying for a grant-writing position, what would make a person stand out as a candidate?

Certainly, a portfolio of past successful proposals would be the primary factor in selection of a potential grant writer. Other considerations might be a demonstrated understanding of the topic area, knowledge of funding agencies and foundations, and samples of other technical writing projects. Written references from past jobs or a conversation with previous employers would also be very helpful.

Chapter 10

Proposals for Endowment Support

G rant proposals for projects or program support comprise the majority of proposal writing for grant writers. However, you may also be called upon to write proposals for endowment support.

It is a good idea to be familiar with how to research and write proposals for endowment support.

Some grant writers, especially those who work in sponsored programs offices or specialize in science research funding, may never write proposals seeking endowment funds. Those who function as the chief proposal writer for a nonprofit organization or educational institution may be called to write endowment grant proposals from time to time. Still other grant writers, especially those working in large development offices, may be assigned this task as a specific job duty, especially if they are working in the context of a capital campaign. Knowing how to research and cultivate endowment grant opportunities and how to write proposals for endowment support are useful skills for a grant writer, especially at an institution or nonprofit aiming to build endowment.

Proposals for Endowment Support

Although relatively few endowment grant awards are given each year, they are very significant in terms of their size and prestige.

The overwhelming number of grants awarded each year do not support endowment. Many private foundations and corporate giving programs do not accept requests for endowment funds and say so upfront in their application guidelines. Most federal agencies (with a few exceptions, notably the National Endowment for the Arts and the National Endowment for the Humanities) likewise do not make endowment grants. However, the picture changes if you look at total dollars as opposed to the number of grants awarded. Each year many of the largest grants awarded in the country are given to establish or supplement an endowment fund at an educational institution or nonprofit organization. At educational institutions, often the most valued and prestigious grants received in a given year are endowment grants, even when they are not the largest grants in dollars.

Endowment gifts are intended to benefit the recipient indefinitely.

Grant proposals for endowment support differ somewhat from other tasks a new grant writer might be asked to undertake. Most grant proposals are for project or program support, and typically the specific term of a project defines the organization's responsibilities to the grant maker. Reporting responsibilities end with the expiration of the term of a project grant. However, in the case of grants awarded to establish new endowment funds or to supplement existing endowment funds, a project, program, or staff position funded by the endowment fund will continue to exist in perpetuity. Logically speaking, the reporting period for endowment grants is forever.

What Is Endowment?

Endowment refers to gift or grant funds that an educational institution or nonprofit organization invests in perpetuity, with the aim of removing a small amount annually to be used for expenses in the forthcoming year. Traditionally, endowments have been managed to grow over the long term so that an invested endowment fund equals or exceeds inflation.

For example, an endowment fund might achieve 12% growth in a given year. This growth might be a combination of income and an increase in capital appreciation. Typically, an organization would draw a specific percentage each year from the endowment for what is called an annual distribution, meaning these funds are placed in the annual budget to be spent. Distribution is usually governed by a policy. The figure 5% is a common distribution figure. Even in years when the endowment may not perform up to 5% in growth, the distribution will still take place. Over the long term endowment growth rates will have been consistently high enough to maintain this rate of distribution, and still expect growth in endowment principle or assets. Endowments have saved many institutions during times of economic hardship.

> An endowment is money invested for the benefit of the organization or institution, which draws down a percentage each year to support the annual budget.

Most organizations "co-mingle" endowment funds for investment purposes. An institution may have hundreds or even thousands of specific endowment accounts that support annual expenses of specific donor or grant-maker interests. These funds are not usually invested individually, but rather pooled to provide the largest possible principle for investment, as that usually provides for greater return and growth.

Endowment gifts and grants can be unrestricted or restricted. Unrestricted endowment distributions can be spent in any way leadership or management wishes. If an endowment is restricted, there is usually a policy in place that requires spending of the distribution funds in any given year according to the grant proposal or gift agreement at the time of the gift or grant.

> Unrestricted endowment income can be spent as the organization's leadership sees fit; restricted endowment income cannot.

Regardless of what type of organization you write for, you should look to higher education institutions if you need models, examples, and other information about endowment. Colleges and universities in the United States have led the way in endowment fundraising and management. Fundraisers in higher education have over time developed programs and methods that are beginning to be widely used in the nonprofit world to build capital and endowment funds.

An educational institution's prestige is directly related to the size of its endowment.

More so than any other single factor that is easy to access, endowment can be used to determine the prestige, financial security, and long-term likelihood of survival of a nonprofit organization. On the American frontier of the 19th century, nearly every new little community in the midwest and northwest established a "college." Most of these educational institutions were church-based, and most had links to Protestant churches in New England. The overwhelming majority of these schools disappeared within a generation. The ones that survived did so because of an endowment fund originally given or managed by the mother church. Over time, these endowments have grown through careful management and by seeking new endowment gifts and grants. Today those colleges and universities in the midwestern and northwestern United States that have grown the largest endowments have evolved as the most prestigious institutions.

You can see this for yourself simply by looking at the list of endowments by market value published annually in the print edition of *The Chronicle of Higher Education*, and available on *The Chronicle's* website. Take a look through the list in Figure 10.1 to note the rankings in multi-billion dollar university endowments. A majority of these institutions began as modest church-sponsored schools in the late 18th and 19th centuries. If you do a selective endowment search on *The Chronicle's* website for colleges and universities in your state, you will find the ranking of institutions by endowment value corresponds to a list of top institutions by any other measure of prestige.

Endowment is the key to long-term success for major nonprofit organizations.

Nonprofit organizations eventually followed higher education in the building of endowments, and those that have thrived over the long-term have developed a substantial endowment. *The Chronicle of Philanthropy* publishes an annual survey of endowments of nonprofit organizations that can be accessed online. You can search this by a variety of categories of nonprofit organizations. A few examples of search categories are arts groups, environmental groups, hospitals and medical centers, social service groups, and religious groups. See Figure 10.2 for the results of a sample search on social services groups.

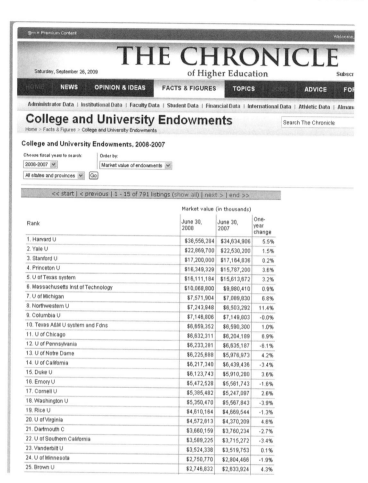

Figure 10.1

Listing of top university endowments from The Chronicle of Higher Education website.

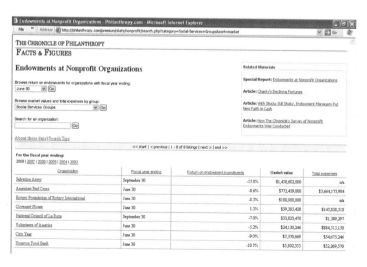

Figure 10.2

Search on The Chronicle of Philanthropy website for top endowments of social services groups.

You can find the endowment value of colleges and universities in *The Chronicle of Higher Education.* The market values of nonprofit endowments are published annually in *The Chronicle of Philanthropy.*

Most mainstream colleges, universities, and nonprofit organizations participate in the annual endowment surveys of *The Chronicles.* However, if you are unable to find an organization listed in either of these sources, you can look to other public records for information. Various membership organizations publish annual endowment surveys of their member organizations. The National Association of Independent Schools surveys the private elementary and secondary schools in its membership, and endowment market value is one of the items listed each year. The National Association of College and University Business Officers (NACUBO) publishes an annual survey of its members' institutions, including the market value of endowments. If you don't find an institution's endowment market value in one of *The Chronicles,* you may find it in a NACUBO survey. Other member organizations for professionals in a variety of nonprofit specializations publish annual financial surveys that include endowment market value.

Learning about Your Organization's Endowment

Management of the endowment is the responsibility of an institution's board of directors.

If you work for a nonprofit that does not yet manage an endowment, you are a significant way from being able to develop a grant proposal for endowment, even if you have identified a good proposal opportunity. An endowment must be created and managed with the oversight of a financial committee of your organization's board of directors. You will need policies in place for the management and distribution of endowment funds, as well as policies and procedures for seeking and accepting gifts and grants for endowment. As important as endowments are to the long-term survival of any nonprofit organization, it would never fall to a grant writer to create the framework for endowment.

Check with your financial officer to find out your organization's policy on sharing endowment information.

However, if your organization has an endowment, it is likely that everything is in place. Your task will be to learn enough about policies so that you can cultivate grant makers and draft proposals. Your financial officer will be able to inform you of the policies in place for endowment management and what information you can reveal in a proposal. Endowment policy is private, although some institutions and organizations make this information freely available to the public. There is no transparency requirement for endowment, so you will want to know the parameters for information you share with the public.

If your organization has a planned giving officer or major gifts officer, that person will likely have prime responsibility for the fundraising of endowment gifts from individuals, and he or she will have advice, gift and grant agreement examples, and appropriate verbiage that can help you to describe your institution's endowment. If you write grant proposals seeking endowment, you will want to establish good working relationships with these individuals.

Major gifts and planned giving officers are usually experts on endowment.

Endowment Proposal Scenario: Endowed Lecture Series

You are a grant writer at The University of the United States charged specifically with supporting the dean of the School of Business. You have a variety of duties as part of the dean's advancement team. The dean and faculty in the School of Business consider you to be their principal proposal writer.

You manage every grant opportunity that the dean and faculty pursue, and maintain the School's proposal log. This is a challenging position because the individuals leading and teaching in the School are demanding, but you enjoy the work and the substantial success that comes with writing grants for dynamic and energetic people. In turn, they appreciate you, as you are well-organized and a hard worker. You are viewed as a highly productive staff person of the School of Business.

Cultivating a Grant Opportunity

In your work with the dean of the School of Business, you have been given grant-writing priorities that support faculty research initiatives. One program you have become intrigued with is the dean's pet project: An annual lecture series in business ethics that brings in leaders in commerce and industry to discuss current business issues.

The dean has funded this program with sporadic discretionary funding for several years, and the lecture series has resulted in quite a bit of positive publicity for the School of Business. A number of business school deans have visited your campus with the express purpose of taking a firsthand look at this program. You have even drawn business school leaders from Europe and Asia who have observed the program and are trying to replicate it.

A successful program with high visibility can be transformed into an endowment opportunity.

As part of your ongoing grants research, you try to keep up on alumni who take on governing roles in corporate giving programs or private foundations. The dean has often said his dream would be to have the lecture series endowed so that it becomes a permanent part of the School of Business graduate program and carries on long after he retires. You have cautioned the dean that private grant-making organizations normally do not make endowment grants, but that you will keep your eye open for any opportunity that may show up.

Endowing a program ensures that it can continue despite economic ups and downs.

One possibility comes to mind. You have learned that Walter Meger, a wealthy alumnus who received his MBA five years ago, has just been appointed to the Wm. Meger Foundation. Walter Meger is of the third generation in the Meger family, and it has become a rite a passage into maturity for a Meger family member to be appointed to the foundation board. You know that Wm. Meger was an alumnus of the School of Business, but since his graduation, no Meger family member attended your institution until Walter pursued his MBA.

Connections to a family foundation are critical to a successful approach for support.

You now make a point of trying to communicate with Walter, and you are successful in getting an appointment to see him in New York. When you meet Walter, he explains that he is very supportive of the School of Business, but since he is new to the foundation board, he doesn't yet know whether he will be able to champion his own charitable interests at the foundation. You thank him for his time, and you keep him up to date on the School of Business with notes and quarterly mailings.

It is important to cultivate relationships when the opportunity to do so presents itself.

Months later, immediately after you have sent him a packet of press clippings on recent School of Business events and faculty, Walter calls to say that he is now in a position to support the school at foundation board meetings. You suggest the dean's dream of endowing the business ethics lectureships, and Walter requests further information. You send him a packet. A week later, you get an email message asking for a time to talk on the phone. Walter is ready to champion the ethics program at the foundation. In your phone call, Walter asks for a draft proposal, saying he would like to read it and then offer suggestions.

You meet with the dean after the call and inform him of the background to your conversation with Walter Meger. The dean tells you to drop everything, write a proposal, and send it off to the

Wm. Meger Foundation. You recommend doing what your contact at the grant maker has recommended because you need his help on the road to success. The dean agrees, and you leave the meeting promising to have a draft proposal for him to review first thing in the morning.

Outlining and Drafting Your Proposal

As you sit down to draft up a proposal outline, you collect your information on the Wm. Meger Foundation. There is very little to go on. The foundation has no website, and it does not publish proposal guidelines. You have the IRS Form 990-PF for the past two years, so you know that the average grant is $1,000,000, and that the foundation has made about 20 such grants over that two-year period. You deduce no pattern to the grant making, and assume that grants are made to charities that are of particular interest to at least one board member. You see the same organizations appearing in the grant list year after year.

Family foundations often do not publish specific guidelines for applications.

As you begin your outline, you are thinking that in order to compete with competitors that have a longstanding relationship with the Wm. Meger Foundation, you must present a very strong case for endowing the ethics in business lecture series. You proceed to outline the sections of the proposal.

1. Executive Summary
2. Background: The University of the United States
3. The School of Business
4. Need
5. Description of Proposed Wm. Meger Endowed Lectureships
6. Budget Summary
7. Donor Recognition

You write the proposal with the aim of being as succinct as possible, while still making clear that the university and the school are worthy of an endowment grant and that the program to be endowed is of national significance. You need to consult with the financial officer of the university for help with the budget summary to ensure everything in it is accurate, true, and doable. The dean reviews and approves the draft, which you then send to Walter Meger. (See Figures 10.3, 10.4, 10.5, 10.6, and 10.7.)

Always try to make your case in as few words as possible; less is more.

SAMPLE ENDOWMENT PROPOSAL (Endowed Lectures), P. 1

University
of the United States

**A Proposal from The University of The United States
School of Business
to
The Wm. Meger Foundation**

February 15, 2013

Executive Summary

> The first sentence establishes the purpose and amount of your grant request.

The University of the United States requests a grant in the amount of $1,000,000 from the Wm. Meger Family Foundation to establish an endowment fund for annual lectures in Ethics and Marketing. Such an endowment fund will ensure that external lecturers who are experts on the subject of ethics will be a permanent part of the academic program in the University's School of Business. Such a fund will also encourage other donors to contribute endowment funds to the School's academic program. Lectures supported by the Wm. Meger Family Foundation will reflect the School's mission, which emphasizes business and commerce for positive social change.

> Make your institution as impressive as possible in the background section.

The University of the United States

Founded in 1776 by earnest pilgrim descendents in Boston, the University of the United States is the country's oldest institution of higher education. Considered by many in the international community to be one of the most respected universities in North America, TUUS draws students from all 50 states and 181 foreign countries. Undergraduate and graduate programs cover liberal arts, medicine, business, engineering and law as well as a seminary of the Puritan faith.

Figure 10.3 *Sample Endowment Proposal (Endowed Lectures), p. 1.*

SAMPLE ENDOWMENT PROPOSAL (Endowed Lectures), P. 2

Proposal to W. Meger Family Foundation, p. 2 of 5
from The University of the United States

TUUS School of Business

> Be specific about the particular organizational unit that will benefit from the endowment, and relate background information to your proposed endowment.

The University of the United States School of Business is the second-oldest graduate school for business and commerce in North America. The School's curriculum is used as a model by countless other graduate institutions in the USA and throughout the world. While ethics has been part of the core curriculum of the undergraduate program at USS since the University's founding, it is not explicitly part of the graduate business curriculum. In recent years, sporadic external funding has provided for a pilot program that hosts business ethics experts to visit the campus, deliver formal lectures, and participate in graduate seminars.

Need

> Make your case for this endowment as compelling as possible.

This pilot lecture program in business ethics has been so successful that many deans of graduate business schools have visited TUUS to observe the program first-hand. Permanent funding of this highly successful and visible program will benefit not only TUUS business students but also to countless students in institutions whose graduate business programs have looked to the TUUS School of Business for curricular and co-curricular leadership and ideas. The School of Business pilot lecture program would the first in the English-speaking world to emphasize positive social change.

Student responses to the pilot program in business ethics have been overwhelmingly positive. Post lecture student surveys show visiting lecturers in ethics to be among the top three academic experiences of business graduate students. MBA graduates consistently rate the visiting ethics lecturers among their most-valued career influences. A majority of business school faculty voted to make visiting lectures in ethics a permanent part of the curriculum if an endowment could be raised to assure its permanent funding.

Figure 10.4 *Sample Endowment Proposal (Endowed Lectures), p. 2.*

SAMPLE ENDOWMENT PROPOSAL (Endowed Lectures), P. 3

In a multi-page proposal, use headings that paginate. Also, be sure to identify the prospective donor and your organization.

Proposal to W. Meger Family Foundation, p. 3 of 5
from The University of the United States

In your description, show your organization's commitment and contribution to the program.

Description of Proposed Wm. Meger Lectures

The proposed endowment will permanently establish the Wm. Meger Ethics in Business Lectures at the University of the United States School of Business. At the beginning of each academic year, the Dean of the School will appoint a committee of senior School of Business faculty to accept nominations and select the next year's invited lecturers. Stipends will be awarded to lecturers to cover their travel expenses to and from the University. All lecturers will receive room and board in University facilities and at the University's expense. TUUS faculty and staff will contribute their considerable expertise and time to organizing and administering this project. No lecture endowment funds will be used for room and board expenses, and no TUUS faculty will receive funds from the proposed endowment.

Wm. Meger Lecturers will be required to spend at least one week on campus, and the faculty nominating committee will approve a lecturer's plan to offer formal lectures, business school seminar participation, and any other curricular or co-curricular activities proposed by a prospective Wm. Meger lecturer. A prospectus for potential nominees will published annually offering business ethics topics of particular interest in a forthcoming academic year.

Budget Summary

Should the Wm. Meger Family Foundation look favorably on this proposal, The University of the United States will create a restricted endowment fund called the "Wm. Meger Endowed Lectures in Ethics." This fund will be comingled with the university's endowment, and no more than 5% of the restricted endowment principle will be used annual to fund the proposed lecture series.

Figure 10.5 *Sample Endowment Proposal (Endowed Lectures), p. 3.*

SAMPLE ENDOWMENT PROPOSAL (Endowed Lectures), P. 4

In a multi-page proposal, use headings that paginate. Also, be sure to identify the prospective donor and your organization.

Proposal to W. Meger Family Foundation, p. 4 of 5
from The University of the United States

Budget Summary (continued)

In your budget summary, describe briefly how endowment funds will be managed.

The endowment of the University is among the nation's best managed according to a recent story in US Business and Capital Reports. Over the past ten years, an annual growth rate averaging 11% has been consistently maintained. Based on the university's time-tested endowment policy, the proposed restricted endowment fund would experience long-term growth exceeding annual inflation rates while funding the proposed visiting lecturer program annually.

Be sure that everything you propose in donor recognition will be welcomed by the foundation.

Donor Recognition

The University of the United States proposes to name this lecture series after William Meger, founding donor of the Wm. Meger Family Foundation, who received his A.B and M.B.A from the University.

The Wm. Meger Family Foundation will be provided with an annual report summarizing each year's events related to the visiting lecturer program. The report will also contain a financial summary of the restricted endowment fund resulting from the Foundation's support. Financial information will include the corpus of the endowed fund and the income received and expended on the visiting lecturer program.

Representatives of the Wm. Meger Family Foundation will be invited to all public events related to the visiting lecturer program. Foundation representatives will also be invited to observe graduate seminars and other curricular activities related to the lecturer program, pending approval of the instructor-in-charge.

Figure 10.6 *Sample Endowment Proposal (Endowed Lectures), p. 4.*

SAMPLE ENDOWMENT PROPOSAL (Endowed Lectures), P. 5

Again, make sure that everything you propose in donor recognition will be welcomed by the foundation.

Proposal to W. Meger Family Foundation, p. 5 of 5
from The University of the United States

All public events, such as lectures, receptions, and other gatherings will acknowledge the support of the Wm. Meger Endowed Lecturer Fund. Such acknowledgement will appear in printed programs, publicity materials, and other publications. The foundation will be sent one copy of every publication citing support of the endowment fund.

Figure 10.7 *Sample Endowment Proposal (Endowed Lectures), p. 5.*

Walter responds as soon as he receives the draft proposal, and tells you to submit it to the foundation. You prepare a final draft and draft cover letter, and together you and the dean make an appointment with the university president to present these documents to him for review and approval. This meeting goes smoothly until the president suggests changing the proposal to a $2 million request for an endowed chair. The dean, having been briefed by you all along, responds quickly to say the School's contact at the foundation is new to the board, and that he is not yet ready to promote multi-million dollar grants. That may come in the future, you add, but a larger request might embarrass Walter Meger as he gains his footing right now on the Meger Foundation board.

You have a quiet sigh of relief to yourself when the president says he understands and then signs the cover letter. As soon as the president has signed off, you do two things: you mail the proposal, and you send a copy of everything sent to the foundation to Walter Meger. Then you note the details in your proposal log.

If the executives in your organization misinterpret or magnify positive indications from a potential funder, gently pull them back to what is realistic.

Endowment Proposal Scenario: Endowed Chair

You are the Director of Corporate and Foundation Relations at a selective liberal arts college. You function as the chief proposal writer at the college. Much of your proposal writing is aimed at securing scholarship support from local and regional foundations and companies. You also assist administrators and faculty in developing proposals for project support, and you oversee any federal grant proposals.

Recently your college began a capital campaign, and you are expected to contribute to the campaign by developing approaches to corporations and foundations for support of capital needs. Much of your work has been developing proposals for building projects. Bricks and mortar projects comprise half of the $100,000,000 capital campaign goal. You've had some success with bricks and mortar. As for endowment, you haven't yet been able to identify a prospective donor for the $10 million campaign endowment goal.

An Opportunity Arises for an Endowment Proposal

One morning you receive a call from the president's assistant, who tells you that the president wants to talk to you in an hour. You sense it has something to do with the board meeting the previous week, but you're not given a hint about the subject of the meeting.

As you sit down for the meeting, both your supervisor (the chief development officer) and the dean of faculty are sitting at the president's conference table. The president states that this is a meeting to follow up on a conversation he had with a board member the previous evening. This board member, who is CEO of the Meger Manufacturing Company, told your president that William Meger is retiring. You know the name. Meger single-handedly started up Meger Manufacturing as a small, privately held industrial firm after World War II. Over the years, the company grew, went public, and eventually joined the industrial ranks of the Fortune 500. You also know that William Meger went to the college sometime in the 1930s. You do not know him as a generous benefactor to the college.

Life transitions such as birth, retirement, and death are often the occasion for endowment gifts.

The president relates his conversation, in which the board member said that the Meger Manufacturing Company wants to do something special to honor William Meger before he retires. Specifically, the board member said, "We'd like to do something big, like name a building after him." The president, who over the past few years has come to know William Meger, suggested that an endowed chair in Latin might be better, since Meger had funded a temporary position in Latin last year with a private gift of stock when the college had cut it from the annual budget. This year the college maintained the position without Meger's funding in the hope that he might consider endowing a position in Latin. The board member said he didn't know about any of this, but that it sounded interesting. He promised to think about it.

Endowment gifts usually reflect the values and interests of the donor.

This morning the board member called your president to say he had discussed the endowed chair idea with his fellow corporate executives and his corporate board, and that they want to proceed as soon as possible. He ended by saying that someone from the college should get in touch with director of the Meger Manufacturing Corporate Foundation.

From Opportunity to Outline

After the president relates his conversation, he instructs you to call the director of Meger Manufacturing's corporate foundation to see what the next step might be. You finally speak up, saying this is great news. You had previously identified Meger Manufacturing's corporate foundation as a prospect for smaller grant but not for an endowed chair. Today's new information makes this grant opportunity your highest priority. The president tells the dean to help you with the proposal, and you leave the meeting.

Next you call Meger Manufacturing's corporate foundation and speak to the director. He tells you he knows about the conversation his CEO had with the president of your college. He tells you that he is expecting a proposal by the end of the week. The foundation needs to be in receipt of proposals at least two weeks in advance of a foundation board meeting, which is three weeks away. You tell him you know the guidelines, and that you will overnight a proposal for his review tomorrow.

Sometimes when things come together for an endowment gift you will have very little time to prepare a proposal.

After you hang up, you send an email to the dean of faculty, with a cc to the president and your supervisor, relating that the college needs to send off a proposal today per your discussion with the director of Meger Manufacturing's corporate foundation. You ask for a time you can meet with the dean to draft up a proposal for the president's review.

As you wait for the dean's reply, you pull out copy of a photocopied document entitled "Application Guidelines" that you requested a few months ago from the Meger Manufacturing Corporate Foundation. You note that proposals require "a statement of the need for support" and proof of tax-exempt status. After re-reading the document, you outline your proposal as follows:

1. Executive Summary

2. Background on Methodius College

3. Statement of Need for an Endowed Chair in Latin

4. Purpose and Duties of an Endowed Chair in Latin

5. Budgetary Summary

From Outline to Proposal

Just as you finish typing your outline, the phone rings. It is the dean, and he says he is available in his office right now. You walk right over to his office, sit down, and offer him your bare outline with a copy of Meger Manufacturing's grant guidelines. You relate the details of your phone conversation moments ago with the director of the Meger Manufacturing Corporate Foundation.

A longstanding and consistent pattern of modest gifts can sometimes be the precursor of a major endowment gift.

You tell the dean that you were not aware of William Meger's interest in the college until this morning, even though you knew his name as one of the college's most prominent alumni. The dean tells you that Mr. Meger maintains a low profile in general, and that he has done the same at the college. He has made modest annual gifts to the college, but has not been a consistent major donor, despite that fact he is a millionaire many times over.

Sometimes a potential major donor will gather information from sources outside your control.

Until two years ago, Meger rarely visited the campus, even though he lives an hour's drive away. But the budget crisis two years ago that prompted some departmental budget cuts caught Meger's attention. The dean then tells you of a phone conversation he had with Meger, and a follow up meeting in which he had to explain why classical languages were being cut from the college's course offerings. The dean learned that even though Meger had rarely visited the college, he meets regularly with Meger Manufacturing employees who are alumni and makes it a point to get to know all undergraduates who do summer internships at the company. Meger has relied on information about the college that has come to him primarily from students.

Endowment gifts are often closely connected to the donor's personal values and interests.

The dean tells you how distressed Meger felt about the abandonment of classical language study, and Latin in particular. Meger went on at some length about how important Latin had been in his education. After several phone calls and a meeting on campus with the dean and the president, Meger was satisfied that the budget cuts were a necessity and asked whether he could fund a teaching position in Latin for one year. The dean and president of the college agreed to accept a gift that would support Latin course offerings pending Meger's funding of the position. The first year went well, with Latin courses filled sufficiently to renew the offerings for another year without the need of a large private gift from Meger.

The dean informs you that everything he is revealing is for background information only, and that William Meger has insisted on remaining anonymous with respect to any gifts he has made to the college. The dean relates that two months ago Meger had called him to say he was interested in establishing a trust of several million dollars for scholarships, and that his attorney will contact the president this year to work out the details.

At this point you ask whether Meger's name can even be mentioned in the proposal, wondering to yourself how you are going to have a chair named anonymously. The dean says that the president has already talked to Meger about naming an endowed chair for him, and that he likes the idea as long as the company is made known to the public as the donor. Meger does not want to be approached personally by other schools and colleges where officials think they might get him to make large endowment gifts to their institutions.

> It is not unusual for individuals with the means to make major endowment grants to prefer anonymity.

At this point, the dean pauses, and you ask whether he and the president had ever asked William Meger whether he would endow a position in Latin. The dean tells you that they had raised the issue after enrollments looked good, but that Meger was more interested in establishing a scholarship endowment. Meger told the dean that he felt it was the college's responsibility to fund its faculty, and that he regarded scholarships as the personal responsibility of an alumnus. Meger also told the dean and president at that time that he had put a $2 million bequest in his will for endowed scholarships to be given to students who take at least one course in Latin. The dean explains that this bequest intention is evolving into a trust and will be great for the long-term situation of classical languages. But, he adds, for the college to truly ensure excellence in teaching, the college needs an endowment to support a tenured classicist.

> Conversations between a prospective major donor and the recipient organization can benefit both parties.

You agree that is just what should be said in the proposal to describe the college's need for an endowed chair in Latin, and you ask the dean to draft a "Purpose and Duties of an Endowed Chair in Latin" section for the proposal. You offer to draft up the other sections needed in this proposal, and to get the draft to him as soon as you finish it. It is early afternoon, and you return to your workstation. You proceed to write a section on background, including the long tradition of classical languages as part of the college's curriculum from the beginning. Then you write a section on the need for an endowed chair based on the details the dean has revealed to you and other information you know of the college's budget crisis two years ago.

Always pay close attention to the donor's wishes when you draft a proposal for endowment support.

You then meet with the college's financial officer to get some budgetary information in order to describe how an endowment will support an academic position. With this information, you craft a budget section for the proposal, add it to your draft proposal, which at this point has a blank executive summary, thinking that can be written after every other section of the proposal is drafted up. You send your draft via email to the dean.

Finishing a Final Draft

The dean responds. By the time he receives your draft, he has drafted three pages describing the proposed endowed chair. You thank him for the material, knowing that having too much detail and information at this point is far better than having too little. You offer to work his material into the proposal. You return to your office and extract information from the dean's description of the position, filling in the only hole left in your draft proposal. You proceed to write an executive summary, and with a draft proposal completed, you send it via email to the dean. (See Figures 10.8, 10.9, 10.10, and 10.11.)

Successful proposals are usually the result of close collaboration.

The dean calls you on the phone telling you that the president needs to look at it. You print a copy and take it to the president's executive assistant, who assures you it will get reviewed within an hour. You return to your office to draft a cover letter from the president to accompany the proposal.

Sometimes you will need to focus 100% of your time and attention to a proposal in order to pull it together quickly enough to meet a deadline.

By the time you finish the draft cover letter, you get a call from the president's assistant saying that the proposal has been reviewed and looks fine. You take the draft cover letter to the president's assistant, and await his signature. It is now about four o'clock and you have two more hours to make the FedEx deadline for overnight shipping. You get a call that the letter is signed and ready for you to pick up. You make photocopies of the signed cover letter, attach the original to the proposal, and send it for overnight delivery. You then note the proposal in your proposal log.

SAMPLE ENDOWMENT PROPOSAL (Endowed Chair), P. 1

A Proposal to the Meger Manufacturing Company Foundation

for The Wm Meger Endowed Chair in Latin

from

Methodius College

> The first sentence establishes the purpose and amount of your grant request.

Executive Summary

Methodius College requests a grant of $2 million from the Meger Manufacturing Company Foundation to create the William Meger Endowed Chair in Latin. Named for William Meger, Methodius College alumnus member of the class of 1937, this chair will honor the retiring chairman of the Meger Manufacturing Company. The broad purpose of this endowed chair is to enhance the development of the teaching of classics in the liberal arts curriculum, and to assure that the study of Latin has a permanent place in education at Methodius College.

Methodius College

Founded in 1855, Methodius College is a traditional four-year selective liberal arts college dedicated to excellence in education. The College's educational program is built on the premise that has always characterized liberal arts learning. This premise holds that no single approach or no single discipline monopolizes the search for truth or the methodology for teaching and learning.

Figure 10.8 *Sample Endowment Proposal (Endowed Chair), p. 1.*

SAMPLE ENDOWMENT PROPOSAL (Endowed Chair), P. 2

In a multi-page proposal, use headings that paginate, and identify the prospective donor and your organization.

→ Proposal to the Meger Manufacturing Company Foundation,
p. 2 of 4
from Methodius College

Methodius is selective in its admissions. As one of only 9 percent of the nation's colleges to host a chapter of Phi Beta Kappa, Methodius College has an above average student body by any national measurement. Typically students at Methodius rank in the upper 25 percent of their high school graduating class, and in college entrance test scores they typically rank in the top 20 percent. It is significant to note that more than 50 percent of Methodius graduates go on to do graduate professional or academic studies and receive post-graduate degrees.

Need for an Endowed Chair in Latin

Select details in your background section that are impressive and easily understood.

In recent years the curriculum at Methodius College has embraced a global model. This change has been embraced by both faculty and students. In general, the global model has improved the college curriculum and co-curricular activities. Expansion has been particularly notable in the Modern Languages, where Chinese and Arabic are now taught. Globalization of the curriculum, however, has resulted in a decline of subjects traditionally studied at Methodius. Most notably this is evidenced in the study of classical languages. Whereas a hundred years ago, every Methodius student studied Latin or Greek, today only a small fraction of the student body study classical languages. Several years ago a budget crisis prompted the temporary suspension of classes in Latin and Greek.

When possible, always show how other contributions and commitments will strengthen the program for which you are seeking support.

The Methodius College long-range plan calls for a re-invigoration of classics. Over the previous two academic years the study of Latin has been reinstated in the College's course offerings. Student evaluations are overwhelmingly supportive, and criticisms largely concern requests for an expansion of offerings. Recently alumni of the college have organized a fundraising drive to honor retired classics professor John Smith with an endowed scholarship for classics students. Other alumni have expressed interest in funding such scholarship support, and the college is optimistic about raising funds to support students of need who study the classics.

Figure 10.9 *Sample Endowment Proposal (Endowed Chair), p. 2.*

SAMPLE ENDOWMENT PROPOSAL (Endowed Chair), P. 3

Proposal to the Meger Manufacturing Company Foundation,
p. 3 of 4
from Methodius College

Need for an Endowed Chair in Latin (cont.)

To assure that classics remain an integral and permanent part of the Methodius curriculum, the college considers an endowed faculty position to be a priority. An endowed chair would resolve all remaining issues related to the restoration of the teaching of Latin at Methodius College. Such endowment funds would provide funding for a permanent, tenured faculty position.

Purpose and Duties of the Endowed Chair in Latin

The Wm Meger Chair in Latin would be selected from a national, competitive search coordinated by the Dean of Faculty. The appointed candidate would enter as a tenure-track faculty member. If the successful candidate has a distinguished academic record in teaching and publication, and holds tenure at another teaching institution, tenure would be offered to the successful candidate.

The Wm Meger Chair in Latin would bear full-time teaching responsibilities and would be expected to teach general education courses for freshman and sophomores as well as advanced courses for Classics and History majors. In addition to underwriting the salary of the chair holder, three modest annual stipends will draw funding with the proposed Wm Meger Chair in Latin endowment. An annual travel stipend would assure that the chair holder has funds for research and professional travel to conferences. A Latin Scholarship fund would award financial aid to at least two Classics majors per year, and a student assistant fund would enable the chair holder to select students to assist in projects related to the study of Latin. With the resources provided by a permanent endowment, the successful candidate for the Wm Meger Chair in Latin will be expected to re-build the classics program at Methodius College to a state that attracts growing numbers of students and results in a need for additional faculty members.

Figure 10.10 *Sample Endowment Proposal (Endowed Chair), p. 3.*

SAMPLE ENDOWMENT PROPOSAL (Endowed Chair), P. 4

Proposal to the Meger Manufacturing Company Foundation,
p. 4 of 4
from Methodius College

Budgetary Summary

Should the Meger Manufacturing Company Foundation look favorably on this proposal, Methodius College would invest grant funds in its permanent endowment as a restricted endowment fund to support the Wm Meger Chair in Latin at Methodius College. Gift and grant funds for endowment at Methodius College are co-mingled in the College's endowment fund, which is managed and governed by policies of the Methodius College Board of Directors. Current endowment policy, which has not changed for the past 47 years, allows for no more than five per cent of endowment principle to be drawn as annual support for endowment gift and grant intentions. This policy has enabled the College's endowment principle to grow at least two points beyond annual inflation rate in any given year and fund programs according to donor's wishes..

> After consultation with your financial officer, you have sufficient information to discuss endowment policy in more detail, including projected distributions over the first three years of the endowment's operation based on data from the College's three previous fiscal years. Your contact at the foundation has indicated that level of detail is not needed in the proposal.

Figure 10.11 *Sample Endowment Proposal (Endowed Chair), p. 4.*

Chapter 11

Federal Grants

- An Introduction to the World of Federal Grants and Cooperative Agreements
- Finding a Federal Grant
- Know Your Regulations
- Building the Application
- Federal Grants Accountability

Thus far, the discussion about grants in this book has focused on the private sector. Philanthropic and corporate interests fuel private-sector grant making. By contrast, federal grant making is driven by legislation and public policy. The official definition of "federal grant" can be found on Grants.gov, the central website for information about United States government grants:

> A federal grant is an award of financial assistance from a federal agency to a recipient to carry out a public purpose of support or stimulation authorized by a law of the United States.

Cooperative agreements are very similar to grants except that they require substantial involvement on the part of the awarding agency. Grants.gov defines "cooperative agreement" as follows:

> An award of financial assistance that is used to enter into the same kind of relationship as a grant; and is distinguished from a grant in that it provides for substantial involvement between the federal agency and the recipient in carrying out the activity contemplated by the award.

There are 26 federal grant-making agencies:

- Agency for International Development (USAID)
- Corporation for National and Community Service
- Department of Agriculture (USDA)
- Department of Commerce
- Department of Defense (DOD)
- Department of Education (USDE)
- Department of Energy (DOE)
- Department of Health and Human Services (DHHS)
- Department of Homeland Security (DHS)
- Department of Housing and Urban Development (HUD)
- Department of the Interior
- Department of Justice (DOJ)
- Department of Labor (DOL)
- Department of State

- Department of Transportation (DOT)
- Department of the Treasury
- Department of Veterans Affairs (VA)
- Environmental Protection Agency (EPA)
- Institute of Museum and Library Services
- National Aeronautics and Space Administration (NASA)
- National Archives and Records Administration
- National Endowment for the Arts (NEA)
- National Endowment for the Humanities (NEH)
- National Science Foundation (NSF)
- Small Business Administration (SBA)
- Social Security Administration

Together, these 26 government agencies administer more than 1,000 grant programs in 21 categories:

- Agriculture
- Arts
- Business and Commerce
- Community Development
- Disaster Prevention and Relief
- Education
- Employment, Labor, and Training
- Energy
- Environmental Quality
- Food and Nutrition
- Health
- Housing
- Humanities
- Information and Statistics
- Law, Justice, and Legal Services
- Natural Resources
- Recovery Act
- Regional Development
- Science and Technology
- Social Services and Income Security
- Transportation

There are many professional opportunities available in federal grant writing.

If it has occurred to you browsing through these lists that there are many and varied job opportunities for federal grant writers, you are right. Prospects are very bright indeed for a grant writer who acquires the knowledge and skills needed to navigate the federal grants process.

An Introduction to the World of Federal Grants and Cooperative Agreements

A beginning grant writer might be called upon to contribute to the preparation of a federal grant application.

It is highly unlikely that you will be called upon to produce an entire federal grant application yourself during your first 90 days as a grant writer. However, it is entirely possible that you might contribute in various ways to the development of a federal grant application. You might be asked to coordinate the submission process or to take the lead on specific sections. Putting together a competitive federal grant application is a big job, and it is usually done collaboratively with program managers and other experts.

Familiarizing yourself with the legal framework that regulates federal grants is essential.

Understanding a bit about the legal and regulatory framework that governs the world of grants and cooperative agreements is essential for anyone participating in the preparation or implementation of a federal grant project. Everything associated with federal grants is regulated, from the proposal stage to closure and the final audit. You need to know which regulations apply to your organization and where to go for information. Fortunately, all the information you will need for a successful start in the world of federal grants is easily accessible on the Internet. The single-most important website is Grants.gov (shown in Figure 11.1).

Finding a Federal Grant

Grants.gov is the place to start searching for information about federal grant opportunities.

Grants.gov is the place to start a search for federal grant programs that match your organization's needs and mission. On the "Find Grant Opportunities" page you will be able to search for suitable grants in a variety of ways. Grants.gov provides links to the three main sources of detailed information about federal grants: the Catalog of Federal Domestic Assistance, agency program announcements, and the Federal Register.

Figure 11.1
Grants.gov is an indispensable resource for writers of federal grants.

Catalog of Federal Domestic Assistance

The Catalog of Federal Domestic Assistance or CFDA (shown in Figure 11.2) contains a comprehensive listing of all federal grant programs. It is searchable by keyword or program number, and contains a downloadable Public User Guide. Save this user guide to your hard drive and print it out so that you can consult it as you navigate the CFDA website. A helpful tutorial on writing grants is also provided on this website.

The CFDA contains information on all federal grant programs.

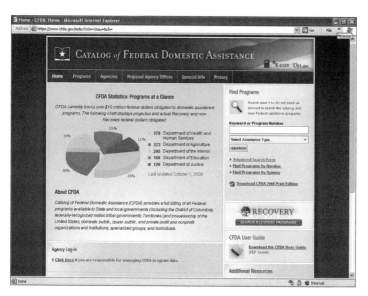

Figure 11.2
The Catalog of Federal Domestic Assistance (CFDA) is a compendium of all federal grant programs.

Agency Program Announcements

Each federal grant-making agency publishes announcements of grant programs.

Another vital source of information about grant opportunities can be found on the website of each of the 26 federal grant-making agencies listed previously. If you know the federal agency most likely to be the appropriate grant-making agency for your organization (for example, it might be EPA if your organization's mission is stream cleanup), you need to study that agency's website carefully. Grant program announcements are routinely posted on agency websites (see Figure 11.3). Most will also provide an opportunity for you to sign up for emails that will notify you of upcoming funding opportunities.

Figure 11.3

Agency program announcements give detailed descriptions of eligibility and program requirements.

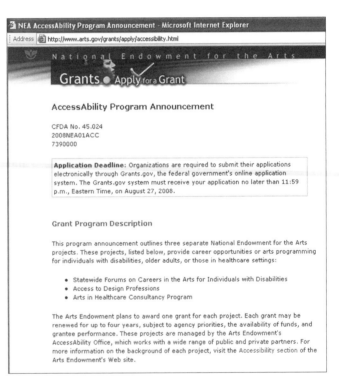

Federal Register

Full announcements of all federal grant opportunities can be found in the Federal Register.

The Federal Register provides the American public with access to all federal laws, regulations, and presidential documents. Because it is updated daily, it is sometimes referred to as "the daily newspaper" of the United States government. The Federal Register contains full announcements of all federal grant opportunities (see Figure 11.4). You can learn about these by searching or subscribing to an RSS feed on the Federal Register website.

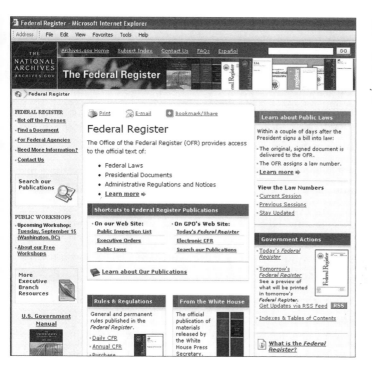

Figure 11.4.
The Federal Register contains full program announcements of all federal grant opportunities.

Know Your Regulations

The federal regulations that apply to your organization are determined by the type of organization it is, not by the federal agency that awards the funds. This makes sense if you think about it, because otherwise an organization that receives grants from more than one federal agency could be caught in a tangle of inconsistent and possibly conflicting regulations.

The regulations that apply to a grant award are determined by the type of recipient.

The basic regulatory framework for grants and cooperative agreements is set down in the cost principles and administrative requirements for each type of grant recipient.

Cost Principles

Federal grants are awards of taxpayer dollars, so it should not be surprising to learn that there are uniform regulations that determine how those taxpayer dollars are spent. When you apply to a foundation for a grant, the foundation will review your budget according to its own rules and standards and either approve or not approve your request. When you apply to a government

Uniform cost principles apply to the recipients of federal grants.

agency for a grant, the standards for use of the money are uniform. These standards are known as the cost principles, and there are three sets of them. Unless you are a freelancer working for a variety of organizations, you will only need to familiarize yourself with the one set that applies to your type of organization. The cost principles affect not only the budget but also every aspect of program development and implementation, so writers as well as finance people need to be aware of them.

The cost principles originated in the Office of Management and Budget and now reside in the Code of Federal Regulations.

All of the cost principles originated in the Office of Management and Budget (OMB). They exist in the form of OMB Circulars, which have been codified or moved to the Code of Federal Regulations (CFR). Therefore, each set is known by two names, which may be confusing until you get the hang of it. Federal grants are authorized by statute and regulated by the CFR, which has the full force of federal law.

Cost Principles for State, Local, and Tribal Governments. If the entity that is to receive federal grant funds is a state government agency, a local government agency such as a county or a school system, or a recognized tribal government, the applicable set of cost principles is OMB Circular A-87, now 2 CFR 225 Cost Principles for State, Local, and Indian Tribal Governments (see Figure 11.5). Most veterans in the grants business still call it A-87, which is a bit easier to say, but you can search for it by either name.

Cost Principles for Nonprofit Organizations. If the recipient of federal grant funds is a 501 (c) (3) nonprofit organization, the applicable set of cost principles is OMB Circular A-122, now 2 CFR 230 Cost Principles for Nonprofit Organizations (see Figure 11.6).

Cost Principles for Colleges and Universities. A great deal of the research, development, and training sponsored by the United States government is actually carried out via grants awarded to institutions of higher learning. If you work for a college or university that receives federal grant funds, the applicable set of cost principles is OMB Circular A-21, now 2 CFR 220 Cost Principles for Educational Institutions (see Figure 11.7). If you work in a university sponsored-research office, you will become very familiar with A-21.

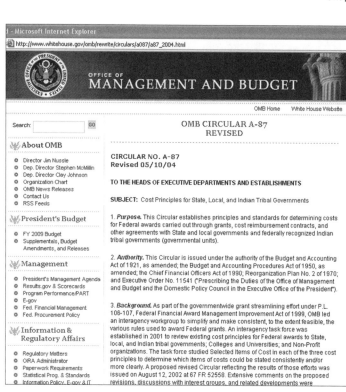

Figure 11.5
OMB Circular A-87 or 2 CFR 225 applies to state, local, and tribal governments.

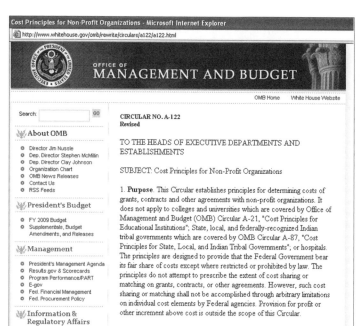

Figure 11.6
OMB Circular A-122 or 2 CFR 230 applies to all nonprofit organizations.

Figure 11.7
OMB Circular A-21 or 2 CFR 220 applies to colleges and universities.

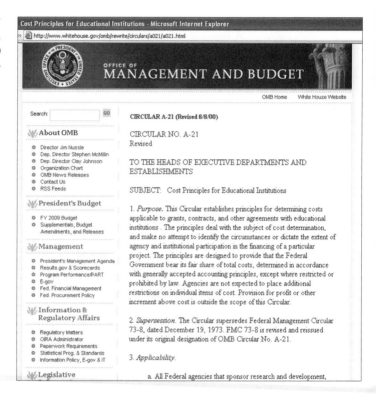

All three sets of cost principles lay out criteria and rules for the use of federal funds. There may be additional legal requirements, but basically whether or not an expense can be charged to a grant is guided by the following considerations:

- **Allowability.** Does the expense meet the criteria for allowable expense set down in the applicable set of cost principles? The purchase of food to be served to indigent clients would be an allowable expense for a soup kitchen, for example, but the purchase of beer to accompany meals would not. Laboratory equipment required to conduct research on climate change would be an allowable expense for a research university, but lobbying Congress based on the results of the research would not.

- **Reasonableness.** Is the expense reasonable? Is it necessary? Would a "prudent person" consider the expense to be both reasonable and necessary? Does your proposed senior day care center need marble-topped sinks? Probably the prudent person would say, "No." Does your proposed senior center need costly chair lifts and resuscitation equipment? The prudent person is likely to say yes to those expenses if they appear to be necessary for the population your center is intended to serve.

- **Allocability.** Is the expense allocable to the grant? In other words, is it linked to a specific objective of the grant? Your organization might need a new furnace, but if that expense is not clearly linked to grant project activities and objectives, it is probably not allocable.

Each set of cost principles is detailed and specific. There is no need for you to memorize what is in your cost principles because they are indexed and searchable. What is most important is that you get a sense of when you need to consult your circular to see if your program ideas are consistent with the cost principles. For example, if you want to include expenses to support employee health and morale, can you do that? If you want the professional development for your project to include attendance at a conference in Las Vegas, can you do that? The important thing for a grant writer or project coordinator to keep in mind is the necessity of always planning in accordance with the applicable cost principles.

> It is important to be aware of when you need to consult the cost principles that apply to your organization to make certain that you do not incur unallowable costs on your grant.

Administrative Requirements

Just as each type of organization has its own set of cost principles, each has its own set of uniform administrative requirements. There are, however, only two sets; nonprofits are subject to the same administrative requirements as colleges and universities. Like the cost principles, these documents originated in the White House Office of Management and Budget. The administrative requirements guide the whole life cycle of the implementation of a federal grant, covering topics such as:

- Pre-award requirements
- Procurement
- Financial management and drawdown of funds
- Time and effort records
- Inventory
- Grant accountability and reporting
- Records maintenance
- Closure procedures
- Consequences related to noncompliance

Administrative Requirements for State, Local, and Tribal Governments. If you work for a state, local, or tribal government agency, your grants will be subject to OMB Circular A-102, popularly known as the Common Rule (see Figure 11.8). If the Common Rule applies to you, it will be necessary to read through it to get a sense of what it covers and how it is organized because it does not have a table of contents.

Figure 11.8
OMB Circular A-102 or the "Common Rule" applies to grants awarded to state, local, and tribal governments.

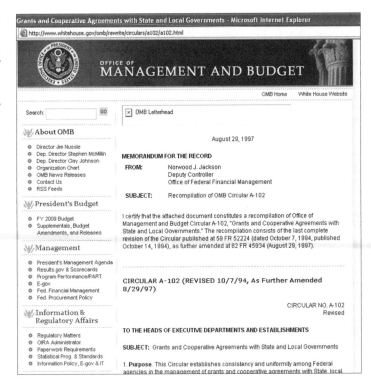

Administrative Requirements for Nonprofit Organizations and Higher Education Institutions. Grants awarded to colleges and universities are subject to the same administrative requirements as nonprofit organizations. These are set down in OMB Circular A-110, now 2 CFR 215 Uniform Administrative Requirements for Grants and Agreements with Institutions of Higher Education, Hospitals, and Other Non-Profit Organizations (see Figure 11.9). Part 215 was revised in 2006 and has a table of contents and subheadings that make it very easy to navigate.

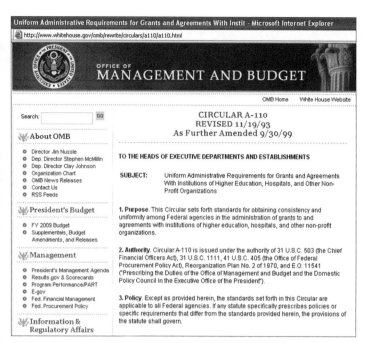

Figure 11.9

OMB Circular A-110 or 2 CFR 215 applies to grants awarded to colleges, universities, and nonprofit organizations.

It is important to remember that all grant funds that have a federal origin are subject to the applicable cost principles and administrative requirements. This means that if your organization is a subrecipient rather than a prime (or direct) recipient of federal grant monies, the requirements still apply. For example, if you are a county that has received a grant from your state for bridge repair, you are subject to A-87 and A-102 if the funds originated at the federal level. The fact that you applied to and received funding from your state does not mean that the funds are subject only to state regulations. The funds you received for bridge repair may well be subject to additional state regulations and requirements, but the federal ones also apply. Federal funds are routinely distributed to states, which then re-grant them. Funds distributed in this way are referred to as "passthrough" funds.

However, if you are a nonprofit organization that has received a passthrough grant from your state to provide programming for children with visual impairment, you are subject to A-122 and A-110. Remember, the cost principles and administrative requirements that apply are determined by the type of recipient you are.

Subrecipients of federal grant funds are subject to the regulations that apply to federal grants, even though they have not received the funds directly from the federal government.

Passthrough funds are subject to the cost principles and administrative requirements that apply to the recipient.

Building the Application

The typical federal grant application contains many of the same components routinely required for private-sector grant proposals. You will need to lay out the need for your project, a description of your project, the goals and objectives, and an evaluation plan. The way you propose to address the needs you present is likely to be quite different, however. Whereas private-sector grant makers tend to require that you present a program or solution that is new and innovative, federal agencies may require that you replicate a program shown through scientifically based research to have been successful elsewhere. For example, if you are applying for a grant to reduce the rate of juvenile crime in your community, you will probably be required to select your strategies and interventions from a list approved by the agency. Unless the grant is for research, government agencies want to serve the public good by funding projects that already have a track record of success.

Federal agencies tend to fund research-proven solutions to problems rather than innovative, new approaches to problems.

The grant program announcement will tell you exactly what your application needs to include and in what order the information must be presented. Usually federal applications are scored by panels of expert reviewers. The review criteria and the number of points assigned to each section of the proposal will be given in the program announcement. Pay close attention to this information.

Federal grant applications are scored by panels of experts according to pre-determined criteria.

Federal grant applications are likely to be longer and more detailed than private sector proposals, and they may call for components that corporations and foundations do not always require. You may need to submit a pre-proposal, for example. You may need to conduct a preliminary survey and submit the results. For community development or human services grants, you will need to submit evidence of extensive planning with stakeholders. Whatever category of support you are seeking, you will undoubtedly need to submit a logic model that depicts graphically the way in which desired outcomes will be achieved (see Figure 11.10).

The requirements for federal grants tend to be extensive and detailed because of the necessity to expend public funds in a responsible manner.

If a federal grant proposal requests support for research, you will need to include a literature review, the resume of the principal investigator, evidence of your institution's capacity to conduct the research, and a full bibliography. If the project involves research using human subjects, there is an extensive protocol that must be followed.

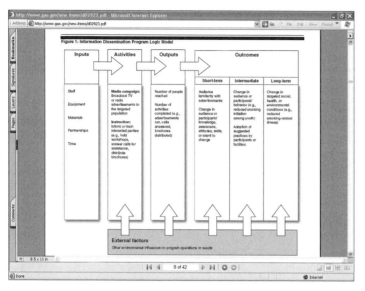

Figure 11.10
Federal grants routinely require that your program's inputs, activities, outputs, and outcomes be displayed on a logic model.

Budgets must be developed in accordance with the applicable cost principles and must be presented on a Standard Form (SF) using the standard federal object class categories: personnel, fringe benefits, travel, equipment, supplies, contractual, construction, other, and indirect costs. See Figure 11.11 for a page of SF 424.

Federal grant budgets must be displayed by category on the required form.

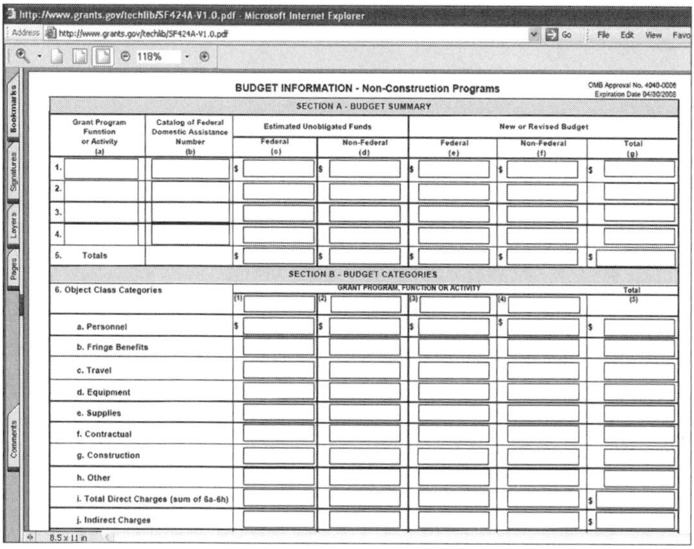

Figure 11.11
Federal grant budgets must be presented on a Standard Form such as SF 424.

Direct costs are those expenses specifically associated with your grant project activities. Indirect costs are those expenses that represent overhead.

Your budget will need to distinguish between direct costs (such as salaries, supplies, equipment, and so on) and indirect costs (overhead expenses) that are negotiated as a percentage of the total award. You may also need to furnish detailed evidence of your organization's financial stability and eligibility to receive the proposed grant assistance. In addition, the awarding agency will require signed certifications and assurances that bind your organization to specific legal requirements.

All of these requirements and many more will be spelled out in detail. The key is to study the application package carefully and do exactly what it says. If it says that funds can only be used in Federal Enterprise Zones, that is exactly what it means. If it says that applications must be received by midnight on a given date, it is not okay to have yours in by the next morning. If it says you must submit your proposal in 12-point font with one-inch margins, don't try to give yourself a bit more space by reducing the font to 11 points or narrowing the margins. Federal applications go through a pre-screening process, and those that don't follow all requirements are usually not reviewed. Violation of a single submission requirement can potentially jeopardize the entire submission.

Follow application requirements to the letter.

Careful coordination is vital if a federal grant application is to be successful. Competition is fierce. You may find yourself competing for an award that will have only 5 successful applications. There may be 500 applicants for this award. Success depends upon coordinating every step of the process.

You will submit your federal grant application on Grants.gov.

Federal Grants Accountability

Accountability requirements for federal grants are an important area of expertise for a grant writer because the person who is the principal writer of a proposal is usually also the person who drafts the required reports. That means you need to have a good grasp of what is contained in the applicable administrative requirements. If your organization is classified as a "low risk" grantee based on past audits, you will only need to submit two reports each year, an interim progress report and a final report. See Figure 11.12 for a view of the first page of the SF-PPR Performance Progress Report form.

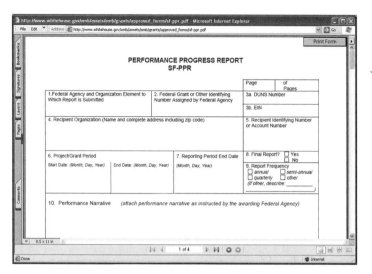

Figure 11.12
The SF-PPR is used to report on federal grant projects.

If your organization is classified as a "high risk" grantee, you may need to submit reports as often as once a month.

Preparing for a Successful Audit

All recipients of federal grants totaling $500,000 or more are subject to an annual mandatory federal audit. The Single Audit Act of 1984 (amended in 1996) ensured that recipients of federal grants from more than one federal agency would not have to go through multiple audits. OMB Circular A-133 lays out the audit regulations for federal grant recipients. It applies to all types of organizations.

It is wise to begin preparing for a successful A-133 audit during the grant-proposal preparation process. The project itself must be structured in such a way that compliance will be ensured. For this reason, it is critical that a federal grant writer be familiar with OMB A-133 (see Figure 11.13).

The results of A-133 audits are public information and must be reported annually to the Federal Audit Clearinghouse (see Figure 11.14).

Reporting for federal grants is outlined in the applicable Administrative Requirements.

Audit regulations for federal grant recipients are set down in the Single Audit Act of 1984 (amended in 1996) and OMB Circular A-133.

Figure 11.13
The Single Audit Act ensures that a grant recipient does not have to go through multiple audits.

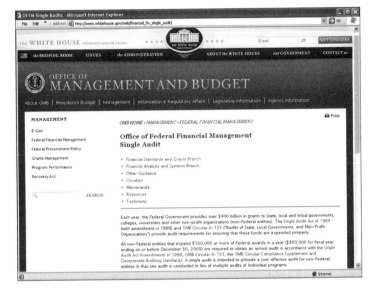

Figure 11.14
An A-133 Single Audit is performed by an independent auditor.

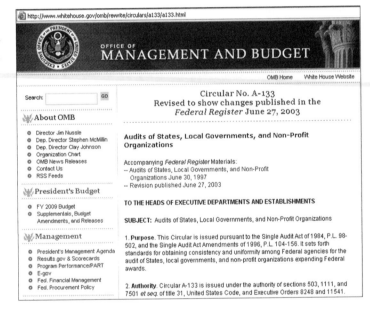

Maintenance of Records

Records associated with federal grants must be maintained for three years following the filing of the last annual financial report, unless there is an open investigation or dispute, in which case records must be maintained for three years following the resolution and closure of the investigation or dispute. If you are a grant writer responsible for accountability reporting, you will need to make certain that grant records are maintained for the required period of time.

Federal grant records must be maintained for three years following the date of the filing of the final financial expenditure report. If there is an open investigation or dispute, they must be maintained for three years following the resolution of the dispute.

Your 90-Day Checklist for Federal Grants

✓ Become familiar with all of the resources available on Grants.gov.

✓ Add the CFDA to your Internet Explorer Favorites and make sure you are able to navigate the site to find the information you need.

✓ Familiarize yourself with the websites of all federal agencies that your organization might apply to for funding, and subscribe to receive alerts of new grant opportunities as they arise.

✓ Subscribe to an RSS feed from the Federal Register.

✓ Identify the cost principles and administrative requirements applicable to your organization and familiarize yourself with both.

✓ Identify a mentor experienced in the federal grant-submission process who can steer you in the right direction.

Chapter 12

Managing Grant Awards

- Managing Successful Proposals
- Publicizing Grant Awards
- Managing Grant Reports

$\mathbf{S}$ ending off a completed proposal does not end your work as a grant writer. Instead, it marks the beginning of a new phase of work. The phrase "post-award" is often used to encompass the various tasks that follow the submission of proposals. Not every one of your proposals will result in a grant award, but even unsuccessful proposals will require some post-submission work on your part.

Managing Successful Proposals

Your work continues after a grant is awarded.

Following the award of a grant, you will be involved in communication with the grant maker. You will also coordinate publicity associated with the grant award. Finally, you will coordinate any reporting required by the grant maker. This will inevitably involve you in monitoring progress over the term of any grant awarded to your organization.

Acknowledgement Letters

Typically, a grant is approved on a timeline that coincides with corporation or foundation board meetings or an agency's governing body meetings. When you are successful, you will receive a letter stating the amount and purpose of the grant award. You may also receive a phone call or email message notifying you of the decision, but generally, the official communication will be in the form of a letter.

Scour a new award letter for details about grant payment and reporting requirements.

Grant award letters also convey other important information. A grant award letter might also tell you when the actual check will be released or whether and when funds will be available by electronic means. It might also include information about reporting requirements. Distribute the grant award letter to everyone in your organization who needs to be apprised of the terms of the award.

If a grant is awarded for a multi-year period, there will probably be information about the planned release of the funds over the grant period, including the dates when you can expect to receive the funds. Sometimes an initial check is included in an award letter; sometimes it is transmitted at a later date.

Since the award letter will be sent to your CEO, make sure that he or she involves you as soon as it is received. You will want to turn around a brief acknowledgement letter from the CEO expressing your organization's gratitude for support and including any information about forthcoming reports expected by the foundation.

The acknowledgement letter from your CEO will serve as the letter of record. It should be brief, and it should convey acceptance of the award and gratitude. Avoid dense verbiage about your institution if it has nothing directly to do with the need or the project. However, if you can make a statement that demonstrates how the award will help your organization to serve its constituencies better, then by all means include it.

If reporting requirements are outlined in the award letter, it is a good idea to restate them in the acknowledgement letter with a vow to submit reports as required. Should there be personal relationships between the foundation and your organization's board members or staff, you might want to orchestrate additional thank you letters with verbiage like, "I wish to add my thanks to those expressed by President Doe…." Handwritten notes on the letters add a gracious touch. If you are drafting and preparing the final copy for the signature of your CEO and any board members, you can help them by attaching a post-it note to the final draft with suggestions for a handwritten note. Design the letter so that there is sufficient space for this note. See Figure 12.1 for an example.

Managing Rejection Among Colleagues, Staff, and Volunteers

Not every proposal is funded. Some are rejected. Some receive partial funding. No one likes rejection, but it is endemic to the nature of grant writing. Rejection is something every good grant writer must learn to deal with creatively.

When you get a rejection letter, there is no need for an immediate response. However, you will want to determine your next steps to find out what went wrong and what you can do in the future to improve your chances of funding. This might involve a variety of things in the coming months, including calling a program officer to discuss your unsuccessful proposal or perhaps even arranging a meeting. In most cases, a rejection letter will not give you detailed information but will simply reflect the decision.

You should regard every rejection as the beginning of a discussion with colleagues on what might have gone wrong and what should happen next. You might renew your strategy for the grant

---

It's important to turn around a brief acknowledgement letter immediately upon receiving notification of a grant award.

A grant-recipient's acknowledgement letter of record accepts the grant and its terms, including reporting requirements.

Rejections are part of the grant-writer's professional life; not all proposals for funding are awarded.

SAMPLE GRANT ACKNOWLEDGEMENT LETTER

January 1, 2022

Ms. Jane Doe
Executive Director
The Jim and Jane Johnson Foundation
125 Park Avenue
New York, NY 10011

> Open your acknowledgment letter with the facts of the grant award.

Dear Ms. Doe:

I write to thank you for the grant of $200,000 in support of Johnson Fellowships in Nursing at The University of the United States. This grant will support outstanding graduates in our School of Nursing as they pursue the master of science degree in the 2022-2023 academic year.

This grant is most welcome and timely. The nation currently suffers from a critical shortage of nurses with graduate degrees. The University of the United States is in the midst of a national initiative in graduate nursing. Recently, the General Foundation awarded our School of Nursing a $1 million grant for an applied graduate nursing initiative to develop new graduate curricula in acute needs areas.

> Include verbiage touting your organization only if it is directly related to the grant being acknowledged.

This year's Johnson Graduate Fellowship will ensure that our most promising nursing graduates can pursue graduate studies in the midst of these major advances in the School of Nursing. I would like to once again extend my gratitude to the Selection Committee of The Jim and Jane Johnson Foundation for this generous grant.

Sincerely,

Timothy Kachinske
President

> *Post-it note*
> *President Kachinske, You may want to write a note to Ms. Doe in this space thanking her for the interesting discussion during your visit to the foundation earlier this year.*

Figure 12.1 *Sample grant acknowledgment letter.*

maker that rejected your proposal, or you may do research to support an approach to other grant makers for a rejected project. Sometimes your organization may need to acknowledge that a project is simply not fundable with grant support.

Each rejection presents an opportunity to reflect and strategize.

It is a good idea to do research before you discuss a rejection with colleagues. If possible, obtain information about the institutions and organizations that received funding during the cycle when your proposal was rejected. Larger foundations and corporate giving programs usually make this information available shortly after board meetings, but smaller grant makers may not publicize their grants, making it a challenge to scope out your successful competitors. Federal grant decisions are public record, but the information is not always available on a timely basis.

Viewed positively and strategically, a rejection can mark the first step toward developing a future approach that will be successful.

It sometimes falls to a grant writer to bolster the egos of individuals who have invested time and effort in the development of a proposal. It's important to keep discussions on a rational plane, especially when stakeholders have emotional ties to project or program development.

Publicizing Grant Awards

It is a good idea to do a press release when you receive a significant grant, because it provides a public document that you and others will find useful even if it doesn't find its way into print or onto a web publication. Press releases need to be coordinated with corporation or foundation staff and should include details about the grant as well as the verbiage used to describe the corporation or foundation. Ideally, grants of interest to the community will be noted in local venues such as magazines, journals, and newspapers. Even if you don't make it in to the print edition, you stand an excellent chance of having your grant noted on a publication's website, as shown in Figure 12.2.

Always coordinate grant project press releases with the donor to make sure that your publicity aligns with their expectations.

Working with Public Information Staff

Your organization may have an internal staffer (a public information officer, for example) who produces and disseminates press releases, in which case you will need to be the conduit of foundation-approved information about the grant award even if you are not the final author. Cultivate a relationship with your public information officer with the aim of maintaining quality control of anything grant-related that is produced by his office.

Grant writers work closely with public information or publication relations officers.

Figure 12.2
Grant award story on local magazine website.

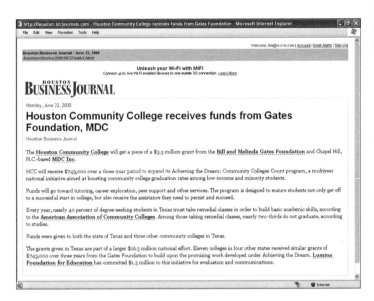

Also, make sure that your grants are publicized in your own internal publications such as newsletters, magazines, and annual reports. It is always good to start with a press release or story on your own organization's website.

Human-interest stories can usually illustrate the impact of a grant project better than factual information.

Your public information officer will probably be able to take on the work of publicizing a grant in your organization's publications. Copy for this type of publicity should always be vetted by the corporation or foundation before publication. Grant makers generally appreciate feature stories about people served through a program they have funded. An article about a grant award that outlines the details of a proposal has nothing like the PR value of a profile or story of a deserving person helped by a grant-funded project.

Writing and Distributing Press Releases

You will need to do your organization's grant-related PR if no one else is available.

If your organization does not have public relations staff, you will need to produce and distribute the releases yourself. *The Chronicle of Philanthropy* publishes a "New Grants" list in each issue. Some corporations and foundations will announce grant award lists in press releases that are submitted to *The Chronicle* and other philanthropic and educational publications. If you want your grants noted in *The Chronicle,* send a notice yourself to make certain it has a chance of being published.

Other publications you contact will vary according to your locale, your organization, and the nature of the project to be funded. As you gain experience, you will develop contacts in local media, electronic media, and trade publications. It is a good idea to nurture these relationships in order to decrease the likelihood that your news releases will end up in a wastebasket or recycle bin. For an example of a print press release, see Figure 12.3.

Corporations, much more so than foundations, have well-oiled PR offices that can be a tremendous help in getting the word out about a grant. They will often be glad to assist, and asking for their guidance and involvement helps to avoid any potential damage-control issues. Never assume that you know what a donor will appreciate. A company that has to do damage control over ill-conceived publicity is not likely to support your organization with future grants.

> Always give corporations and foundations the opportunity for advance review of news releases and other publicity about a grant award. You don't want your well-intentioned efforts to put you in damage-control mode.

Internal Releases on Grant Awards

From time to time, you may need to publicize a grant award within your organization for a specific internal audience. This can happen when a grant-funded project requires participation from staff or volunteers in your organization. For example, if you are working at an educational institution, and you are awarded a faculty development grant to support projects that are to be competitively selected from among your faculty, it would be appropriate to develop a special internal release significantly different from a press release for the general public. If you were working for a nonprofit organization that receives a grant for volunteer development, it would be appropriate to prepare a special internal release to be shared only with volunteers who are potential participants in the grant project.

> Internal releases are used to publicize grant awards within your organization.

An internal release is similar to press releases in one important respect: you should prepare a draft to be reviewed by the grant maker before distributing it. Nothing you prepare for broad dissemination among colleagues and volunteers is confidential, so you should approach the task of writing an internal release as though it were a press release for the general public.

Because an internal release is prepared for a specific audience, it will not contain general information on the background of your organization. In that sense, it differs considerably from a press release. An internal release might go into greater detail about the project than would be found in a release for the general public.

> Like press releases, internal releases should be reviewed by the grant maker before dissemination.

SAMPLE GRANT PRESS RELEASE

**Fr. Meger Center for Social Justice receives grant to
build volunteer support for people with arthritis in King County.**

For Immediate Release
January 1, 2022

Contact: Jane Doe
Phone: (direct) 301-555-1224
(main) 301-555-1200

The Jim and Jane Johnson Foundation has awarded a grant of $135,000 to Fr. Meger Center for Social Justice for a new model of support for people with arthritis in southern King County.

This grant will enable Fr. Meger Center for Social Justice to develop a model community living partnership and an interfaith network of volunteer supports to help close the gap left by insufficient federal, state, and county services.

"In southern King County, people with severe arthritis and their families have a great need for basic help," said Timothy Kachinske, President of the Fr. Meger Center. "It is critical that we develop a volunteer core of support now."

Volunteers will be recruited and trained specifically in the following areas of need: transportation, respite, case management, and advocacy.

The Jim and Jane Johnson Foundation, based in New York, NY, is the nation's largest philanthropy devoted exclusively to health care for people with arthritis. The Arthritis Action program is based on the ideal of community volunteerism and neighbors helping neighbors.

The Fr. Meger Center for Social Justice provides life-span educational and human services in the King County region in support of people with all types of disabilities.

Figure 12.3 *Sample grant press release.*

Also, the contact person on an internal release is likely to be the project director of the grant-funded project, who may not be the person coordinating public relations for the grant noted on a press release.

It's important that internal releases be drafted with the same care you would take on a piece prepared for the general public. Your colleagues are an important constituency and they may be very judgmental. Internal releases should look every bit as professional as press releases. You may want to consult with your public information officer when you draft up an internal release, but the facts and presentation should be driven by persons responsible for the substance of the project funded by the grant. See Figure 12.4 for a sample internal release disseminating information about a faculty development grant that seeks innovative course development ideas from faculty.

Internal releases should be every bit as professional as publicity prepared for public release.

Managing Grant Reports

As a grant writer, you are the point person for any reports that must be filed as a condition of a grant award. Making sure that all reporting deadlines and requirements are met will be your responsibility. You will need to have a good handle on these activities because in many cases you will be dependent on other people (e.g., financial, program, and executive staff) to provide you with information. The availability of your CEO to sign off on reports is another consideration. All of this requires that you have a grasp of calendars and schedules other than your own.

Grant writers are responsible for any reporting associated with successful grants.

The first rule in reporting on a grant is to know your grant-maker's reporting requirements. The complexity of reporting requirements tends to depend upon the size of the grant award and the nature of the project. Expect each grant maker to have different reporting requirements, even if you notice common threads among various guidelines. Grant reports can range from a straightforward letter to complex matching requirements that require detailed financial information on gift and grant revenue from donors supporting a challenge. A large grant involving many people outside your organization may necessitate a significant investment of time and effort to satisfy reporting requirements.

Each grant maker has its own set of grant-reporting requirements.

Methodius College Launches Blueprint for International Relations

January 21, 2014
For Immediate Internal Release

Contact: Todor Jivkov
Phone: (direct) 301-555-1224
E-mail:deanfaculty@methodius.edu

President Jerome B. Benedict announced today that The General National Foundation has awarded a grant of $200,000 to Methodius College. This grant supports "Blueprint for International Relations," a project to develop new models of international relations study for the liberal arts curriculum.

This grant will enable faculty members to travel and study abroad as they develop specific curricular materials and new liberal arts courses related to international relations.

"The General National Foundation recognizes the need to develop international relations courses for the benefit of the country, and they have chosen Methodius to lead the way," said Jerome B. Benedict, President of Methodius College. "Blueprint for International Relations will help us develop liberal arts courses that make our students competitive in the world arena."

Travel and study grants up to the amount of $4,000 will be awarded to faculty teams that present the most competitive course ideas. Funds may be used for travel or the purchase of study materials. Guidelines will be available on January 30, 2014 at the office of the Dean of Faculty. Proposed projects approved for funding will undergo a rigorous evaluation, and decisions will be made on Mar 1, with funding available for the summer of 2014.

"We are encouraging teams comprised of several disciplines to propose projects for this important faculty development initiative," said Todor Jivkov, Dean of Faculty.

Since 1956 the General National Foundation has supported innovation in higher education in the United States.

###

Figure 12.4 *Sample internal release.*

Tracking Reports

Keeping track of due dates for reports is essential. As you receive grant awards, you should develop a fool-proof system to keep track of reports that are due to grant makers. Initially you may be able to keep a simple list of due dates, but as your productivity increases, you will want to maintain a reporting calendar as shown in the sample timeline in Figure 12.5.

Keep in mind that when you work with a timeline of due dates, you will always be projecting backward for time to prepare and deliver a report. You will need to plan for the time it will take to pull together details, draft the report, get it reviewed, make necessary revisions, and obtain approval and signatures. You also need to consider the time it will take for the report to get to a grant maker by the deadline. Because of all that is involved prior to send off, the date you mark on your personal calendar to begin working on a report will be much earlier than the report due date.

Eventually, if you produce many successful proposals, you will want to consider developing a database that works with a calendar so that you can keep track of all the tasks or activities needed for successful grant implementation and reporting. See Chapter 13 for a discussion of tracking reports using Microsoft Outlook and Microsoft Dynamics CRM.

> Constructing a grant-reporting calendar requires taking into consideration the time needed for all aspects of report preparation.

> Create a timeline for tracking grant report due dates. Consider developing a database that works with your personal calendar to track the work you need to do to get reports to a grant maker.

Project Implementation

As a grant writer, you probably will not have project implementation included in your responsibilities. This does not mean that once a proposal is written and submitted that your involvement with the project is over. You will need to track the project implementation from the beginning to end. For one thing, reporting requirements typically include tracking project implementation and expenditures in terms of percentages (as in % completed or % expended) or adherence to timelines. Also, of course, keeping tabs on the implementation will enable you to write about it with confidence.

Even when all grant funds are expended and all obligations of the proposal are complete, you will still want to stay abreast of the work undertaken on a grant project for a variety of reasons. You may in the future want to return to a grant maker that has previously awarded grants to your organization, and at the very least, you will need evidence to show that your organization continues

> Even though you are not the grant project manager, you will need to be thoroughly familiar with the implementation of grant-funded projects.

Sample Grant Reporting Timeline

JAN	FEB	MAR
Jan 15: Interim report due to General National Fdn on faculty development project Blueprint for International Relations Jan 22: Final report due Meger Family Fund grant for renovation of dormitory Jan 30: NSF Biol grant final report	Feb 1: Preliminary report due to Stanley Meger Fdn on scholarship endowment Feb 28: Final report due Grand Fdn grant for president's discretionary fund	Mar 1: Interim report due Beagle Foundation on writing lab grant Mar 31: Quarterly Progress Report on Kresge Foundation challenge grant Mar 31: Final report due Waldorf Trust on sidewalk renovation

APR	MAY	JUN
Apr 1: Final report due to Midwest Power Co. for scholarship support-- need description of recipients. Apr 15: Interim (half-year) report Stanley Fund due on writing laboratory grant	May 25: Interim report due to Noble Fdn on graduate fellowships--need names of recipients. May 30: Final report due Robust Co. grant for research in sawdust recycling	Jun 31: Quarterly Progress Report on Kresge Foundation challenge grant Jun 31: May 30: Final report due NSF grant for research in insect communication

JUL	AUG	SEP
Jul 10: Annual restricted endowment performance reports due to: - Noble Foundation - Herbert Sherbert Fund - John Doe Trust - National Lug Nut Corp Fdn. - Meger Family Foundation - The General National Foundation - Lake Superior Oil Co.	Aug 12: Final report due Ralph Mortimer Trust for environmental project Aug 15: Courtesy report to National Nail Co.for scholarship grant 2 yrs ago Aug 27: Interim report (half-year) Donato Family Trust scholarship grant	Sep 15: Final report Stanley Fund report due on writing laboratory grant Sep 31: Quarterly Progress Report on Kresge Foundation challenge grant

OCT	NOV	DEC
Oct 1: First year report due Wend Fdn for 3 yr grant on communications research Oct 26: Final report due General National Fdn on faculty development project Blueprint for International Relations	Nov 1: Final report due to Noble Fdn on graduate fellowships- need info on theses titles/subjects. Nov 15: 1st year report due to NEH Challenge Grants Div. Nov 30: Courtesy report due to Lake Superior Oil on infrastructure grant two years ago.	Dec 1: Preliminary report due Light Industry Assn. grant for workforce retraining project Dec 10: Courtesy report Jane Fdn grant last year for writing laboratory Dec 31: Quarterly Progress Report on Kresge Foundation challenge grant

Figure 12.5 *Sample grant-reporting timeline.*

to reap benefits from that previous investment. As a cultivation strategy, you may even want to provide grant makers with informal reports long after any required reporting period has finished.

A record of completing successful projects for one funder can often be used as an example to a new funding source to show that your organization has a documented track record of success in grant-funded projects. The fact that you track grant project results long after their completion will assure other grant makers that you take such investment in your organization seriously.

Grant reports can pave the way for future grants.

Using Interim Reports for Cultivation

At the point that you are awarded a grant, research and strategizing for your next approach for funding should begin. Normally, you can't approach a foundation for another grant until a previously funded program has been completed. For example, if you were awarded a scholarship or project grant for the current year, you would not be able approach the grant maker again for at least 12 months. Nevertheless, you should be thinking 12 months ahead to formulate your strategy for the next grant cycle.

Think of reporting as a means of cultivating your grant makers for future support, and consider going above and beyond their minimal reporting requirements. If you have a grant that supports a project over 12 or 24 months, identify significant events or milestones during the period that could serve as content for update letters to the grant maker. These news items can function as an informal interim report.

Reporting can be used for cultivation.

Consider this scenario. Your institution receives a grant for faculty development that involves competitive projects for new courses proposed by your teaching staff. Your academic leadership will select the best projects and provide teachers with modest travel funds from the grant, as illustrated by the sample internal release in Figure 12.4. Even though the grant maker only requires one report upon completion of the project, you should not necessarily wait until the project is complete to report on the grant.

In such a situation, you would have information about the faculty members and their new course projects long before the completion of the grant project. Correspondence from your organization relating this information would likely be welcomed by the grant maker. You should consider drafting an update letter for your chief executive officer's signature, as shown in Figure 12.6.

Interim reports can strengthen your organization's relationship with a grant maker.

SAMPLE INTERIM REPORT

Methodius College

May 15, 2014

Ms. Jane Doe
Executive Director
The General National Foundation
125 Park Avenue
New York, NY 10011

> Open your interim report letter expressing gratitude for the recent grant, and then lead into the purpose of providing an update.

Dear Ms. Doe:

I write to thank you once again for your recent grant in support the Blueprint for International Relations project at Methodius college. As you know, this grant will support a faculty development project aimed at enhancing the teaching of international relations in a liberal arts context. I am pleased to report that we have selected faculty travel to be supported by this grant, and I am providing you with selected details.

Course Proposed	Countries to be Visited	Faculty
Commerce and Law in The Middle Ages	Italy, Spain & France	P. Hogan (History), R. Bohdan (Politics)
Post-Soviet Intl. Relations in E. Europe	Russia, Poland	A Tarnow (Mod. Langs.), L. Hall (History)
Arts Exchange in Asia	China, Japan, Korea	I. Ching, (Mod. Langs.), T. Berman (Art)
New Dimensions in Australasia	New Zealand	H. Bloom (Politics), E. Everage (Sociology)
Sub-Artic Societies in Change	Canada, Russia	D. Asp (Anthrop.), N. Dortmon (History)
US-Mongolian Relations Since WWII	Mongolia	V. Newburg (History), T. Elmwood (Econ.)

Should you want further details about these proposed new courses, please contact me.

On behalf of the students and faculty of Methodius College, I once again express gratitude for the generous support of the General National Foundation, and your marvelous investment in our curriculum.

Sincerely,

> If space permits, you may want to suggest placing a personal, hand-written note here.

Timothy Kachinske
President

Figure 12.6 *Sample interim report.*

Showing progress with an informal interim report, even when it is not required, presents your organization as a conscientious steward of grant support.

When preparing interim reports, use enclosures to add substance and interest. News clippings about a grant-funded project would serve as excellent attachments to a report. If a grant supports events, attach publicity materials. A profile of a grant-supported project carried in your organization's magazine or newsletter is an ideal enclosure.

Carefully-chosen enclosures enhance the effectiveness of your grant reports.

Preparing Final Reports

As you prepare interim reports, keep in mind that you will need to submit a final report once the term of the grant is completed. You should plan your interim reports so that they provide update information but do not present a conclusion to the successful completion of a grant project. The final report will do that.

Deadlines for final reports should be anticipated well in advance so that you have collected monitoring information and potential supplementary enclosures long before they are needed. Also, a final report should be outlined well ahead of the due date so you can anticipate any difficulties that might arise in obtaining program or financial information. If you have a number of successful grant-funded projects in progress, you may want to have a paper chronological file for each report you know to be in the chain. Create your files from your master list of reports due, as shown in the sample timeline in Figure 12.5. This will give you a place to store information related to carrying out a grant project as you receive it.

Report deadlines must be flagged well in advance of the due date to ensure that sufficient time is available to prepare for submission.

Prior to outlining a final report, review the grant-maker's grant application guidelines as well as any other information published about reporting requirements. Be aware that sometimes grant makers include additional reporting information with a letter notifying you of a grant award. Keep this information in your reports folder as well. You will also want to have a copy of the proposal handy, as well as any correspondence, interim reports, or copies of anything else you might have sent to the grant maker since the grant was awarded.

Your final report should be structured according to what the grant maker wants to see. Expect each grant maker to have different requirements. Some may not offer any details about requirements, other than the fact that a final report is required by a specific date. Final reports can vary from a simple one- or two-page letter summarizing what you did with grant funds, to reports containing complicated financial and activity information. The rule of thumb is to present a report that shows everything your research indicates would be expected by the grant maker.

> *Final reports should give the grant maker all information required in grant guidelines.*

As you collect and consider materials to be included with interim reports, keep in mind that you will want to attach supplementary materials to final reports as well. If you have sent a clipping or two in an interim report, but were able subsequently to garner more publicity, consider binding all the clippings with a descriptive cover referring to the grant. You should not, however, send inclusions that are identical to what you have sent earlier. Always try to send supplementary materials with final reports.

> *Final reports, like interim reports, should include supplementary materials if at all possible.*

Most grants require a final report to be submitted after grant funds are expended and a project is complete. Even if your grant award does not require a final report, it is best practice to prepare one.

Reporting for Challenge Grants

Corporations, foundations, and federal agencies can require a challenge to raise additional funds as a condition of a grant award. Some grant makers have special programs exclusively devoted to challenge grants. A challenge connected to a grant award generally means that your organization is expected to raise or contribute funding, materials and equipment, or personnel services as part of a project. This may involve reporting on fundraising progress to date before you can even apply for a challenge award.

> *Don't neglect to investigate the possibilities for challenge grants.*

Sometimes funding to meet a challenge can come from an organization's existing resources and current funds available. Alternatively, a challenge might stipulate that the resources be raised in new gift or grant dollars to an organization. A requirement such as this can complicate and expand a grant-writer's scope of work. Very often, federal grant challenges require that additional funds raised must come from private sources such as corporations, foundations, or individual donors. Projected funds for a challenge will always be quantified in the proposal budget, and reports should follow the framework established in the proposal.

Challenge grants are worth researching because of their potential to yield a significant return on your investment of effort. If, for example, your organization is planning to undertake building construction or a capital campaign, your vital contribution as a grant writer might be your expertise on challenge grant opportunities.

Most challenge grants require that you raise new matching gifts and grants toward a project before you can be awarded funds from a challenge grant. Grant makers that award challenge grants tend to view their support as a strategic means to complete the fundraising of a project or need. For example, you could be halfway to completion of a fundraising campaign for a new building. Funds received thus far have come from trustees and other major gift donors. A foundation challenge grant could be used effectively to fund the next 25% of the total need, as a matching challenge presented to all the donor constituencies in your organization beyond the trustees. Once your fundraising achieves 75% of the goal, the challenge grant maker would award a grant to complete your fundraising campaign. A successful foundation challenge grant can often push you over the top by increasing the giving of current donors and bringing new donors on board.

Challenge grants can provide the motivation for other potential donors.

Challenge grant proposals that promise to raise new funds require more planning than a conventional grant proposal. Reporting after a grant award is complex, too. A special fundraising program designed for a challenge must be carefully fitted into an organization's highest priorities and long-range planning. Leadership of the fundraising is undertaken by executive officers and board members, and usually all development staff are mobilized to meet a challenge.

Reporting on challenge grants can be complicated because of the need to account for matching contributions.

Historically, The Kresge Foundation has led the nonprofit sector in awarding challenge grants. For more than 50 years, this foundation has awarded so many bricks and mortar grants that literally hundreds of colleges and universities can point to buildings built or renovated with a Kresge Foundation Challenge. In recent years, the Kresge Foundation has had a similar impact on nonprofit organizations in human services delivery, the arts, and community development. Studying the Kresge Foundation's guidelines for applications and reporting will give you a good understanding of the grant proposal and reporting tasks required for challenge grants. Go to the Kresge Foundation's website and search "challenge grant," to begin your study, as shown in Figure 12.7.

A visit to the Kresge Foundation website will give you an idea of the issues involved in challenge grants.

Figure 12.7

Go to www.kresge.org and search "challenge grant" for detailed information about applying for and reporting on a Kresge Foundation challenge.

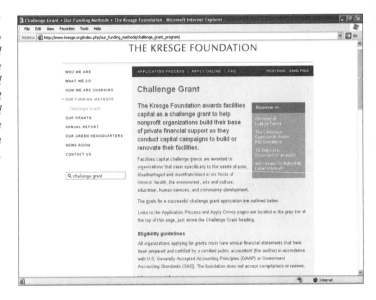

Challenge grants are complicated, but they can be very rewarding and can bring additional dollars to your organization.

You can also search for "challenge grants" online or in the indexes of directories. Keep in mind that foundation challenge grants will probably involve going beyond your own areas of responsibility to involve annual fund staff or capital campaign staff.

Challenge grants can be a complicated undertaking that requires considerably more planning and reporting than a typical proposal grant project, but the rewards can be commensurate with the time and effort expended.

Your 90-Day Checklist for Managing Grant Awards

✓ Establish a good working relationship with the public relations or public information officer in your organization.

✓ Establish good working relationships with the program managers who are implementing active grant projects in your organization.

✓ Familiarize yourself with the "New Grants" section of *The Chronicle of Philanthropy.*

✓ Familiarize yourself with the internal and external publications you might use for publicizing grant project activities.

✓ Review the past news releases and internal releases associated with grants awarded to your organization.

✓ Organize all grant-reporting requirements for current grants awarded to your organization, and develop a method for collecting and retrieving information and materials that can be included with grant reports.

✓ Develop a system for tracking due dates for grant reporting.

✓ Conduct thorough background research on challenge grants and be prepared to articulate how the time invested in pre-award reporting on a challenge grant program can reap benefits for your organization.

✓ Write as many interim and final grant reports as your organization needs.

Chapter 13

Tracking Your Successes

- CRM and xRM
- What Is Microsoft Dynamics CRM?

Microsoft Dynamics CRM is a powerful tool for grant writers because it integrates with Outlook.

For computer automated tracking of grants, you have many options. You could use an Excel spreadsheet to keep track of goals, proposals, grants, and reports. You could use an industry-specific software, like DonorPerfect or Blackbaud. Or you could use a more generalized contact database, like Microsoft Dynamics CRM. In this chapter, we will focus on Microsoft Dynamics CRM, since it is one of the fastest growing databases in its class and offers complete integration with Microsoft Office Outlook.

CRM and xRM

Figure 13.1

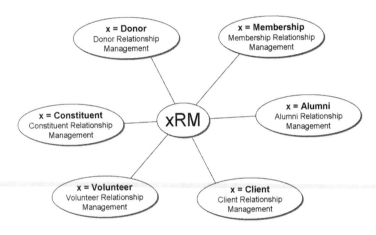

The "x" in xRM could stand for anything that needs relationship management.

CRM refers to "Customer Relationship Management."

CRM stands for "Customer Relationship Management" and is a class of software. CRM software was originally developed for use by people in sales and service as a tool to maximize productivity by organizing and retaining information in a searchable database.

The "x" in "xRM" can stand for any type of relationship management. The "x" can represent management of alumni, students, donors, clients, members, or organizations.

In recent years, though, CRM software has been adapted for use in industries beyond sales. This adaptation is commonly referred to as xRM. CRM has traditionally dealt with customer management. If you take the "c" out of CRM, you have xRM. The "x" could stand for anything. In the educational sector, xRM could be Alumni Relationship Management, Donor Relationship Management, or Student Relationship Management. In a not-for-profit organization that provides the delivery of social services, xRM could be Client Relationship Management or Donor Relationship Management. In a membership organization, xRM could be used to track Member Relationship Management or Organization Relationship Management.

So while traditional CRM software has been used for for-profit marketing, sales, and service industries, you should consider using Microsoft Dynamics CRM as a platform for creating an xRM solution to manage the types of relationships that are critical to your organization's success.

Today, many fundraising professionals use CRM software to track the contact they have with grant makers, prospects, and colleagues. Microsoft Dynamics CRM is the best solution for most of these not-for-profit professionals because it generally costs less than a comparable implementation of a system like Blackbaud, and it offers full integration with Outlook, relatively easy customization, and many options for remote access including handheld device access.

> Microsoft Dynamics CRM can be customized and will give you remote access on your handheld.

Traditional databases, like Microsoft SQL or Microsoft Office Access, can help you keep track of basic name and address information. CRM databases (and the xRM solutions built on them) allow you to house the same basic contact information, but CRM software has many built-in features that facilitate the communication you have with the people with whom you are working.

A CRM database can:

- Keep track of appointments and tasks scheduled with your contacts
- Send mail merges, print labels, and facilitate written communication
- Send personalized email merges and facilitate electronic communication
- Track important notes for your contacts
- Integrate with third-party social networking sites like Twitter and Facebook

Using Microsoft Dynamics CRM, you will never lose track of your contacts. Best of all, since CRM implementations are generally shared department or organization wide, your colleagues will have instant access to your communication history. Since all of your information is consolidated into one common area, generating reports for funders, managers, and board members is simple.

What Is Microsoft Dynamics CRM?

Microsoft Dynamics CRM differs from all other CRM products in that it is fully integrated with Microsoft Office Outlook.

Microsoft Dynamics CRM is one of the fastest growing database applications on the market. The reason for this is simple: Microsoft Dynamics CRM is built entirely into Microsoft Office Outlook. It uses the Microsoft Office Outlook calendar to track activities. It lets you track grants, proposals, and report deadlines all within Microsoft Office Outlook. Because almost every hand-held device available works with Microsoft Office Outlook, any contact details recorded in your CRM database will be available on your phone. This full Microsoft Office Outlook integration makes Microsoft Dynamics CRM different from any other product on the market. Microsoft Dynamics CRM is also fully integrated with all other software in the Microsoft Office suite, like Microsoft Office Word and Microsoft Office Excel. Since Microsoft Dynamics CRM is a web-based system, you can access your data from any computer through Internet Explorer.

Why Would a Grant Writer Use CRM?

Grant writers must manage many overlapping relationships and a vast amount of information.

CRM software is ideal for tracking grants because it is focused on organizing the contact you have with people. The success of any nonprofit organization or educational institution depends in large part on managing relationships and information effectively. The activities you track in Microsoft Dynamics CRM ultimately turn on human relationships and therefore must be carefully orchestrated. These activities include:

- Membership management
- Volunteer management
- Alumni, parent, student, and staff relations
- Public relations
- Donor management
- Foundation and corporate relations
- Annual fund, major gift, and planned giving programs
- Social service delivery and client relations
- Government relations

Microsoft Dynamics CRM can simplify the management of the relationships and information a grant writer is required to be on top of at all times.

A grant writer is potentially in the center of activity with all of these, and you will definitely need a tool like Microsoft Dynamics CRM to simplify the consolidation of this information, to be able to retrieve the information quickly, and to create reports easily for yourself and managers.

By harnessing the power of Microsoft Dynamics CRM, non-profits and educational institutions are able to take advantage of the tremendous financial investment that has been made to develop software to help companies maximize profits. In comparison, software applications developed specifically for nonprofit applications such as fundraising have minuscule R&D resources behind them.

Sometimes advances in technology turn out to have uses that extend far beyond their original intention. For example, software developed by the gaming industry has greatly improved the delivery of rehabilitation services for people with disabilities. Similarly, the military's huge investment in battlefield medicine is responsible for major advances in private sector telemedicine. The use of Microsoft Dynamics CRM in the nonprofit world is yet another instance of a software application that is transferrable to multiple settings.

> Software developed for one purpose sometimes turns out to be tremendously useful in another context.

What Can a Grant Writer Do with Microsoft Dynamics CRM?

Grant writers have a great deal to keep track of. The professional life of a grant writer is a complex web of information, activities, and due dates. If you are to be successful, you must have a system for organizing the following:

- Prospect research
- Grant opportunities
- Submission guidelines and requirements
- Grant proposal submissions and reports
- Correspondence
- Email traffic
- Telephone contacts
- Meetings
- Notes that need to be associated with a contact or organization
- Internal and external publicity
- Calendars and timelines
- Deadlines
- Information on grant makers
- Information on competitors
- Important documents

You can start out doing all of this on paper, but it will quickly turn into a nightmare. You can of course manage information far more efficiently using Microsoft Office Word, Microsoft Office Excel, and Microsoft Office Outlook, but you will still face challenges when it comes to retrieval and reporting. Microsoft Dynamics CRM integrates all of these functions. Using Microsoft Dynamics CRM, you can design your own customized database for storing and retrieving everything—including your calendar.

Microsoft Dynamics CRM is fully customizable, which means that you can set it up to meet the unique circumstances of your grant-writing position.

The advantages of maintaining a Microsoft Dynamics CRM database are many. It will enable you to search for information easily. For example, you can track your emails by clicking a Track in CRM button and then retrieve them by contact or organization (see Figure 13.2).

You can do a mail merge to organizations or individuals by clicking the Microsoft Office Word button in a Microsoft Dynamics CRM view (see Figure 13.3).

Anything in your Microsoft Dynamics CRM database can be instantly exported into Excel, as shown in Figure 13.4. You should aim to do as much reporting as possible in Microsoft Dynamics CRM views because Microsoft Office Excel is the easiest and most flexible report writer available. You can create dynamic spreadsheets so that your reports are automatically updated as you add or change data in Microsoft Dynamics CRM.

Figure 13.2
Track in CRM Button for tracking emails in Microsoft Office Outlook.

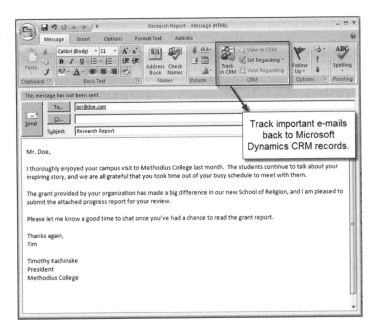

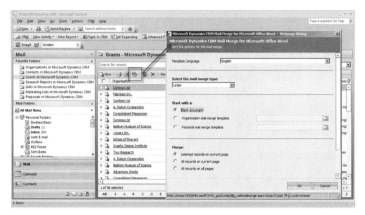

Figure 13.3
Direct Access to Microsoft Office Word templates and merge functions.

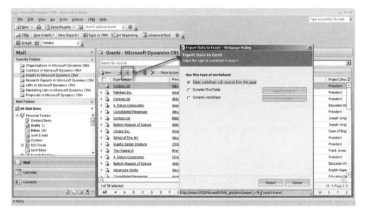

Figure 13.4
Microsoft Office Excel button for instant exports to blank worksheets, dynamic worksheets, or dynamic pivot charts and tables.

You can access your database from your desktop, or if you have a laptop you can access it remotely. This can be done directly within Microsoft Office Outlook or Internet Explorer. All contact and calendar information synchronizes via Microsoft Office Outlook to your handheld device.

Grant writing can be very stressful. Everything you can do to maximize your organization and efficiency will lower your stress level and free you up to enjoy the aspects of the job that are truly rewarding.

Storing all of your information in Microsoft Dynamics CRM means you can access it almost anywhere.

How Can Microsoft Dynamics CRM Be Used to Document Productivity?

Grant writers need to be able to provide evidence of productivity on a regular basis. Why? Because you have to prove that you bring in more money than it costs the organization to employ you. A grant writer who appears to be a drain on the organization's

Grant writers must justify their salary, benefits, and the square footage they occupy in terms of dollars raised.

resources quarter after quarter is in a weak position. You want to be able to demonstrate your productivity and be in a position of strength from Day 1.

A complete, chronological record of the submission of grant proposals during your employment is the single most important tool for assessing your productivity. A proposal log contains essential information such as:

- Name of the grant maker
- Dollar amount of the grant
- Purpose of the grant
- Submission date
- Anticipated decision date
- Status or outcome
- Totals

The principal means for documenting a grant-writer's productivity is the proposal log.

Your proposal log will serve to document your productivity as a grant-writing professional.

You should start your proposal log your first day on the job. Since most nonprofit boards meet quarterly, you should anticipate submitting a proposal log in your first 90 days as a grant writer. It may be some weeks before you are actually sending out proposals. However, within the first week or two, after some research, you will be able to enter potential submissions and deadlines on your log.

A grant-writer's proposal log is typically submitted before each board meeting.

At the very beginning, it will suffice for you to have mostly projected proposal submissions in this report. See Figure 13.5 for an example of a Microsoft Dynamics CRM proposal log done during the first quarter on the job.

Soon you will be submitting proposals, and your proposal log will be comprised of a combination of projected and submitted proposals. Once you have a number of proposals under your belt, your log will contain only submitted proposals to show actual proposal productivity, as shown in Figure 13.6. You may want to develop another "proposal opportunity" report to track planned submissions that project potential productivity.

SAMPLE PROPOSAL LOG (First Quarter on the Job)

CONFIDENTIAL

Report to the Vice President of Development
Timothy Kachinske, Director of Corporate and Foundation Relations

Projected Proposal Submissions – Current Fiscal Year
Mar 15, 2013

Corporation	Amount	Purpose	Anticipated Submission Date	Anticipated Decision Date
Alpha Corporation	25,000	Minority Scholarships	4/12/2013	9/30/2013
Beta Company	45,000	Summer Internships	4/30/2013	10/30/2013
Gamma Corporation	67,000	Recycling Curriculum	5/1/2003	12/30/2013
Delta Foundation	5,000	Biology Lab Support	5/30/2013	9/30-2013
Epsilon Corporation	6,000	Undergrad. Internships	6/13/2013	12/1/2013
Zeta Foundation	15,000	Faculty Regengeration	6/30/2013	4/1/2014
Eta Trust	454,000	New Library Computers	7/15/2013	9/30/2013
Theta Corp. Fdn.	125,000	Publication: Nature & Art	7/15/2013	10/1/2013
Iota Corporation	53,000	K-12 Social Studies Curr.	7/30/2013	1/15/1014
Kappa Company	100,000	Faculty Development	8/10/2013	10/1/2013
Lambda Inc.	33,220	National Student Conference	8/25/2013	9/15/2013
Mu Foundation	1,500,000	Matching Grant: Renovation	9/1/2013	2/2/2024
Nu Company	25,000	Book: Current Env. Policy	9/15/2013	10/15/2013
Xi Corporation	39,560	Laptops for Professors	10/1/2013	11/30/2013
Omicron Inc.	27,990	Education Equality Study	10/1/2013	3/15/2014
Pi Company Fnd.	62,500	Corporate Internships	10/15/2013	12/1/2013
Rho Corporation	33,110	Scholarships	10/15/2013	11/15/2013
Sigma Foundation	25,000	Emergency Student Aid	11/1/2013	2/1/2014
Tau Company	10,000	Winter Break Study Travel	11/15/2013	3/15/2014
Upsilon Foundation	25,680	Scholarships	11/30/2013	2/1/2014
Omega Corporation	14,200	Curriculum Overhaul	12/10/2013	2/1/2014

Figure 13.5 *Sample proposal log (first quarter on the job).*

SAMPLE PROPOSAL LOG (First Year on the Job)

CONFIDENTIAL

Civil Policy Association

Report to the Vice President of External Relations
Timothy Kachinske, Senior Grant Writer

Proposal Log – Current Fiscal Year

Proposal $ Amount Totals Since Jan 1, 2020			Number of Proposals		
Planned	Submitted/Pending	Awarded	Planned	Submitted/ Pending	Awarded
$2,200,000	$1,100,000	$246,000	36	24	6

Corporation	Amount	Purpose	Submission Date	Decision Date	Outcome
Alpha Corporation	25,000	Immigrant Studies	1/15/2020	3/1/2020	Declined
Beta Company	45,000	Medical Costs Policy	2/15/2020	1/1/2021	Hiatus
Gamma Corporation	67,000	Recycling Survey USA	2/16/2020	3/1/2020	67,000
Delta Corporation	5,000	Env.Engineering Conf.	3/1/2020	1/1/2021	5,000
Epsilon Corporation	6,000	Undergrad. Internships	8/15/2020	1/1/2021	6,000
Zeta Foundation	15,000	New Soil Regengeration	8/15/2020	1/1/2021	15,000
Eta Corporation	454,000	Downward Econ Mobility	7/15/2020	1/1/2021	Declined
Theta Company Fdn.	125,000	Publication: Env. Handbook	8/15/2020	1/1/2021	Declined
Iota Corporation	53,000	K-12 Social Studies Curr.	7/15/2020	1/1/2021	53,000
Kappa Company	100,000	State Capitol Measurements	8/15/2020	1/1/2021	100,000
Lambda Inc.	33,220	New Congress Conference	7/23/2020	3/15/2021	Pending
Mu Corporation	12,000	Graduate Fellowships	7/15/2020	2/1/2021	Pending
Nu Company	25,000	Book: Current Env. Policy	7/25/2020	3/15/2021	Pending
Xi Association	39,560	Laptops for Teachers Prog.	7/26/2020	2/1/2021	Pending
Omicron Foundation	27,990	Health Equality Study	7/30/2020	3/15/2021	Pending
Pi Company	62,500	Animal Rights Conference	8/1/2020	3/15/2021	Pending
Rho Corporation	33,110	Manufacturing Survey	8/2/2020	4/1/2021	Pending
Sigma Inc	25,000	Corporate Advisory Group	8/8/2020	2/1/2021	Pending
Tau Company	10,000	Winter Conference	8/16/2020	3/15/2021	Pending
Upsilon Inc	25,680	Winter Conference	8/23/2020	4/1/2021	Pending
Omega Corporation	14,200	Graduate Fellowships	8/27/2020	2/1/2021	Pending

Continued...

Figure 13.6 *Sample proposal log (first year on the job).*

Microsoft Dynamics CRM makes the task of creating a proposal log very simple. All you need to do is design a grants entity that will house the information you need, and then design a view that will enable you to see the information in Microsoft Office Outlook. With a click on the Microsoft Office Excel icon, the information will export instantly to a Microsoft Office Excel spreadsheet. You can then paste it into a Microsoft Office Word document, send it as an email, or store it wherever you wish to keep it. Figure 13.7 displays a view in Microsoft Office Outlook showing a Microsoft Dynamics CRM grants entity.

It is simple to create a proposal log using Microsoft Dynamics CRM.

Figure 13.7
Microsoft Dynamics CRM Grants Entity view in Microsoft Office Outlook.

> **NOTE**
>
> Customer Relationship Management (CRM) software is used to manage sales productivity. The author has created a customized Microsoft Dynamics CRM system specifically for fundraising professionals. If you would like a copy of it, send an email to tim@is-crm.com.

Index